The Complete Whole Grain Cookbook

Aveline Kushi
Wendy Esko

Japan Publications
Tokyo • New York

Published by Japan Publications, Inc., Tokyo and New York.

Distributors:
UNITED STATES: Kodansha America, Inc., through Farrar, Straus & Giroux,
19 Union Square West, New York, N.Y. 10003. CANADA: Fitzhenry & White-
side Ltd., 195 Allstate Parkway, Markham, Ontario L3R 4T8. UNITED KING-
DOM & EUROPEAN CONTINENT: Premier Marketing Ltd., 1 Gower Street,
London WC1E 6HA. AUSTRALIA AND NEW ZEALAND: Bookwise International, 54 Crittenden Road, Findon, South Australia 5023. THE FAR EAST
AND JAPAN: Japan Publications Trading Co., Ltd. 1-2-1, Sarugaku-cho, Chi-
yoda-ku, Tokyo 101.

First edition: January 1997

LCCC No. 96–79069
ISBN: 0–87040–898–4

PRINTED IN THE UNITED STATES OF AMERICA

Contents

Foreword

For me personally, the idea of naturalness has been a life-long bias, from my boyhood days on the family farm immersed with nature, to and through the more than thirty years of my professional research and teaching career. A twelve-year diet, lifestyle, and disease study in rural China, which we have been conducting, was intentionally designed to obtain a more comprehensive understanding of the "natural order of things," to borrow from the title of Jim Mason's thought provoking new book, *An Unnatural Order.*

While there is enormous appeal in this concept, I also find confusion and tension existing between it and its relative, high-tech science. The underlying experimental concepts of modern, so-called rational science used to study the causes and cures of diseases connect poorly, in my view, with the concept of natural foods and natural products. High-tech science emphasizes, for example, the very simple and obviously appealing notion that factor X causes biological response Y. Indeed, research funding institutions virtually demand that proposed research be done in this way if funds are to be granted.

Although this simplistic X-Y notion of high-tech science lends itself to fundable research projects, career advancement, and lots of research publications and media attention, it is nonetheless dangerously superficial. How many readers know that the so-called wonder drugs and vaccines alleged to have reduced the major diseases of the past (including tuberculosis, pneumonia, diphtheria, typhoid, measles, etc.) actually were introduced after these diseases were far in decline? Similarly, how many readers know that most of the widely publicized causes and cures of chronic degenerative diseases (e.g., cancers and cardiovascular diseases) also do not act in such simplistic ways as X to Y? Many, many serious blunders have occurred because of this naive view and many still lurk about. In contrast, the natural foods and natural products concept is more likely to emphasize the wholistic effects of multiple causes upon multiple biological responses.

My point is this: reducing our understanding of the underlying biology of health and disease to explanations of single chemical causes and single chemical cures and single mechanisms is, at best, extraordinarily simplistic and superficial. Within such a paradigm, chaotic information abounds. I do not say that investigation of these highly sanitized events in the laboratory is without merit–they may be very important. But this importance emerges only when we appreciate, perhaps even understand how these singular events fit within their larger context. Application of isolated bits of research information into real life settings, without consideration of nature's synergy, borders on mindlessness. Synthesis and integration of isolated observations into a more wholesome view of nature is much more sensible, reliable, and health enhancing.

Based on an overwhelming body of scientific evidence, the natural norm for optimal nutrition is that provided by diets which are comprised of a wide variety of reasonably unaltered plant foods, including whole cereal grains. Variety ensures adequate intake of all nutrients while retention of natural form tends to limit nutrient losses. The greater the alteration of this food matter by human hands, the greater is the deviation from naturalness.

The idea of near-perfect naturalness, although supported by substantial scientific evidence, is too rigorous and unreasonable for most people to use in their everyday lives, unless they wish to stress themselves with the struggle for purity. Indeed, some alteration, such as that provided by cooking, has been shown to expand the availability and palatability of certain whole foods.

This idea, in general, suggests the following. The most comprehensive health benefits will be provided by a comprehensive selection of foods, that is, a good wholesome diet. The next most comprehensive health benefits are provided, in decreasing order, by mixtures of foods, single whole foods, crude extracts of foods, and lastly by individual chemicals of foods. From whole diets to single chemicals, health benefits become less and less comprehensive and more and more problematic. That is, consuming food in an ever more piecemeal way becomes increasingly unnatural and more and more unpredictable and problematic for long term health. It represents irregular wandering from nature and, in my experience, such wandering results, in considerable measure, from reductionist scientific research the results of which cast an enormous shadow over public understanding of health.

In *The Complete Whole Grain Cookbook*, Aveline Kushi and Wendy Esko, two pioneers in natural foods cooking, present a unique cookbook in which whole grains or their products are used in each recipe. Synthesizing the traditional and the modern, they present a wealth of recipes and culinary suggestions that meet contemporary scientific and medical dietary guidelines as well as satisfy aesthetic and spiritual standards of cooking of East and West.

Whole grains are especially rich in dietary fiber. The cancer-prevention properties of dietary fiber are hardly a secret. Indeed, in modern times the late Dr. Denis Burkitt (of Burkitt's Lymphoma fame) made the so-called "fiber story" famous in his work among native Africans. This British researcher, with his colleagues Alan Walker and Hugh Trowell, spent many years in Africa tirelessly working to better understand why diseases typically found in Western countries were rare in Africa. What he discovered made worldwide news. Diets high in fiber appeared to be associated with reduced cancer incidence of the large bowel, as well as the incidence of many other diseases common to Western countries.

In rural China, we took this lead to further explore the fiber-cancer association among people who were consuming very large amounts of fiber compared to Americans. In so doing, we incorporated two other understandings. First, dietary fiber is not a single chemical entity. There is an almost unlimited variety of dietary fibers. Second, our knowledge about the unique effects of specific fibers was, and still is, very sparse. So, to get a better feel for the big picture, we measured the consumption of fourteen different kinds of dietary fiber.

As expected we first noted that the average intake of dietary fiber was at least double, perhaps even triple, the intake in the U.S. Second, the rates of colon and rectal cancers in China were only about one-half the rates in the U.S., although in some areas, this cancer was almost non-existent.

Also as expected, we did not see any special differences in the cancer related effects of these different fibers. Each of the fourteen different fiber types was inversely correlated with cancers of the large bowel. That is, the higher the fiber intake, the lower the rates of colon and rectal cancers, although almost all of these correlations were somewhat less than statistically significant.

In conclusion, it is our view that Burkitt's dietary fiber theory remains intact and it is worthwhile to consume high-fiber diets, not just to prevent large bowel cancers but also to promote a variety of other positive health conditions. And finally, remember that dietary fiber can only be found in foods of plant origin, once again pointing to the value of consuming plant-based diets.

The Complete Whole Grain Cookbook is an excellent way to put these scientific and medical research findings into practice to ensure the health of your family.

T. Colin Campbell
Jacob Gould Schurman Professor of
Nutritional Biochemistry at
Cornell University
Ithaca, New York

Dr. T. Colin Campbell, the internationally known dietary researcher at Cornell University, is director of the acclaimed China Health Study, the landmark epidemiological project jointly conducted by the U.S. and Chinese governments.

Preface

Nearly a half century ago, a young woman arrived in America from Japan who, along with her husband, would change the face of modern society. Over the years, Aveline and Michio Kushi spearheaded the organic, natural foods revolution, reintroducing the concept of whole foods after several generations of modern food refining, processing, and artificialization.

At the heart of the standard macrobiotic diet which they popularized was a way of eating centered on whole cereal grains. During the last century, whole wheat berries, barley, whole oats, rye, brown rice, millet, and other cereal crops that formed the staff of life for our ancestors and all previous civilizations have progressively declined in the modern way of eating.

It was the Kushis' who rediscovered these staple foods and proclaimed them as the answer to our contemporary ills. Now, a generation later, modern science and medicine are confirming that whole grains are the key to reversing heart disease, cancer, diabetes, and the other degenerative diseases of modern civilization. Ecologists, economists, and other researchers are also finding that a return to a grain-based agriculture and food system is the key to preserving the earth's natural environment. A grain-centered diet would help reverse decades of soil erosion, water pollution, air contamination, and even forestall the onset of global warming–an unparalleled catastrophe that is fast approaching as the world's traditional farmlands and rain forests are transformed into cattle pasture for producing beef for hamburgers and other fast foods.

The Complete Whole Grain Cookbook is the culmination of Aveline Kushi's fifty-years of devotion to creating healthful foods for individuals and families. Through thousands of macrobiotic cooking classes and seminars, she has trained a generation of whole foods cooks, restaurant and hotel chefs, and food preparers at schools, hospitals, prisons, and other institutions how to cook with whole grains and their products, preparing delicious, nourishing, satisfying meals.

Wendy Esko, one of Aveline's first students, has gone on to become the premier macrobiotic cooking teacher and author in North America. Through her cooking classes at the Kushi Institute in Becket, Mass., countless seminars and classes across the country and abroad, and her fifteen earlier cookbooks, she has brought the good news of whole grain cooking to a new generation.

As we enter a new millennium, *The Complete Whole Grain Cookbook* is a fitting climax to the first century of modern macrobiotics. Its nearly 500 recipes will serve as a faithful compass and trusted guide to countless families and communities in the years to come.

Through healthful food, prepared in a spirit of love and peace, we shall be able to recover our balance at all levels and create a world of joy and harmony that will long endure.

Alex and Gale Jack
Becket, Massachusetts
October 2, 1996

Alex and Gale Jack are the authors of *Amber Waves of Grain: American Macrobiotic Cooking* (Japan Publications, 1992) and many other books on macrobiotics and holistic health.

Food for Humanity
The Uniqueness of Cereal Grain

Our world is compact and solid, and yet it was produced from greatly expanded space. Non-matter changed itself into matter; the great infinite expansion created the small geometric point on which we are living. From this point
vegetables began to grow. Expanded space produced the contracted earth; the
earth produced vegetables, which in turn are more expansive in their growth;
then vegetables produced a very contracted food in the form of seeds. Expansion changes into contraction, and contraction into expansion in the eternal
rhythm of life. These cereal grains became the food of humanity.

Plants grow from a very contracted beginning. When the plant reaches its
most expanded stage, a flower is produced which begins to discharge perfume
and radiations. Insects are attracted from miles away to eat from this. Compact
seeds develop from these expanded flowers. Because seeds are so compact,
they fall to earth and begin to grow once again. Their contracted condition ena-
bles them to survive in cold winter weather.

Leaves and flowers will try to adapt themselves to the cold by making
themselves more contracted; they change their color from green to yellow, red,
and finally brown, expel water, and become dehydrated. These adaptations
serve for mildly cold weather; however, if more cold arrives they cannot con-
tract any further and begin to fall. Seeds, however, live comfortably through
the winter, becoming even more contracted from the coldness. When spring
comes and rain begins to fall, they attract this water very quickly and begin to
expand, sending out roots and stems.

Cereals grow in the same way, except that their fruits and seeds are combined. Ordinary fruits have a very clear separation between the seeds and
fruits. The uniqueness of grains is this compact combination of both into one

edible form. In other words, the beginning (seed) and the end (fruit) have been made into one unity. When we eat grains, we eat the entire world of vegetables and we can see the wholesomeness of the entire universe.

Other fruits are very watery and liable to spoil and decay rather easily. Cereal grains have such vitality that they can be kept for two years or two thousand years, and still grow when they are planted.

Another uniqueness of cereal grains is that they receive energy mainly from heaven. Most fruits are formed by the interaction of forces coming from both heaven and earth. An apple is a good example. The navel at the bottom serves to receive the expansive force from the earth; this mingles with the force from heaven, and spiral forms are made which produce the apple. The seed is formed at the center as the last transformation of the fruit. Many vegetables, such as pumpkins and squash, are made in this manner.

Most vegetables receive this force from the earth. Cereal grains, however, are very unique in this respect for their force comes mainly from heaven. The fruit of the cereal plant does not hang down as do most fruits, but stands upright. Their solid nourishment comes from the stem, while their tassels reach upward to receive the electromagnetic energy from heaven. Seeds and fruits form together at the periphery.

Cereal grains are unique among all the products of heaven and earth, and it was by eating them that humanity developed. Those who ate these cereal grains for millions of years as their main food stood up, just as grains do, and they began to receive the electromagnetic vibrations from heaven and their nourishment from the earth. Their head came to be shaped like a grain and their intelligence, sensitivity, and spirituality began to develop. For this reason, cereal grains are the true food of humanity.

Michio Kushi

Introduction
Cooking with Whole Grains

Whole grains have constituted the primary food of humanity for tens of thousands of years. Every civilization prior to our own recognized whole grain as the staff of life, and the different types of grain, growing methods, cooking, and ways of preparation gave rise to the wonderful diversity and richness of the earth's cultures and societies. Cooked whole grains and grain products have constituted humanity's staple food for centuries. Until modern times, they were eaten as the main food throughout the world. Rice and millet were principal foods in the Far East; wheat, barley, oats, and rye in Europe and the Middle East; buckwheat in Russia and central Asia; sorghum in Africa; and corn in the Americas. The consumption of whole grains in bread form was more prevalent in the West, while in the East, noodles were often used as a supplement to the main whole grain dish. Although corn and buckwheat are members of a different botanical family than other grains, we include them in this general category as sub-cereal plants.

Whole cereal grains contain a balance of protein, carbohydrates, fat, and vitamins and minerals. Beans and legumes contain proportionally less carbohydrates and more protein than grains, while meat, chicken, cheese, and other forms of animal food lack carbohydrates. Fruits and vegetables contain carbohydrate, but lack protein. Eating whole grains helps us secure a natural balance of energy and nutrients. Whole grains are ideally suited as principal foods in the human diet.

The complex carbohydrates, or polysaccharides, in whole grains are gradually and smoothly assimilated through the digestive organs, providing the body with a slow and steady source of energy. In the mouth, an enzyme in saliva initiates predigestive activity and is the main reason why all foods, but especially whole grains, need thorough chewing. In contrast to the gradual burning of complex carbohydrates in grains, the simple sugars in fruits, milk and other dairy food, sugar, honey, and other highly refined sweeteners, burn faster, contributing to rapid and uneven digestion, fluctuations in levels of physical activity, and wide swings in mood and emotions.

Whole grains are also high in niacin and other B-vitamins, vitamin E, and vitamin A. The B vitamins, in particular, along with complex carbohydrates, contribute to mental clarity and stability. The B vitamins in whole grains act as the agent for glutamic acid in the brain to produce two opposite organic chemical compounds that signal "proceed" or "stop," "activate" or "inhibit." The smooth functioning of this mechanism contributes to mental health and clarity. Whole grains and other foods high in complex carbohydrates increase the brain's supply of serotonin, a neurotransmitter believed to induce calm and relaxed mental states. Low levels of this neurotransmitter have been linked to impulsive and erratic behavior.

Many scientific studies have shown that whole grains strengthen the heart and circulatory system, protecting against heart attack, stroke, high blood pressure, and other cardiovascular disorders. Reviewing the the medical data, Jeremiah Stammler, M.D., an international authority on heart disease, concluded:

> People subsisting on cereal-root diets have low levels of serum cholesterol and little atherosclerotic coronary disease. This correlation has been consistently observed in every [traditional society studied] to date.

In an editorial "Sensible Eating," the *British Medical Journal* commented:

> Few nutritionists now dispute that Western man [and woman] eats too much meat, too much animal fat and dairy products, too much refined carbohydrate, and too little dietary fiber. Epidemiology studies of heart disease suggest that some at least of the deaths in the middle ages from myocardial infarction [heart attack] could be cut by a move toward a more prudent diet--which means more cereals and vegetables and less meat and fat.

A wide range of studies also show that as a part of a balanced diet whole grains protect against many forms of cancer. The Senate Select Committee's report *Dietary Goals for the United States* (1977), the Surgeon General's document *Healthy People* (1979), the National Academy of Science's report *Diet, Nutrition and Cancer* (1982), and many others all call for substantial increases in the daily consumption of whole grains. The new Food Pyramid produced by the U.S. Department of Agriculture reflects this new emphasis on whole grains and other plant foods, while de-emphasizing meat, dairy, and other animal foods.

Brown rice, barley, whole wheat, oats, rye, corn, and other whole grains contain compounds known as protease inhibitors. These substances are believed to inhibit the action of proteases, enzymes suspected of promoting cancer. Researchers theorize that protease inhibitors block the activity of oncogenes which are thought to stimulate normal cells to turn cancerous.

Researchers at the Harvard School of Public Health have experimented with protease inhibitors and have found that they prevented cells damaged by carcinogens from turning cancerous, and cause carcinogen-damaged cells to return to normal.

Laboratory studies also show that cereal grains protect against cancer. Rice bran, the outer coating of brown rice, has been shown to reduce the incidence of cancer of the large intestine. Japanese scientists have isolated several substances in rice bran that have cancer-inhibiting properties, and have found that these substances suppressed the growth of solid tumors in mice.

The benefits of a grain-based diet extend beyond personal health. A diet based on whole grains also benefits our planetary environment, while a diet based on animal food damages it. Cattle ranching, for example, is a leading cause of destruction of tropical rain forests. In *Healing Planet Earth* (One Peaceful World Press, 1996) Edward Esko discusses the relationship between a grain-based diet, personal health, and the environment:

> As we move up the food chain from plant to animal foods, the amount of energy required to produce, transport, and store foods increases dramatically. Grains and other plant foods are lower on the food chain and require much less energy to produce. Researchers at Ohio State University compared the amounts of energy required to produce plant and animal foods and discovered that the least energy-efficient plant food was nearly ten times as efficient as the most energy-efficient animal food. A grain-based diet reduces the use of fossil fuels and eases the pollution burden entering the environment. Eating whole grains is something each of us can do to restore not only our personal health, but the health of our planetary environment.

A Grain-Based Diet

Whole grains are ideal as principal foods for a number of reasons. They complement our unique physical structure. Our teeth, for example, reveal the ideal composition of the human diet. Of the thirty-two adult teeth, twenty are molars or premolars. These teeth are well-suited to crushing and grinding whole grains, beans, seeds, and other fibrous plant foods. The eight incisors located in the front of the mouth are ideally suited to cutting vegetables, while the four canine teeth can be used for tearing animal food. As we can see, according to our tooth structure, whole grains and other plant foods should comprise the majority of our diet.

The dietary practices of traditional cultures around the world have reflected this overall pattern. For thousands of years, humanity based its diet around whole grains. Plant foods such as beans, fresh local vegetables, sea vegetables, and others were eaten as secondary foods. Animal food was eaten much less often that it is at present. It was not until the twentieth century that the shift away from this traditional pattern of eating began. During that time, the consumption of whole grains declined, while the intake of meat, chicken, dairy food, sugar, and processed food increased dramatically. It was during this time that the rates of chronic illness, especially heart disease and cancer, increased as well. Public health agencies around the world now agree that whole grains are an essential part of a healthful, preventive way of eating.

In the macrobiotic diet, whole grains are the centerpiece of a way of eating based primarily on plant foods. Along with whole grains and their products, the macrobiotic diet includes such secondary foods as beans and bean products, fresh local vegetables, sea vegetables, seeds and nuts, temperate fruits, and a variety of natural seasonings, condiments, and beverages. Increasingly, scientific research is discovering the power of these balanced natural foods to prevent sickness. For a complete listing of foods in the macrobiotic diet, including modifications for different climatic conditions, refer to *Standard Macrobiotic Diet,* by Michio Kushi, published by One Peaceful World Press.

Equipping Your Kitchen

The type of knifes, cookware, serving dishes, and other utensils used in your kitchen has a great influence on the quality of food you prepare. Aluminum cookware is best avoided, as is teflon or cookware coated with plastic. In this section are guidelines for selecting high-quality cookware. Artificial cookware scratches or chips easily, and can release toxic metals and plastic into your foods. Cookware coated with plastic is chemically treated and not recommended for health and well-being. Glass pots and skillets make it harder to cook foods properly. These devices cook food at temperatures that are much higher than stainless steel. When you remove your pots from the burner, food continues cooking in them. Utensils such as these are made by bonding plastic particles with glass.

It is better to avoid electric skillets, cooking pots, and stoves. Electric current disturbs the natural energy of food, and has been recently linked to cell changes associated with cancer. Foods heated by electricity are not recommended for optimal health and are tasteless and lifeless in comparison to those cooked with the natural energy of gas or wood.

Stainless Steel Pressure Cooker Pressure cookers are essential items in

macrobiotic kitchens. A pressure cooker is used to prepare brown rice and other whole grain dishes. They are available at most natural food stores and come-
in both stainless and enameled steel. A small five-liter cooker is often sufficient
for beginning use.

Flame Deflector Flame deflectors are metal discs with wood handles. They
contain hundreds of tiny holes and are placed under pots on the stove. They
evenly distribute the flame during cooking, and reduce the chance of your food
burning. A flame deflector is usually placed under the pressure cooker when
brown rice is being cooked, and under the pot when food is being kept warm.
They are inexpensive and available in natural food and hardware stores.

Stainless Steel Cookware High-quality stainless steel cookware makes
your cooking easy and efficient. You can start with several large or medium
sized pots, several smaller saucepans, and one or two skillets.

Cast Iron Cookware A cast iron skillet is also a useful item. When properly
seasoned and treated with care, it will last for many years.

Deep-frying Pot A cast iron Dutch oven is very useful for deep frying vegetables, tofu, and other foods. Treat it with as much care as you do your cast
iron skillet.

Oil Skimmer This utensil is useful for removing deep-fried foods from hot
oil, or for removing blanched or steamed vegetables from a pot. Skimmers are
inexpensive and come in fine or large mesh varieties.

Stainless Steel Baking Ware Baking ware is useful for when you roast
seeds, nuts, sea vegetables, or other foods in the oven for use in condiments
and garnishes.

Wood Utensils Spoons, forks, spatulas, ladles, rice paddles, and cooking
chopsticks are often used in macrobiotic cooking. They help keep your metal
cookware from becoming scratched or chipped, and make it easier to handle
your food in a gentle, natural way. They are inexpensive and available at natural food and kitchenware stores.

Vegetable Brush Natural bristle brushes from Japan are ideal for scrub-
bing root or ground vegetables. They are inexpensive and can be found in

 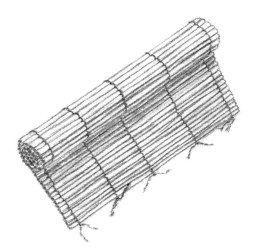

natural ral food stores.

Vegetable Knife Japanese vegetable knives are excellent for cutting vege tables. They have sharp blades that make it easy to slice vegetables smoothly and elegantly, with full control. They come in stainless steel, carbon steel, and high-grade carbon steel varieties. Wash and dry your knife after each use and store it in a wood knife rack. Carbon steel knives may be oiled from time to time to prevent rusting. Japanese knives come in different sizes and shapes for a variety of uses.

Paring Knife A stainless steel pairing knife is useful for mincing and peeling vegetables and fruits, and for making fancy garnishes.

Sharpening Stone Japanese vegetable knives need to be kept sharp for maximum efficiency. Stones for sharpening your knives are available in natural food and hardware stores. Whet stones are moistened with water before use, while oil stones are rubbed with oil. Sharpening rods are not recommended for Japanese knives.

Wood Cutting Boards Wood cutting boards make it easy to slice vegetables, sea vegetables, tofu, tempeh, and other foods. If you eat fish or seafood, it is better not to use your vegetable cutting board for cutting these foods. Use a separate board to cut fish and seafood. To season your cutting board, rub the surface with corn or light sesame oil. Let the board sit for several hours so that it absorbs the oil. Wipe the board dry with paper towels, completely removing surface oil. Cutting boards last longer when oiled once a month in this manner. To clean your board, simply wipe it with a wet sponge after each use. Soap can be absorbed by wood boards and cooking utensils, and is best not used.

Colander or Strainer It is helpful to have one colander and two strainers: one larger mesh and one finer mesh (for small grains such as millet). These utensils are helpful when washing, rinsing, and draining whole grains, beans, seeds, and other foods. They are inexpensive and can be found in natural food and kitchen specialty stores.

Flat Grater Flat metal or porcelain graters from Japan are useful for finely grating ginger, daikon, and other vegetables. They are inexpensive and

available at natural food stores.

Box Grater Stainless steel box graters are useful when grating vegetables for salads and other dishes.

Tamari Soy Sauce Dispenser Tamari soy sauce is packaged in bottles that are not so convenient to use in the kitchen. Glass soy sauce dispensers are therefore invaluable when you wish to season dishes with soy sauce one drop at a time. They are available in natural food stores and come in several sizes.

Suribachi and Surikogi A suribachi is a grooved, earthenware bowl used to purée and grind foods by hand. It is useful in preparing gomashio and other condiments, dips, and sauces, and in making soft foods for babies and persons with special needs. A surikogi is the wood pestle that comes with the suribachi. They are available in natural food stores.

Serving Bowls Serving bowls enhance the presentation of your whole grain and other dishes. They come in various shapes and sizes, and are made of a variety of natural materials, including wood, earthenware, bamboo, and porcelain.

Mixing Bowls Wood, glass, or stainless steel bowls are useful when mixing foods or kneading bread or noodle dough. They can also be used as serving bowls.

Containers Glass, ceramic, or wood containers are ideal for storing whole grains, beans, sea vegetables, and other dried foods. They are inexpensive and well worth the investment. It is better to avoid storing food in plastic containers, as plastic detracts from the natural energy and taste in food.

Bamboo Sushi Mat These flexible mats are made of thin strips of bamboo. They are wonderful for covering leftovers and keeping food warm prior to serving. They allow air to circulate and help food retain moisture, thus slowing the rate at which food spoils. They can also be used when making whole grain sushi. They are inexpensive and it is well worth purchasing several.

Steamer Basket Steamer baskets are useful for reheating foods and steaming vegetables for side dishes. They come in two varieties: collapsible stainless steel steamers that fit inside your pots, and bamboo steamers that are placed on

top of the pot. They are available in natural food and kitchen specialty shops.

Stainless Steel Hand Food Mill A hand food mill is useful when you wish to purée foods. They can also be used when making seitan, or whole wheat gluten. Mills are available in most natural food or kitchen supply stores.

Wood Bowls Wood bowls are useful for kneading bread and noodle dough and for serving brown rice and other whole grain dishes. Wood is porous and lets food breathe. It imparts natural energy to food. You will probably need at least one medium-sized bowl at the beginning. They come in different sizes and shapes and are made of different types of wood. Wood bowls need to be seasoned from time to time with oil to ensure long life.

Organic Soap High-quality, biodegradable soap is helpful for removing oil from your pots, pans, and skillets. Soap is often not necessary for most dishes. A simple washing in hot water will usually suffice.

Electric Appliances Electricity interferes with the natural energy in food. It is better to minimize or avoid the use of electric appliances. For optimal health, convert from electric to gas cooking as soon as it is convenient. Electric blenders, waffle irons, popcorn poppers, food processors, and similar devices are best reserved for use on special occasions only. Microwave ovens are not recommended for cooking or heating foods or beverages.

Prepping Your Foods

Washing foods properly greatly enhances their taste and visual appeal. Cutting vegetables before you wash them is not recommended. Once you slice a vegetable, there is more exposed surface from which nutrients and flavor can escape. It is also harder to remove soil from cut vegetables than it is from whole ones.

Washing Grains, Beans, and Seeds Before you wash your grains, beans, or seeds, place them on a plate a handful at a time and sort and remove the damaged pieces, stones, or other debris. After sorting, place your grains, seeds, or beans in a bowl and cover with cold water. Using one hand, stir in one direction. Wash these foods quickly, as this helps prevent nutrient loss. Pour off the water and repeat once or twice more until the water is clean. Finally, place the grains, beans, or seeds in a wire mesh strainer or colander with the appropriate sized mesh and quickly rinse under cold water to remove any remaining dust. Allow to drain for a minute or two. Your grains, beans, and seeds are now ready to cook.

Washing Sea Vegetables Kombu and other sea vegetables are used often in whole grain cooking. Kombu needs only to be gently wiped on both sides with a clean damp sponge before being soaked and sliced. Flat sheets of nori do not require washing; simply toast and use them as is. (Fresh nori that is not in sheet form must be washed as above in advance of soaking and cooking.) All other sea vegetables can be washed in the following manner: Place the sea vegetable on a plate or table and sort out any hard clumps, stones, shells, or other debris. Then place in a bowl and cover with cold water. Quickly rinse by moving the sea vegetable around with your hand. Pour off the rinsing water and cover again with cold water. Rinse again, quickly, with your hand, and pour off the water. Place the sea vegetable in a colander or strainer and quickly rinse under cold water from the faucet. The sea vegetable is now ready to be soaked, sliced, and cooked.

Washing Root and Ground Vegetables The skin of these vegetables is usually firm and soil can be difficult to remove completely by simply rinsing. Root or smooth round vegetables can be scrubbed with a natural bristle vegetable brush to properly remove soil. Place the vegetables in the sink and run cold water over them. Gently but firmly scrub with the vegetable brush, making sure not to damage the nutrient-rich skin.

Washing Leafy Greens To wash your greens, begin by sorting through the leaves and removing any yellowed or damaged leaves or grass that may be mixed in with the greens. Discard them. Place the greens in a large bowl or pot and cover with cold water. Soak the greens for several seconds, then wash them by swishing them around in the cold water. Remove the leaves and pour off the water. If the leaves have soil or sand on them, you may have to wash them several times. Then, take the leaves one at a time and wash them under cold running water.

Washing Dried Foods Foods such as dried daikon, dried lotus root, and lotus seeds require a quick rinsing under cold water before you wash them. Place them in a colander, quickly rinse, and pour off the water. Dried chestnuts need to be sorted before you wash and rinse them. Shiitake mushrooms and dried tofu can simply be soaked, without being washed, prior to use. Nuts roast more evenly if they are quickly rinsed and drained prior to roasting.

Other Preliminaries

Some of the whole foods used in preparing grain dishes need to be soaked, puréed, diluted, ground, or roasted. Below are guidelines for these preliminary steps.

Soaking The following foods need to be soaked prior to cooking in order to allow them to cook properly or make them soft enough to cut: beans, sea vegetables, dried chestnuts, lotus seeds, dried lotus root, dried daikon, dried tofu, and dried shiitake.They are soaked for various lengths of time, but the procedure for soaking them is basically the same. First wash or rinse the dried food as instructed above. Place in a bowl and cover with cold water. Soak the food for the amount of time indicated in the recipe, or in the following chart. Shiitake mushrooms and dried tofu are best soaked in warm water.

Soaking Times for Foods

Beans	6 to 8 hours
Sea vegetables	3 minutes
Dried chestnuts	4 hours
Lotus seeds	4 hours
Dried lotus root	20 minutes
Dried daikon	10 minutes
Dried tofu	10 minutes
Shiitake mushrooms	15 to 20 minutes
Fu	10 minutes

In most cases, the soaking water can be included as a part of the water measurement in the recipe. The water left from soaking fu, shiitake mushrooms, dried chestnuts, lotus seeds, and dried lotus root can be saved and used in the recipe. The water left from soaking sea vegetables is salty and can be discarded. The soaking water from most beans, with the exception of azuki beans and black soybeans, is also discarded. When dried daikon is soaked, the water sometimes comes out dark brown, at other times, light yellow. Dark brown water can be discarded, as it has a bitter taste. The water used to soak dried tofu has an unpleasant taste and can also be discarded.

Grinding Foods by Hand Your suribachi can be used to grind seeds and other food items and to mash foods to a soft consistency. Place the ingredient in the suribachi. Hold the wood pestle (surikogi) securely with one hand while holding the suribachi with the other. Use an even, circular motion to grind, preferably in one direction. The grooved sides of the bowl make it possible to grind to the desired consistency. A hand food mill can also be used to purée items such as tofu, soft-cooked vegetables, fruits, or grains, and can be used to prepare sauces and dressings. Place the mill on top of a bowl so that it fits securely and put the food into the mill. Hold the handle with one hand and turn the hand grinder with the other. Continue until the food becomes smooth and is squeezed through the holes in the bottom of the mill.

Diluting Foods Kuzu, a dried chalky powder made from the root of the kuzu (or kudzu) plant, needs must be diluted before you add it to your dishes. Place the kuzu in a cup or small bowl and add slightly more cold water than kuzu. Stir to dilute so that the lumps dissolve and the kuzu becomes liquid. Miso is also puréed before being added to soups and other dishes. Place the miso in a suribachi. Add slightly more water than miso, and use the surikogi to purée. Use an slow, even circular motion. Continue until the miso become smooth and creamy.

Grating A flat grater can be used for fine grating, and a box grater for coarse grating. To finely grate ginger, daikon, or other foods, set the flat grater on a flat surface. Hold it securely with one hand, and use the other hand to move the food across the teeth of the grater. Box graters can be stood upright in a bowl or over a plate or cutting board. Hold the handle firmly and grate in a downward motion.

Roasting Certain recipes call for roasted seeds, nuts, grains, sea vegetables, and other foods. Foods can be roasted in the oven or in a pan on top of the stove.

Seeds, dried chestnuts, grains, beans, and nuts tend to roast more evenly when placed in a dry skillet and roasted on top of the stove. Wash, rinse, and drain the food first, and then place the damp food in a skillet over a high flame. Use a wood rice paddle to move the food quickly back and forth to ensure even roasting. When the moisture has evaporated, lower the flame to medium and continue roasting until golden. Seeds and grains will often begin to pop when done and release a nutty fragrance. Roast beans only until the skin splits slightly. Shake the skillet back and forth during roasting to make sure the food roasts more evenly.

Cutting Vegetables

Cutting vegetables properly enhances the flavor, energy, and appearance of your whole grain dishes. Below are several techniques that can help you cut vegetables in an attractive and efficient way.

The proper use of your knife is essential in smooth and effortless cutting. Grip the handle firmly with either hand. If you are right-handed, curl your fingers firmly around the right side of the handle. Place your thumb firmly against the opposite side of the handle. Grip the handle firmly but not too tightly. Use your thumb and index finger to apply the most pressure; your other fingers can be used to balance the handle, thus making control of the knife easier. When holding the vegetables that are being cut, curl your fingers slightly inward at the first joint. This reduces the risk of cutting yourself. Tilt the blade slightly away from your fingers so that the upper portion of the blade rests gently against the middle or end joint of your middle finger. Position the blade on the vegetable and slide it firmly but gently forward through the vegetable, with a slight downward pressure. Cut with the entire length of the blade. It is best not to saw or push down too hard to the extent that the knife tears through the vegetable. This produces jagged slices that are not attractive or harmonious in terms of energy balance.

When slicing long vegetables or leafy greens, you can use a method known as the "drawing motion." Place the tip of the knife on the vegetable and draw the blade back toward you until the entire length of the vegetable is cut. With continual practice, your technique and speed will improve, so that you are able to cut vegetables quickly, artistically, and efficiently. Several common methods for cutting vegetables are shown in the illustration below.

Cutting Techniques

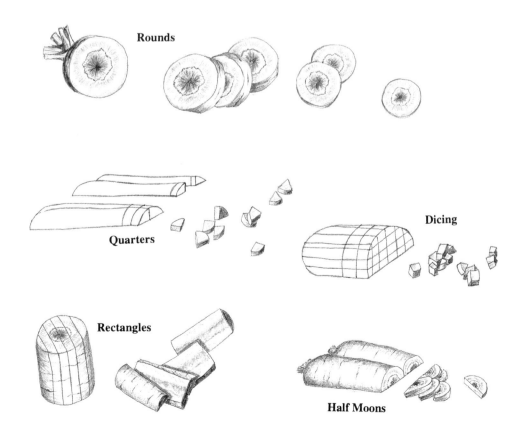

Rounds

Quarters

Dicing

Rectangles

Half Moons

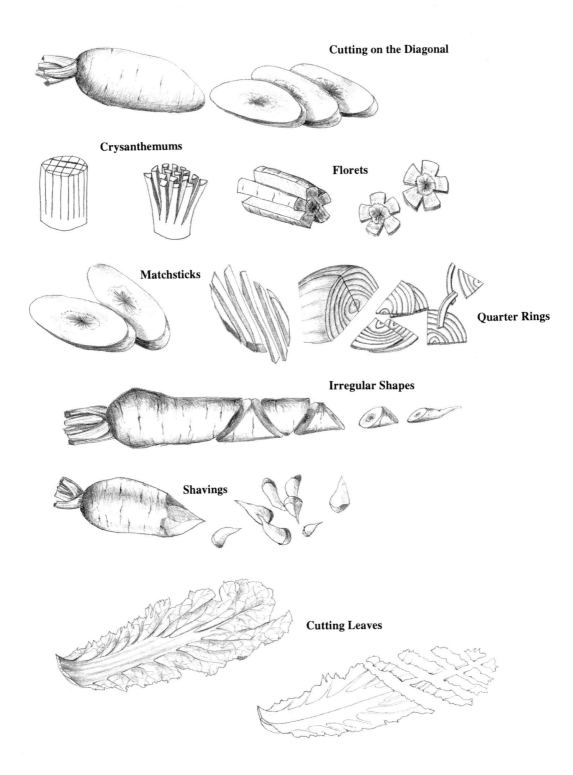

Cutting on the Diagonal

Crysanthemums

Florets

Matchsticks

Quarter Rings

Irregular Shapes

Shavings

Cutting Leaves

Chapter 1
Brown Rice

Brown rice, now grown virtually around the world, is divided into three types. Short-grain rice is the smallest and hardest of the three, and contains the most minerals and a high amount of gluten (the protein factor in whole grains). It is naturally sweet and the most suitable for daily use in a temperate climate. Medium-grain rice is slightly larger and cooks up slightly softer and more moist. It too is excellent for daily consumption. Long-grain rice, a longer variety, is light and fluffy when cooked. It is prepared more in tropical and semitropical areas or during the hotter time of the year in temperate climates.

There is another type of rice called sweet rice. It is more glutinous than regular brown rice and slightly sweeter to the taste. It is primarily used in making mochi, amazake, cookies, crackers, and other special preparations. Brown rice products include puffed brown rice, used as an occasional breakfast cereal or in rice cakes; brown rice flour or sweet brown rice flour used in baking; and brown rice flakes. Wild rice, an uncultivated cereal grass used by Native Americans, is not a member of the same species as regular rice but shares similar qualities. Because of its scarcity and price, it is used sparingly, usually in holiday or festive cooking.

Brown rice and other whole grains are delicious when eaten with condiments such as gomashio (ground toasted sesame seeds and sea salt), umeboshi (pickled salt plum), pickled shiso (perilla) powder, green nori (sea vegetable) flakes, toasted sesame seeds, and tekka (a black roasted powder made from minced burdock, lotus root, carrot, miso, sesame oil, and ginger.) Condiments allow you to adjust the taste and nutritional value of your grain dishes. Natural sauekraut and pickles also complement rice and other grain dishes. Please refer to *Introducing Macrobiotic Cooking*, published by Japan Publications, for guidelines on the preparation and use of condiments and pickles.

Pressure-Cooking Brown Rice

In China, Mesoamerica, and other parts of the ancient world, whole grains were traditionally cooked under pressure in heavy pots or cauldrons. Stones set on top or thick lids often provided additional weight. When the boiling water started to produce high pressure from steam within the heavily covered pots, the fire was slowed down. This way of cooking preserved the energy and nutrients in the grain and made for easier digestion. In modern times, grains have been increasingly refined of their harder, outer layers, requiring lesser time for boiling, steaming, and other cooking. Moreover, modern forms of cooking often allow food substances to stream out of the pot, further reducing the final quality of the grain.

Pressure-cooking is the most thorough and efficient modern way to prepare brown rice. The natural sweetness of the grain is fully brought out under this method, and rice prepared in this way is uniformly well-cooked, easily digested and assimilated by the body, and calm and peaceful to the mind. The entire process of pressure-cooking takes about an hour, depending upon the amount of grain cooked. Soaking the rice for several hours prior to cooking, or overnight if time permits, further softens the hard outer layers of the grain, making each grain softer and slightly reducing the actual time needed for cooking. It is also traditional to add a pinch of sea salt to the pot at the beginning of cooking. This further strengthens the quality of the rice, contributing to a slightly alkaline effect in the blood.

Brown rice may be pressure-cooked with other grains. Brown rice is delicious when combined with barley, pearl barley, millet, wheat berries, and fresh corn. Usually 10 to 20 percent of the other grain can be cooked along with rice in the pressure cooker. Rice and other whole grains may also be prepared with beans, chestnuts, lotus and other seeds, nuts, winter squash and other vegetables. When a pressure cooker is not available, or for a lighter grain dish, rice and other whole grains may be boiled.

The quality of water used in preparing whole grains and other foods has a tremendous effect on the flavor and energy of the dishes you prepare. The best quality water is good, clean well or spring water which is free of chemical pollutants or additives. If well water is not available, good quality spring water can usually be purchased in natural food stores or from spring water companies. Distilled water is lifeless and unnatural, and is not recommended for cooking or drinking.

Usually a small, two-finger pinch of sea salt (less than 1/8 teaspoon) is recommended for each pot of grain. In some cases, a small piece of kombu can be used instead. The kombu is first soaked for 3 to 5 minutes and then diced before you place it in the cooking pot. A piece of kombu the size of a postage stamp (about 1 inch square) can be added to each pot of grain cooked.

Pressure-Cooked Brown Rice (Quick Soaking Method)

The quick soaking method allows short grain brown rice to soften somewhat before cooking. The rice cooks more thoroughly and has a naturally sweet taste. In this method, place your washed rice in an uncovered pressure cooker along with water. Do not add sea salt. Place the cooker on a low flame until the water begins to bubble. If sea salt is added at the beginning, it interferes with the complete expansion of each grain. As the water gradually heats up, the rice expands thoroughly, producing a well cooked, sweet dish with nice calming energy. Once the water has started to boil, add a pinch of sea salt and cover the pressure cooker. Bring the flame up to high and let the rice come up to pressure. Below is a recipe for cooking short grain rice in this manner.

3 cups organic short grain brown rice, washed
4 1/2 cups spring or well water
pinch of sea salt or small piece of kombu

Place the washed rice in the pressure cooker and add water and kombu if you are using it instead of sea salt. Place the uncovered cooker over a low flame until the water just starts to boil. This will take 10 to 15 minutes, depending on the amount of rice in the cooker. Add sea salt (but not with kombu), and place the lid on the cooker. Turn the flame to high, and bring up to pressure. Reduce the flame to medium-low, and place a flame deflector under the cooker. Cook for 45 to 50 minutes.

When the rice is done, take the cooker off the burner. Let the rice sit for about 5 minutes. Place a chopstick under the gauge on the lid of the pressure cooker, thus releasing pressure more rapidly. Remove the lid and use a wooden rice paddle to scoop the rice into a wooden serving bowl. Cover with a bamboo sushi mat until you are ready to serve. When serving, use the rice paddle to scoop individual portions of brown rice onto each person's plate, or the serving bowl can be passed from person to person and each person can help themselves. Cover leftover rice with a bamboo mat. It can be stored overnight in the pantry or on a kitchen counter.

Pressure-Cooked Brown Rice (Non-Soaking Method)

This method can be used if you do not have time to use the quick soaking method described above. Because the rice is brought up to pressure right away, it has a stronger, more condensed quality of energy. This method is thus more appropriate in colder seasons when you need stronger energy from your foods. Below is a recipe for cooking brown rice in this way.

3 cups organic short grain brown rice, washed
4 1/2 cups spring or well water
pinch of sea salt or small piece of kombu

Place the washed rice, water, and pinch of sea salt or kombu in the pressure cooker. Fasten the lid on the cooker and place the cooker over a high flame. When the pressure comes up, place a flame deflector under the cooker and lower the flame. Cook for 45 to 50 minutes.

When the rice is done, remove the cooker from the stove and let the pressure come down. Remove the lid and use a wooden rice paddle to scoop the cooked grain into a serving bowl. Cover with a bamboo mat before serving.

Pressure-Cooked Brown Rice (Pre-Soaking Method)

In this method, the rice is soaked from 6 to 8 hours or overnight. Water causes the rice to become expanded and fluffy. The finished grain has a lighter, less glutinous quality than rice that has not been soaked or soaked for only a short time. This more expansive quality of brown rice can help balance a dry hot climate. Below are guidelines for using the pre-soaking method.

3 cups organic short grain brown rice, washed
4 1/2 cups spring or well water
pinch of sea salt or small piece of kombu

Place the washed brown rice in a bowl and cover with the amount of water mentioned above. Add kombu at this time if you are using it instead of sea salt. Cover the bowl to prevent dust from entering and set it aside to soak for 6 to 8 hours or overnight.

Place the soaked rice, soaking water, and sea salt (if you have not used kombu) in a pressure cooker. Fasten the lid on the cooker and set over a high flame. When the pressure comes up, reduce the flame to medium-low, and place a flame deflector under the cooker. Cook for 45 to 50 minutes.

When the rice is done, remove the cooker from the stove and let it sit for 5 minutes. Let the pressure come down naturally or place a chopstick under the pressure gauge. Remove the lid, and use a wood rice paddle to scoop the cooked rice into a serving bowl. Cover with a bamboo mat before serving.

Pressure-Cooked Brown Rice (Roasting Method)

Roasting the grain before you cook it produces a drier, fluffier dish of brown rice. Roasting concentrates energy in the grains. It is not necessary to use this method on a regular basis, although it can be used to help balance humid weather or on special occasions. Below are guidelines for cooking brown rice with this method.

3 cups organic short grain brown rice, washed
4 1/2 cups spring or well water
** pinch of sea salt or small piece of kombu**

Heat a stainless steel skillet over a high flame. When hot, place the washed and drained rice in the skillet. Use a wooden rice paddle or spoon to dry roast the rice, moving it constantly back and forth until most of the water has evaporated. Reduce the flame to medium, and continue roasting for several minutes until the rice releases a nutty fragrance and turns slightly golden. (Be careful not to scorch the grains.) When the rice has been thoroughly roasted, remove from the skillet and place in a pressure cooker. Add water and sea salt or kombu, and fasten the lid on the cooker. Turn the flame to high, and let the pressure come up. Reduce the flame to medium-low and place a flame deflector under the cooker. Cook for 45 to 50 minutes on a low flame, then remove the cooker from the stove and let the rice sit for 5 minutes. Let the pressure come down and remove the lid. Serve as described above.

Basic Brown Rice

Although pressure-cooking is usually the preferred method of preparing short grain brown rice, you can also boil your rice on occasion if you wish a lighter, fluffier dish. Boiled rice can be used during the summer or if you live in a hotter climate. It can also be prepared at any time in order to create variety in your cooking. The basic method for preparing boiled rice is discussed below.

3 cups brown rice, washed
6 cups spring or well water
pinch of sea salt or small piece of kombu

Place the rice, sea salt (or kombu), and water in a heavy pot. Cover with a heavy lid. Bring to a boil on a high flame. Reduce the flame to medium-low and simmer for approximately 60 minutes. Remove with a wooden rice paddle and place in a serving dish. Cover with a bamboo mat while waiting to serve.

Brown Rice with Other Grains

Brown rice is very delicious and nourishing by itself. It is also very satisfying and delicious when combined with other whole grains. By combining brown rice with other grains you can create a variety of energies in your primary grain dish, while also providing a variety of different flavors and textures. Some grains, such as whole corn or hato mugi, have a slightly bitter flavor. Other grains, such as fresh sweet corn, sweet brown rice, millet, and whole oats, have a mild, subtly sweet flavor, while others, such as whole barley, wheat, and rye, have a more chewy texture. Other grains also add protein, minerals, and other nutrients to your brown rice dishes.

The usual proportion of rice to other grains in combination dishes is 3/4 to 2/3 brown rice to 1/4 to 1/3 of the other grain. For optimal variety and balance, it is recommended that you combine your rice with other grains on a regular basis. When combining other whole grains with brown rice, it is sometimes necessary to soak, roast, or boil them first. Below are suggestions for combining brown rice with other whole grains.

Brown Rice with Whole Barley

Barley has a light, upward quality of energy. Adding it to brown rice makes the dish fluffier and less glutinous. Barley can be cooked with brown rice on a regular basis.

2 cups organic brown rice, washed
1 cup whole barley, washed and soaked for 6 to 8 hours
4 1/2 cups water, including water used to soak barley
pinch of sea salt or small piece of kombu

Place the brown rice, barley, and water in a pressure cooker. If you are using kombu, add now. Place the uncovered cooker over a low flame until the water starts to boil. If you are using sea salt instead of kombu, you may add it at this time. Cover the cooker, turn the flame to high, and bring up to pressure. Reduce the flame to medium-low and place a flame deflector under the cooker. Cook for 45 to 50 minutes. Remove from the flame, and allow the pressure to come down. Remove the cover and allow to sit for 4 to 5 minutes. Remove the rice and barley from the cooker and place in a serving bowl.

Brown Rice with Hato Mugi (Pearl Barley)

Pearl barley is valued in Oriental countries for its power to neutralize the harmful effects of animal food. It adds a wonderful light quality to your brown rice dish and can be used often.

2 cups organic brown rice, washed
1 cup organic hato mugi, washed
4 1/2 cups water
pinch of sea salt or small piece of kombu

Place the brown rice, hato mugi, and water in a pressure cooker. Place the uncovered cooker over a low flame until the water just begins to boil. Add the sea salt, cover, and turn the flame up high. Reduce the flame to medium-low after the pressure comes up, and place a flame deflector under the cooker. Cook for 45 to 50 minutes. Remove the cooker from the flame and let the pressure come down. Remove the cover and let the grains sit for 4 to 5 minutes before placing in a serving bowl.

Brown Rice with Wheat or Spelt

The different types of wheat berries available in natural food stores can all be combined with brown rice. Hard, red winter wheat berries are more chewy and hard. These are usually better if soaked 6 to 8 hours prior to cooking in order to soften them. Soft, spring or pastry wheat berries can also be soaked in the same way. They are also very delicious if you dry-roast them prior to cooking. Spelt, an ancient variety of wheat, can also be combined with brown rice by either soaking or roasting prior to combining and cooking with brown rice.

2 cups organic brown rice, washed
1 cup organic wheat berries, washed and soaked 6 to 8 hours
4 1/2 cups water, including water used to soak wheat
pinch of sea salt

Place the brown rice and wheat berries in a pressure cooker. Add the water (including the soaking water from the wheat berries), and place the uncovered cooker over a low flame until the water just begins to boil. Add the sea salt, cover the cooker and raise the flame to high. When the pressure is up, place a flame deflector under the cooker and cook for approximately 45 to 50 minutes. Remove from the flame, allow the pressure to come down and remove the cover. Allow the rice to sit for 4 to 5 minutes in the uncovered pot. Remove the rice and place in a serving bowl.

Brown Rice with Whole Oats

For a slightly more warming, sweet and rich flavor with a subtle creamy texture try combining whole oats with brown rice. Whole oats like wheat berries
can either be soaked or dry roasted in a skillet prior to combining them with
brown rice.

3 1/2 cups organic brown rice, washed
1/2 cup whole oats, washed and soaked for 6 to 8 hours
4 1/2 cups water, including water used to soak oats
pinch of sea salt

Place the brown rice, whole oats, and water in a pressure cooker. Mix and
place the uncovered cooker over a low flame just until the water begins to boil.
Add the sea salt and cover the cooker. Place over a high flame and allow to
come to pressure. Reduce the flame to medium-low and place a flame deflector
under the cooker. Allow to cook for approximately 45 to 50 minutes. Remove
the cooker from the flame and allow the pressure to come down. Remove the
cover and allow the rice and oats to sit for 4 to 5 minutes before placing in a
serving bowl.

Brown Rice with White Rice

2 cups organic brown rice, washed
1 cup organic white rice, washed
4 cups water
pinch of sea salt

Place the rice and water in a pressure cooker without the salt or the lid.
Place on a low flame until the water just begins to boil. Add the sea salt, cover,
and turn the flame up to high. When the pressure comes up, reduce the flame
to medium-low. Place a flame deflector under the cooker and cook for 45 to 50
minutes. Remove from the flame and allow the pressure to come down. Remove the lid and let the rice sit for 4 to 5 minutes. Remove the rice and place in
a wooden serving bowl.

Brown Rice with Fresh Sweet Corn

For a deliciously sweet flavor and a delightful upward energy try removing the
corn kernels from the cobs of fresh sweet corn and combining them with brown

rice. Sweet corn is especially sweet during its peak harvesting time. It can be used often when sweet corn is in season. Because sweet corn is soft and not dry and hard like other grains, you do not need to add extra water when cooking it with rice.

3 cups organic brown rice, washed
1 cup fresh sweet corn, removed from the cob
4 1/2 cups water
pinch of salt

Place the brown rice, sweet corn, and water in a pressure cooker. Add the water and place the uncovered cooker over a low flame just until the water begins to boil. Add the sea salt and place the cover on the cooker. Raise the flame to high and bring up to pressure. When the pressure is up, reduce the flame to medium-low and place a flame deflector under the cooker. Cook for 45 to 50 minutes. Remove the cooker from the flame and allow the pressure to come down. When the pressure is down, remove the cover and allow the rice and corn to sit for 4 to 5 minutes before placing in a serving bowl.

Brown Rice with Sweet Rice

Sweet brown rice is a variety of rice that has more gluten in it, which means that it is higher in protein. Because sweet rice is more glutinous it has a sticky texture and a more rich, sweet, and warming effect.

2 cups organic brown rice, washed
1 cup organic sweet brown rice, washed (you may soak if you
    want a softer texture, for 6 to 8 hours)
4 1/2 cups water
pinch of sea salt

Combine the brown rice, sweet brown rice, and water in a pressure cooker and mix. Place the uncovered cooker over a low flame just until the water begins to boil. Add the sea salt, cover, and turn the flame to high. When the pressure is up, reduce the flame to medium-low and place a flame deflector under the cooker. Cook for 45 to 50 minutes. Remove from the flame and allow the pressure to come down. Remove the cover and allow the rice and sweet rice to sit for 4 to 5 minutes before placing in a serving bowl.

Long Grain Rice with Millet

You may cook millet with short, medium, long, or sweet brown rice for a variety of flavors, textures, and energies.

2 1/2 cups organic long grain brown rice, washed
1/2 cup organic millet, washed
6 cups water
pinch of sea salt

Place the brown rice, millet, and water in a heavy pot without a cover. Place on a low flame until the water just begins to boil. Add the sea salt, cover, and turn the flame to high. Reduce the flame to medium-low when the water is at a full boil. Place a flame deflector under the pot. Cook for approximately 1 hour. Remove from the flame and place the brown rice and millet in a serving bowl.

Long Grain Rice with Buckwheat

2 1/2 cups long grain brown rice, washed
1/2 cup buckwheat groats, washed
6 1/2 cups water
pinch of sea salt

Place the brown rice, buckwheat, water, and sea salt in a heavy pot. Cover and bring to a boil over a high flame. Reduce the flame to medium-low, place a flame deflector under the pot, and simmer for approximately 1 hour. Remove from the flame and place in a serving bowl.

Long Grain Rice with Wild Rice

Although wild rice is not an official grain but the seed of a wild grass, it can be considered an honorary grain as it was by Native Americans of the Northeast and Midwestern states. As commercial wild rice is one of the most heavily chemically-fertilized grains it is recommended that you purchase organic wild rice at a natural or macrobiotic food store. Wild rice has a wonderful nutty flavor and gives grain dishes a delightful upward or light energy. It is especially popular around holiday time but may be used on occasion throughout the year for variety in your grain dishes.

2 cups organic brown rice, washed
1 cup organic wild rice, washed
4 1/2 cups water
pinch of sea salt

Place the brown rice, wild rice, and water in an uncovered pressure cooker. Place over a low flame until the water just begins to boil. Add the sea salt, cover the cooker, and turn the flame up to high. When the pressure is up, reduce the flame to medium-low and place a flame deflector under the cooker. Cook for approximately 45 to 50 minutes. Remove from the flame and allow the pressure to come down. Remove the cover and allow the rice and wild rice to sit for 4 to 5 minutes before placing in a serving bowl.

Brown Rice with Beans

Cooking brown rice with beans creates a rich, satisfying, and nutritionally complete dish. Because beans usually require longer to cook than grains, they often need some advance preparation. They are usually soaked for several hours, roasted in a dry-skillet, or par-boiled for several minutes prior to combining them with brown rice. All beans may be soaked prior to combining with rice, giving the beans a softer texture and making them easier to digest. Some beans, such as black or yellow soybeans, produce foam when cooked. If you roast them first in a dry skillet, foam will not appear and the beans stay firmer during cooking. This method produces a deliciously sweet dish. If you par-boil the beans for 20 minutes prior to combining them with brown rice, and use the cooking water as part of the final water measurement, this produces a brightly colored dish. An example of this is azuki bean rice, in which the rice takes on an attractive red color. In Japan, they refer to azuki-rice as "red rice."

Brown Rice with Azuki Beans (Soaking Method)

2 cups organic brown rice, washed
1 cup organic azuki beans, washed and soaked 6 to 8 hours
4 1/2 cups water, including water used to soak beans
pinch of sea salt

Drain the water from the soaked azuki beans and set aside. Place the beans and brown rice in a pressure cooker. Add the soaking water from the beans plus additional fresh water, according to the amount suggested above. Mix the brown rice and beans. Place the uncovered pressure cooker over a low flame until the water just begins to boil. Add the sea salt, cover, and turn the flame to high. Reduce the flame to medium-low when the pressure is up. Place a flame deflector under the cooker and cook for 45 to 50 minutes. Remove from the flame, allow the pressure to come down, and remove the cover. Allow the rice and beans to sit for 4 to 5 minutes before placing in a wooden serving bowl.

Brown Rice with Azuki Beans (Par-Boiling Method)

2 cups organic brown rice, washed
1 cup organic azuki beans, washed
4 1/2 cups water, including boiling water from beans
pinch of sea salt

Place the beans in a saucepan and add cold water to cover. Cover the saucepan and bring to a boil over a high flame. Reduce the flame to medium-low and simmer the beans for 20 minutes. Remove from the flame. Drain the beans, reserving the cooking water. Place the beans and rice in a pressure cooker. Add the above water measurement, including the cooking water from the beans. Mix the rice and beans and place the uncovered cooker over a low flame until the water just begins to boil. Add the sea salt, cover, and turn the flame to high. When the pressure is up, reduce the flame to medium-low, and place a flame deflector under the cooker. Cook for 45 to 50 minutes. Remove from the flame and allow the pressure to come down. Remove the cover, allow the rice and beans to sit for 4 to 5 minutes, and place in a wooden serving bowl.

Brown Rice with Azuki Beans (Combined and Soaked)

2 cups organic brown rice, washed
1 cup organic azuki beans, washed
4 1/2 cups water
small piece of kombu

Place the rice, azuki beans, water, and kombu in a pressure cooker. Cover the cooker with a bamboo mat, set aside, and soak for 6 to 8 hours or overnight. Remove the bamboo cover, place the lid on the cooker, and place over a high flame. When the pressure is up, reduce the flame to medium-low, and place a flame deflector under the cooker. Cook for 45 minutes. Remove the cooker from the flame and allow the pressure to come down. Remove the cover and let the rice and beans sit in the cooker for 4 to 5 minutes before placing in a wooden serving bowl.

Black Soybean Rice (Roasting Method)

This deliciously sweet combination of beans and rice is often served at holidays in Japan, especially during the New Year holidays. It can be enjoyed throughout the year. Because the skin on black soybeans is thin and delicate, the beans need to be washed in a different manner than other beans to prevent the skin from becoming loose. Take a clean, damp kitchen towel and place the beans in the middle of it. Fold the towel over the beans so that they are completely covered with the towel. Rub the beans with a back and forth, side to side motion. Pour the beans in a bowl. Rinse the towel under cold water to remove soil and dust, and squeeze it out. Place the beans in the towel again and rub as before. Repeat this process one or two more times to completely clean the beans. They are now ready to dry-roast.

2 1/2 cups organic brown rice, washed
1/2 cup organic black soybeans, washed
4 1/2 cups water
pinch of sea salt

After washing the beans, place them in a strainer to drain. Heat a stainless steel skillet and add the beans. With a wooden spoon or bamboo rice paddle, roast the beans by moving them back and forth and side to side. Start with a high flame, and when the water from washing evaporates, reduce the flame to medium-low. Continue roasting until the skin of the beans becomes very tight and splits slightly, showing a small white streak or split in the skin. Remove the beans from the flame and place them in the pressure cooker. Add the rice and water measurement. Mix the rice and beans. Place the uncovered cooker over a low flame until the water just begins to boil. Place the sea salt in the cooker and place the lid on the cooker. Turn the flame up to high and bring up to pressure. Reduce the flame to medium-low and place a flame deflector under the cooker. Cook for 45 to 50 minutes. Remove the cooker from the flame and allow the pressure to come down. Remove the cover and let the rice and beans sit for 4 to 5 minutes before placing in a wooden serving bowl.

Black Soybean Rice (Soaking Method)

This method gives the beans a slightly softer texture. Wash the beans as described above.

2 1/2 cups organic brown rice, washed
1/2 cup organic black soybeans, washed as described above
4 1/2 cups water

pinch of sea salt

Place the brown rice, beans, and water in a pressure cooker and mix. Cover the cooker with a bamboo mat and set aside to soak for 6 to 8 hours or overnight. Remove the mat and place the uncovered cooker over a low flame until the water just begins to boil. Add the sea salt, place the lid on the cooker, and turn the flame up to high. When the pressure is up, reduce the flame to medium-low, and cook for 45 to 50 minutes. Remove the cooker from the flame and allow the pressure to come down. Remove the cover and allow the rice and beans to sit for 4 to 5 minutes before placing in a wooden serving bowl.

Brown Rice with Kidney Beans (Soaking Method)

2 1/2 cups organic brown rice, washed
1/2 cup organic kidney beans, washed and soaked for 6 to 8 hours or
   overnight, discard soaking water
4 1/2 cups water
pinch of sea salt

Combine the brown rice, beans, and water in a pressure cooker, mixing thoroughly. Place the uncovered pressure cooker over a low flame until the water just begins to boil. Add the sea salt, place the lid on the pressure cooker, and turn the flame up to high. When the pressure is up, reduce the flame to medium-low and place a flame deflector under the cooker. Cook for 45 to 50 minutes. Remove the cooker from the flame and allow the pressure to come down. Remove the cover and allow the rice and beans to sit for 4 to 5 minutes before placing in a wooden serving bowl.

Brown Rice with Kidney Beans (Par-Boiling Method)

If you par-boil kidney beans prior to combining them with rice, and use the cooking water from the beans, your dish will have an attractive red color like that of azuki rice.

2 1/2 cups organic brown rice, washed
1/2 cup organic kidney beans, washed
4 1/2 cups water, including water used to cook beans
pinch of sea salt

Place the beans in a saucepan, add cold water to cover, and cover the pan. Bring to a boil on a high flame. Reduce the flame to medium-low and simmer for 20 minutes. Remove from the flame and place the beans in a strainer. Drain the cooking liquid and set aside. Place the beans and rice in the pressure cooker and mix. Combine the cooking water with fresh cold water so as to obtain the above water measurement. Place the water in the cooker. Place the uncovered cooker over a low flame until the water just begins to boil. Add the sea salt and place the lid on the cooker. Turn the flame to high and bring up to pressure. Reduce the flame to medium-low and place a flame deflector under the cooker. Cook for 45 to 50 minutes. Remove the cooker from the flame and allow the pressure to come down. Remove the cover and allow to sit for 4 to 5 minutes.

Brown Rice with Pinto Beans

2 1/2 cups organic brown rice, washed
1/2 cup organic pinto beans, washed and soaked 6 to 8 hours or
    overnight, discard soaking water
4 1/2 cups water
pinch of sea salt

Place the brown rice, soaked beans, and water in a pressure cooker. Place the uncovered cooker over a low flame until the water just begins to boil. Add the sea salt and place the cover on the cooker. Turn the flame to high and bring up to pressure. Reduce the flame to medium-low, place a flame deflector under the cooker, and cook for 45 to 50 minutes. Remove from the flame and allow the pressure to come down. Remove the cover and allow the rice and beans to sit for 4 to 5 minutes before placing in a wooden serving bowl.

Chickpea Rice

2 1/2 cups organic brown rice, washed
1/2 cup organic chickpeas, washed and soaked for 6 to 8 hours or overnight,
    discard soaking water
4 1/2 cups water
pinch of sea salt

Combine the brown rice and chickpeas in a pressure cooker. Add the water and place the uncovered cooker over a low flame until the water just begins to boil. Add the sea salt, place the lid on the cooker, and turn the flame up to high. When the pressure is up, reduce the flame to medium-low and place a flame deflector under the cooker. Cook for 45 to 50 minutes. Remove from the flame and allow the pressure to come down. Remove the cover and allow the rice and beans to sit for 4 to 5 minutes before placing in a wooden serving bowl.

Brown Rice with Whole Wheat and Chickpeas

Whole wheat berries add a firm, chewy texture to this dish, while chickpeas provide a rich, satisfying flavor. This dish makes great fried rice if you have leftovers on the following day.

2 cups organic brown rice, washed
1/2 cup organic whole wheat berries, washed, soaked, or dry-
    roasted, reserve soaking water
1/2 cup organic chickpeas, washed and soaked 6 to 8 hours or
    overnight, discard soaking water
4 1/2 cups water
pinch of sea salt

Combine the rice, wheat berries, and chickpeas in a pressure cooker and add the water. Place the uncovered cooker over a low flame until the water just begins to boil. Add the sea salt and place the lid on the cooker. Turn the flame to high and bring up to pressure. Reduce the flame to medium-low and cook for 45 to 50 minutes. Remove from the flame and allow the pressure to come down. Remove the lid and allow the rice and beans to sit for 4 to 5 minutes before placing in a wooden serving bowl.

Boiled Brown Rice with Black Turtle Beans

2 1/2 cups organic brown rice, washed
1/2 cup black turtle beans, washed and soaked 6 to 8 hours or
    overnight, discard soaking water
6 cups water
pinch of sea salt

Place the rice, beans, and water in a heavy pot. Mix and place the uncovered pot on a low flame until the water begins to boil. Add the sea salt, cover the pot, and reduce the flame to medium-low. Place a flame deflector under the pot and simmer for 60 minutes. Remove from the flame and allow the rice and beans to sit for 4 to 5 minutes before placing in a serving bowl.

Brown Rice with Blackeyed Peas, Seitan, and Vegetables

2 1/2 cups organic brown rice, washed
1/2 cup organic blackeyed peas, washed and soaked 6 to 8 hours

1/4 cup cooked seitan, cubed or diced
2 Tbsp celery, diced
2 Tbsp onion, diced
2 Tbsp carrot, diced
1 Tbsp parsley, minced, for garnish
4 1/2 cups water

Place all ingredients except the parsley in a pressure cooker. Cover the cooker and place over a high flame. When up to pressure, reduce the flame to medium-low and place a flame deflector under the cooker. Pressure cook for 45 to 50 minutes. Remove from the flame and allow the pressure to come down. When the pressure is down, remove the lid and let the rice and beans sit for 4 to 5 minutes before serving.

Brown Rice with Nuts or Seeds

Combining brown rice with nuts or seeds produces a deliciously rich-tasting, high protein dish. Depending on the type of nut or seed you use, you can create dishes with a sweeter or slightly bitter taste, and a more crunchy texture. Beans or vegetables can also be added to these dishes.

Chestnut Rice (Soaking Method)

Soaking causes the chestnuts to become very soft and produces a sweet and rich grain dish. Chestnuts are low in fat and deliciously sweet and satisfying.

2 cups organic brown rice, washed
1 cup dried chestnuts, washed and soaked for 2 to 4 hours, reserve soaking
    water
4 1/2 cups water, including water used to soak chestnuts
pinch of sea salt

Place the brown rice and soaked chestnuts in a pressure cooker and mix. Add the water and place the uncovered cooker over a low flame until the water just begins to boil. Add sea salt, place the lid on the cooker, and turn the flame to high. When the pressure is up, reduce the flame to medium-low and place a flame deflector under the cooker. Cook for 45 to 50 minutes. Remove the cooker from the flame and allow the pressure to come down. Remove the lid and allow the rice and chestnuts to sit for 4 to 5 minutes before placing in a wooden serving bowl.

Chestnut Rice (Dry-Roasting Method)

Dry-roasting the chestnuts prior to cooking produces a very sweet flavor. It causes the chestnuts to retain a firmer consistency.

2 cups organic brown rice, washed
1 cup organic dried chestnuts, washed and drained
4 1/2 cups water
pinch of sea salt

Heat a skillet and place the damp chestnuts in it. Dry-roast by stirring with a wooden spoon or bamboo rice paddle, in a back and forth and side to side motion, until the chestnuts become slightly golden in color and release a sweet, nutty fragrance. Place the roasted chestnuts in the pressure cooker. Add the brown rice and water. Mix the chestnuts and rice. Place the uncovered cooker over a low flame until the water just begins to boil. Add the sea salt, place the lid on the cooker, and turn the flame to high. When the pressure is up, reduce the flame to medium-low and place a flame deflector under the cooker. Cook for 45 to 50 minutes. Remove the cooker from the flame and allow the pressure to come down. Remove the lid and allow the rice and chestnuts to sit for 4 to 5 minutes before placing in a wooden serving bowl.

Brown Rice with Almonds

This dish is very nice when served during holidays or on special occasions. It has a slightly crunchy texture and sweet flavor.

2 1/2 cups organic brown rice, washed
1/2 cup organic almonds, washed
4 1/2 cups water
pinch of sea salt

Place the almonds in a saucepan, cover with cold water, and bring to a boil. Boil for 1 to 2 minutes. Remove from the flame and place the almonds in a strainer to drain. Discard the cooking water. With your thumb and index finger, squeeze the almonds. The skin will come off the almond very easily. Discard the skins. Repeat until all of the skins have been removed. Combine the par-boiled, skinned almonds with the brown rice in a pressure cooker. Add the water. Place the uncovered pressure cooker over a low flame until the water begins to boil. Add the sea salt, place the lid on the cooker, and turn the flame to high. When the pressure comes up, reduce the flame to medium-low and place a flame deflector under the cooker. Cook for 45 to 50 minutes. Remove the cooker from the flame and allow the pressure to come down. Remove the lid and allow the rice and almonds to sit for 4 to 5 minutes before placing in a wooden serving bowl.

Brown Rice with Lotus Seeds

In Oriental medicine, lotus seeds are believed to promote strength and longevity. They are usually found with their skins removed, giving the seeds a white color. They can occasionally be found in their more natural form with their red skins still attached. Both types of seeds are cooked in the same manner.

2 1/2 cups organic brown rice, washed
1/2 cup organic lotus seeds, washed and soaked for 1 to 2 hours, reserve the
   soaking water
4 1/2 cups water, including water used to soak lotus seeds
pinch of sea salt

   Combine the rice and lotus seeds in a pressure cooker. Add water and place the uncovered cooker over a low flame until the water just begins to boil. Add the sea salt, place the lid on the cooker, and turn the flame to high. When the pressure is up, reduce the flame to medium-low, and place a flame deflector under the cooker. Cook for 45 to 50 minutes. Remove from the flame and allow the pressure to come down. Remove the cover and let the rice and lotus seeds sit for 4 to 5 minutes before placing in a wooden serving bowl.

Brown Rice with Sesame Seeds

Either tan or black seeds can be used in this recipe.

3 cups organic brown rice, washed
1/4 cup sesame seeds, washed
4 1/2 cups water
pinch of sea salt

   Mix the rice and sesame seeds in a pressure cooker. Add the water and place the uncovered cooker over a low flame until the water begins to boil. Add the sea salt, place the lid on the cooker, and turn the flame up to high. When the pressure is up, reduce the flame to medium to low and place a flame deflector under the cooker. Cook for 45 to 50 minutes. Remove the cooker from the flame and allow the pressure to come down. Remove the lid and let the rice and sesame seeds sit for 4 to 5 minutes before placing in a wooden serving bowl.

Chestnut Rice with Walnuts

2 1/2 cups organic brown rice, washed
1/2 cup organic dried chestnuts, washed and dry-roasted
1/2 cup organic walnuts, washed and coarsely chopped
4 1/2 cups water
pinch of sea salt

Mix the brown rice, roasted chestnuts, and chopped walnuts in a pressure cooker and add the water. Place the uncovered cooker over a low flame until the water begins to boil. Add the sea salt, place the lid on the cooker, and turn the flame to high. When the pressure is up, reduce the flame to medium-low and place a flame deflector under the cooker. Cook for 45 to 50 minutes. Remove the cooker from the flame and allow the pressure to come down. Remove the cover and let the rice sit for 4 to 5 minutes before placing in a wooden serving bowl.

Other Combinations

Brown rice can be combined with a variety of other ingredients. Below are some suggestions for adding variety to your staple dishes.

Brown Rice with Umeboshi

Umeboshi, or pickled salt plums, give your rice a slightly salty, sour flavor. Since umeboshi are pickled in sea salt, it is not necessary to add salt to this dish.

3 cups organic brown rice, washed
1 small umeboshi plum
4 1/2 cups water

Place the brown rice, umeboshi, and water in a heavy pot, cover, and bring to a boil. Reduce the flame to medium-low, place a flame deflector under the pot, and simmer for 1 hour. Remove from the flame. Remove the cover and place the rice in a serving dish.

Brown Rice with Bancha Tea

Brown rice can occasionally be cooked with bancha tea and tamari soy sauce (shoyu) for a slightly stronger flavor.

3 cups organic brown rice, washed
4 1/2 cups mild bancha twig tea, strained and twigs removed
1 tsp tamari soy sauce
1/4 cup parsley, scallion, or chives, chopped, for garnish

Place the rice in a pressure cooker and add the bancha tea and tamari soy sauce. Cover the cooker and place over a high flame. Let the pressure come up. Reduce the flame to medium-low and place a flame deflector under the cooker. Cook for 45 to 50 minutes. Remove from the flame and allow the pressure to come down. Remove the lid and let the rice sit for 4 to 5 minutes before mixing in the chopped parsley, scallion, or chives. Place the rice in a serving bowl.

Brown Rice with Dried Shiitake

Dried shiitake mushrooms add a nice light energy to your brown rice dishes.

3 cups organic brown rice, washed
3 to 4 dried shiitake, soaked for 10 to 15 minutes
4 1/2 cups water, including water used to soak shiitake
pinch of sea salt

After soaking the shiitake mushrooms, remove from the bowl, squeeze out the water, and remove the woody tip of the stem with a knife. Dice the shiitake. Place the brown rice, shiitake, and water in a pressure cooker and mix the shiitake evenly with the rice. Place the uncovered cooker over a low flame until the water begins to boil. Add the sea salt, place the lid on the cooker, and turn the flame to high. When the pressure comes up, reduce the flame to medium-low and place a flame deflector under the cooker. Cook for 45 to 50 minutes. Remove from the flame and allow the pressure to come down. Remove the lid and allow the rice and shiitake to sit for 4 to 5 minutes before placing in a serving bowl.

Shiso Rice

Shiso leaves are available in two different varieties: red and green. They are sometimes referred to as "beefsteak leaves" in English. Fresh green shiso leaves can be finely chopped and mixed with cooked rice. Red shiso leaves are found mostly in pickled form or in the form of a delicious powdered condiment. Red shiso is also found in containers of umeboshi plums. The red leaves are used to give umeboshi their characteristic color. To serve them with rice, simply rinse them under cold water to remove salt and chop. They can then be mixed with cooked brown rice.

3 cups organic brown rice, washed
4 1/2 cups water
pinch of sea salt
1/4 cup red, green, or pickled shiso leaves, finely minced

Pressure cook the brown rice as described earlier. When is it done and the pressure comes down, remove the lid of the pressure cooker and mix the minced shiso leaves with the rice. Remove the rice and place in a serving bowl.

Brown Rice with Fresh Mint

3 cups organic brown rice, washed
4 1/2 cups water
pinch of sea salt
1/4 cup fresh mint, washed and finely minced

Cook the rice as instructed previously, either in a pressure cooker or boil in a heavy pot. When the rice is done, mix in the minced mint and place in a serving bowl.

Brown Rice with Squash or Hokkaido Pumpkin

Any kind of hard winter squash, peeled or with the skin left on if the skin is not too tough, may be combined with brown rice to give the dish a delicious, naturally sweet flavor and an attractive orange color. Hokkaido pumpkin, sometimes referred to by the Japanese name *kabocha*, is especially delicious because it is very sweet and stays firm during cooking.

3 cups organic brown rice, washed
1 cup organic winter squash or Hokkaido pumpkin, sliced in
1-inch cubes
4 1/2 cups water
pinch of sea salt

Place the brown rice and squash or pumpkin cubes in the pressure cooker. Add the sea salt and water and mix. Cover the cooker and place over a high flame. When the pressure is up, reduce the flame to medium-low and place a flame deflector under the cooker. Cook for 45 to 50 minutes. Remove from the flame and allow the pressure to come down. Remove the cover and gently mix the rice and squash. Let sit in the cooker for 4 to 5 minutes before placing in a serving bowl.

Brown Rice with Parsley, Chives, or Scallions

3 cups organic brown rice, washed
4 1/2 cups water
pinch of sea salt
1/2 cup parsley, chives, or scallions, finely minced

Cook the rice as explained previously. When the rice is done, mix in the minced parsley, chives, or scallions. Remove and place in a serving bowl.

Gomoku

The Japanese word *Gomoku* means "five-variety rice" or "mixed rice." It normally includes five or more ingredients. Gomoku is something like a Japanese version of the Spanish dish, paella. It may be pressure-cooked or boiled. A variety of vegetables, sea vegetables, and foods such as shiitake, dried tofu, seitan (whole wheat gluten), tempeh, fried tofu, beans, and nuts can be combined with brown rice. Gomoku can also be made with grains such as sweet brown rice, millet, or barley.

Seitan and Vegetable Gomoku

2 cups organic brown rice, washed and dry-roasted
2 square inches of kombu, soaked and diced
4 pieces dried tofu
1 ear of sweet corn, removed from cob
1/2 cup carrot, diced
1/3 cup seitan, cubed
1 stalk celery, diced
1/4 cup daikon, diced
1/4 cup burdock, diced
3 cups water

Place all ingredients in a pressure cooker and mix thoroughly. Add the water, place the lid on the cooker, and place over a high flame. When the pressure is up, reduce the flame to medium-low and place a flame deflector under the cooker. Cook for 40 to 45 minutes. Remove from the flame and allow the pressure to come down. Remove the cover and let the rice and vegetables sit for 4 to 5 minutes before placing in a serving bowl.

Tofu and Vegetable Gomoku

2 cups organic brown rice, washed and soaked 6 to 8 hours
1 cup firm style tofu, cubed and deep-fried until golden brown
1/4 cup fresh sweet corn, removed from the cob
1/4 cup fresh green beans, sliced in 1 inch lengths
1/4 cup carrot, diced
2 Tbsp daikon, diced
2 Tbsp burdock, diced
2 Tbsp celery, diced
2 1/2 to 3 cups water per cup of rice, include water used to soak rice
2 square inches kombu, soaked and diced

Place all ingredients in a pressure cooker, add water, and thoroughly mix. Place the lid on the cooker and turn the flame up to high. When the pressure is up, reduce the flame to medium-low and place a flame deflector under the cooker. Cook for 40 to 45 minutes. Remove from the flame and allow the pressure to come down. Remove the lid and allow the rice and vegetables to sit for 4 to 5 minutes before placing in a serving bowl.

Rice Balls

Rice balls are are easy to make and a great way to use leftover rice. They are wonderful for travel, as brown rice stores very well when coated with nori and stuffed with umeboshi or pickles. When making rice balls for travel, it is best to use leftover rice rather than warm, fresh rice. Leftover rice will keep longer. Rice balls generally come in four shapes: circles, triangles, spheres, and cylinders. In Japan, rice balls are referred to as *musubi* or *onigiri*. Different types of rice balls are shown in the diagram on the next page.

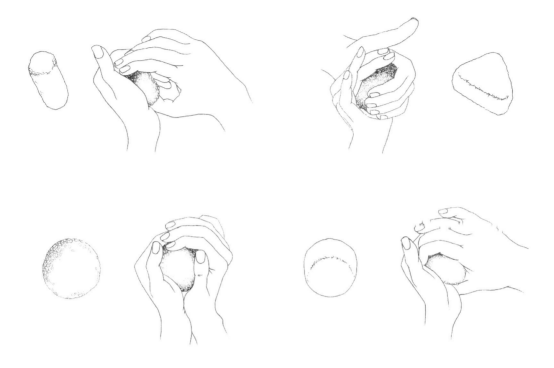

Rice Balls (yields 2)

2 cups (or 2 handfuls) cooked brown rice
1 sheet nori
1 medium umeboshi plum

Roast the nori with the shiny, smooth side up over a flame. Hold it 10 to 12 inches above the flame, and rotate it until the color changes from black to green (about 3 to 5 seconds). Fold the nori in half and tear along the fold. Then fold in half again and tear so that you have 4 equal-sized pieces of nori (about 3-inches square).

Wet your hands slightly in a dish of water. Take half of the rice in your hands and form in a ball, as if your were making a snowball, or in a triangle by cupping your hands in a V shape. Pack the rice to form a solid ball or triangle. Using your index finger, press a hole in the center of the ball, and place half of the umeboshi plum inside. Then pack the rice again to close the hole. Place 1 square of the toasted nori on the rice ball. Wet your hands slightly and press the nori onto the ball so that it sticks. Take another square of toasted nori and place it on the other, uncovered side. Wet your fingers and press the ball again so that the nori sticks. The rice ball should be completely covered with nori. Repeat until the rice, nori, and umeboshi are used up.

Sesame Rice Balls (yields 2)

2 cups cooked brown rice
1/4 cup tan or black sesame seeds, roasted
1 medium umeboshi plum

Form the rice into two balls or triangles as instructed above. Poke a hole in the center of the rice ball or triangle with your index finger. Place half of the umeboshi plum in each hole. Press the balls with your hands to close the holes. Roll each ball or triangle in the roasted sesame seeds until completely coated.

Shiso Rice Balls

2 cups cooked brown rice
4 shiso leaves (special ones for making rice balls), rinsed

Divide the rice in four equal portions. Mold the rice into circles, triangles, spheres, or cylinders. Take 1 shiso leaf and wrap it around each rice ball and press until it adheres. Repeat until all ingredients are used up.

Deep-Fried Rice Balls

2 cups cooked brown rice
light sesame or safflower oil, for deep-frying
1/4 cup tamari soy sauce
1/2 cup water
1 tsp fresh ginger, grated

Form the rice into small balls about the size of a golf ball. Place the oil in a heavy pot suitable for deep-frying. Be sure you have about 2 to 3 inches of oil in the pot. Heat the oil. To test the temperature of the oil, drop a grain of rice in it. If the rice sinks to the bottom and stays there, the oil is not hot enough. When the rice sinks to the bottom and rises to the top almost immediately, the oil is ready to use for deep-frying. Be careful not to let the oil become too hot, other-wise, it will start to smoke. When the oil has reached the correct temperature, drop several rice balls in it and fry until golden. Remove and place on a paper towel to drain.

To make a dipping sauce, place the soy sauce, water, and ginger in a sauce-pan and bring almost to a boil. Turn the flame to very low, and simmer 1 to 2 minutes. Pour the dipping sauce in a small bowl or individual bowls. The rice balls can be placed in the dipping sauce before eating.

Rice Salads

Brown rice can be combined with other natural ingredients to make light and delicious salads. Below are several traditional rice salad recipes.

Chirashi Zushi or Gomoku Zushi
(Rice Salad or Mixed Rice)

This dish is light and refreshing, and is wonderful during the summer. Most of the ingredients are cooked for a short time just prior to mixing.

4 cups cooked brown rice
1 cup deep-fried tofu, cut in very thin slices
1/2 cup carrot, cut in thin matchsticks
1/4 cup burdock, shaved
5 shiitake mushrooms, soaked 10 to 15 minutes and sliced thin
1/2 cup green string beans, sliced in thin matchsticks
1 sheet nori, toasted and cut in thin strips
2 Tbsp tan sesame seeds, toasted
water
tamari soy sauce
sesame oil
rice syrup
lemon juice

Place a small amount of water in a saucepan and bring to a boil. Place the carrot matchsticks in the water, cover, and simmer 1 minute. Remove and place on a plate. Place the green beans in the water, cover, and cook for 1 to 1 1/2 minutes. Remove and place on the plate with the carrots, keeping them separate. Place the tofu strips in a saucepan with enough water to just cover. Season the water with a little soy sauce for a mild salt taste. Cover and simmer for 10 minutes, then remove and drain. Place the tofu on a plate with the vegetables. Place the shiitake in a saucepan with enough water to just cover. Season with a little soy sauce and brown rice syrup for a mild salty-sweet flavor. Simmer for several minutes until all the liquid has evaporated. Remove and place on the plate with the other ingredients. Place a small amount of sesame oil in a skillet and heat. Add the burdock and sauté' for 1 to 2 minutes. Add enough water to half-cover. Cover and simmer for several minutes until tender. Season with a little soy sauce and simmer for another 4 to 5 minutes. Remove and place on the plate with the other ingredients.

Place the fresh cooked rice in a serving bowl. Attractively arrange the vegetables, tofu, and shiitake on top of the rice. Sprinkle the roasted sesame seeds on top. Take 1/2 fresh lemon and squeeze the juice over the vegetable topping. Serve.

Gomoku Zushi (Mixed Rice Salad)

1 cup organic brown rice, washed
1 cup organic white rice, washed
4 Tbsp brown rice vinegar
3 Tbsp brown rice syrup
pinch of sea salt
2 1/2 to 2 3/4 cups water
1/4 cup pickled ginger slices, chopped very fine
1 sheet nori, toasted
2 Tbsp tan sesame seeds, toasted
2 Tbsp bonito flakes (optional)

Place the rice, water, and sea salt in a pressure cooker, cover, and bring up to pressure. Reduce the flame to medium-low and place a flame deflector under the cooker. Cook for 45 minutes. Remove from the flame and allow the pressure to come down. Remove the cover and allow the rice to sit for 4 to 5 minutes. Remove the rice and place in a mixing bowl. In a saucepan, heat the brown rice vinegar and rice syrup. Allow to cool. Mix the vinegar and rice syrup mixture in with the cooked rice.

Add the chopped ginger slices, toasted sesame seeds, bonito flakes, and mix. Tear the nori in small pieces and mix with the rice. Place the mixed rice in a serving bowl.

Fried Rice

Fried rice makes a delicious quick snack. It is a wonderful way to use leftover rice and other foods. The preparation of fried rice can be adjusted to reflect seasonal change. Below are examples of fried rice dishes for the four seasons, along with several fried rice variations:

Fried Rice and Wild Vegetables (Spring)

3 cups cooked brown rice
2 Tbsp sesame oil
1/2 cup chives, finely chopped
1/2 cup dandelion greens, par-boiled 1 minute, finely chopped
1/2 cup burdock, shaved or cut in very thin matchsticks
tamari soy sauce

Heat the sesame oil in a skillet. Add the burdock and sauté for 1 to 2 minutes. Add the rice, mix, and add several drops of tamari soy sauce. Cover, reduce the flame to low, and cook until the rice is warm. Stir occasionally to cook evenly. Add the chopped chives and dandelion. Stir, cover, and cook for 1 to 2 minutes. Add a little more tamari soy sauce for a mild salt flavor. Cover and cook for another minute or so. Mix and place in a serving dish.

Fried Rice and Sweet Corn (Summer)

3 cups cooked brown rice
3 ears sweet corn, removed from the cob
1/2 cup green beans or green peas, sliced thin
1/4 cup carrot, diced
2 Tbsp sesame seeds, roasted
1 sheet nori, toasted
2 Tbsp sesame oil
tamari soy sauce

Heat the oil in a skillet. Add the rice and sprinkle several drops of soy sauce over it. Place the corn, beans, and diced carrots on top of the rice. Cover the skillet and reduce the flame to low. Cook until the rice is hot. Mix the rice and vegetables. Add several more drops of soy sauce for a mild taste, mix in the sesame seeds, and cook for another 2 to 3 minutes. Remove and place in a serving dish.

Fried Rice with Lotus Root (Autumn)

3 cups cooked brown rice
1 cup fresh lotus root, sliced in thin quarters
1/4 cup carrot, sliced in thin quarters
1 cup turnip, mustard, or daikon greens

2 Tbsp dark (roasted) sesame oil
1 tsp ginger juice
tamari soy sauce

    Heat the oil in a skillet. Add the lotus root and sauté for 1 to 2 minutes. Place the sliced carrot on top of the lotus root. Place the rice on top of the vegetables. Reduce the flame to low, sprinkle several drops of soy sauce over the rice, and cover. Cook until the vegetables are done and the rice is hot. Stir occasionally. Place the chopped greens on top of the rice and add a few more drops of soy sauce. Cover and cook over a medium flame until the greens are tender but still bright green. Sprinkle the ginger juice over the rice and mix well. Remove and place in a serving dish.

Azuki Fried Rice (Winter)

3 cups cooked brown rice and azuki beans
1 sheet nori, toasted and torn in small pieces
2 Tbsp tan sesame seeds, roasted
1/4 cup onion, diced
1/4 cup squash or pumpkin, diced
1/2 cup scallion or leek, finely chopped
2 Tbsp dark sesame oil
2 to 3 Tbsp water
tamari soy sauce

    Heat the oil in a cast iron skillet. Add the onion and sauté for 1 to 2 minutes. Place the squash or pumpkin and rice on top of the onion. Add several drops of water and several drops of soy sauce. Cover and reduce the flame to low. Steam the rice and vegetables until hot. Remove the cover, and place the scallions or leeks on top of the rice. Add several more drops of soy sauce. Cover and cook 1 to 2 minutes until the scallions or leeks are tender and bright green. Remove the cover, mix in the sesame seeds, and place in a serving dish.

Brown Rice and Vegetable Burgers

4 cups cooked brown rice
2 Tbsp parsley, finely minced
1/2 cup onion, finely diced
1/4 cup carrot, finely diced
1/4 cup celery, finely diced
1/4 cup sesame seeds, toasted

tamari soy sauce
sesame or corn oil, for frying

Place the rice, parsley, onion, carrot, celery, and sesame seeds in a mixing bowl and mix thoroughly. Form the mixture into 4 to 6 burger-shaped patties. Oil a skillet or griddle with oil and heat. Place the burgers in the hot skillet. Sprinkle 2 to 3 drops of tamari soy sauce on top. Fry until golden brown. Turn the burgers over, sprinkle 2 to 3 drops of tamari soy sauce on the other side, and fry until golden brown. Turn the burgers one more time. Remove and place on a serving platter.

Brown Rice Croquettes with Vegetable-Kuzu Sauce

4 cups cooked brown rice
sesame or safflower oil, for deep-frying

Form the cooked rice into 4 to 6 balls or triangles like you would if making rice balls. Heat 2 to 3 inches of oil in a deep-frying pot. Place the rice balls in the hot oil and deep-fry until golden brown. Remove, place on paper towels, and drain.

Vegetable-Kuzu Sauce

1/2 cup onion, sliced in thick wedges
1/2 cup carrot, sliced in thin diagonals
1 cup broccoli, sliced in florets
1/4 cup celery, sliced in thin diagonals
2 cups water
4 to 5 Tbsp kuzu, diluted in a little cold water
tamari soy sauce
ginger juice

Place the water in a pot, cover, and bring to a boil. Add the onion, carrot, and celery. Cover and boil 1 minute. Add the broccoli, cover, and boil 1 minute. Remove the cover. Add the diluted kuzu, stirring constantly to prevent lumping. When the liquid is thick and translucent, reduce the flame to low and season with several drops of tamari soy sauce for a mild salt flavor. Simmer without a cover for 2 to 3 minutes. Turn the flame off. Squeeze a little fresh ginger juice over the vegetables and mix in. Place 1 to 2 croquettes in each serving bowl. Ladle the vegetable-kuzu sauce over each serving of croquettes and serve.

Brown Rice Stuffings

Brown rice can be combined with vegetables and other ingredients to make a delicious stuffing. Below are recipes that can add variety and nutrition to your day to day cooking.

Stuffed Deep-Fried Tofu

2 cups cooked brown or brown and white rice
5 slices firm style tofu, sliced in 1/2 inch thick slices, drained
sesame or safflower oil, for deep-frying
1 cup water
1 strip kombu, 2 inches long
3 Tbsp brown rice syrup
2 Tbsp natural mirin (sweet cooking sake)
tamari soy sauce
1/2 cup burdock, sliced in very thin matchsticks
1/2 cup carrot, sliced in very thin matchsticks
1 1/2 Tbsp black sesame seeds, toasted
sesame oil, for garnish
3 Tbsp brown rice vinegar

Heat the oil for deep-frying. Place the drained tofu slices in the hot oil and fry until golden brown. Remove and drain on paper towels. Place the tofu in a saucepan with 1 cup water, kombu, brown rice syrup, mirin, and enough tamari soy sauce for a slightly salty flavor. Cover and bring to a boil. Reduce the flame to medium-low and simmer for about 10 minutes. Remove, drain, and allow to cool. Cut the deep-fried tofu slices in half, forming a triangular shape. Take a knife and insert it in the sliced edge of the tofu to open up the triangle. With a spoon, carefully scrape out all of the tofu inside the triangle so that only the deep-fried shell of the tofu remains.

Place a small amount of sesame oil in a skillet and heat. Place the burdock in the skillet and sauté for 2 to 3 minutes. Add enough water to cover the burdock. Lay the carrots on top of the burdock. Cover the skillet and bring to a boil. Reduce the flame to medium-low and simmer for about 7 to 10 minutes until the burdock is tender. Season with several drops of soy sauce, cover, and cook another 3 to 5 minutes. Remove the cover and turn the flame up. Cook off the remaining liquid.

Place the rice in a mixing bowl. Mix the cooked burdock and carrots, roasted sesame seeds, and brown rice vinegar with the rice. Take a small amount of the rice mixture in your hands and form it into a ball or bale as if making a rice ball. Stuff the rice mixture into one triangular slice of the deep-fried tofu. Place on a serving platter. Repeat until all tofu triangles have been stuffed.

Stuffed Cabbage

4 to 6 cabbage leaves, hard stem at base of the leaf removed
2 cups cooked brown rice
1/2 cup seitan or tempeh, finely diced
1/2 cup onion, diced
1/2 cup carrot, diced
1/4 cup celery, diced
1 Tbsp parsley, minced
1 cup sauerkraut
1/2 cup sauerkraut juice
1/2 cup water
1 strip kombu, 4 inches long
tamari soy sauce

Thoroughly mix the rice, seitan or tempeh, onion, carrot, celery, and parsley in a mixing bowl. Shape the grain and vegetable mixture into oblong rounds or bales. Roll the stuffing up inside the cabbage leaves and fasten with a toothpick to hold the rolls together.

Place the kombu in the bottom of a heavy skillet or shallow pot. Add the sauerkraut juice and water. Place the stuffed cabbage rolls in the skillet. Place the sauerkraut between the rolls. Add a few drops of tamari soy sauce, cover, and bring to a boil. Reduce the flame to low and simmer for 15 to 20 minutes until soft and tender. Remove the toothpicks from the rolls. Arrange the stuffed cabbage and sauerkraut on a serving platter.

Baked Stuffed Acorn Squash

1 acorn squash, cut in half, seeds removed
1/2 cup cooked rice and wild rice
1/2 cup whole wheat bread, cubed
1/4 cup onion, diced
1/4 cup celery, diced
2 Tbsp mushroom, minced
1/4 cup water
tamari soy sauce
corn oil, for garnish

Place a small amount of corn oil in a skillet and heat. Sauté the onion for 1 minute. Add the mushroom and celery. Sauté for another 1 to 2 minutes. Sprinkle 4 to 5 drops of soy sauce over the vegetables. Place the vegetables in a mixing bowl. Add the rice, whole wheat bread, and water. Mix well. Fill each squash half with the stuffing. Place in a baking dish. Cover and bake at 450 degrees F. for about 35 to 40 minutes or until done. Poke with a fork to test. Remove and place on a serving platter.

Chapter 2
Sweet Rice and Mochi

Sweet brown rice is a somewhat sticky, glutinous variety of rice traditionally grown in Asia and now in the United States. It can be found in most natural food stores. There are two types of sweet brown rice currently available in the United States: regular, tan sweet rice and black sweet rice. The regular, tan variety is used most often in the recipes in this chapter.

In Japan sweet rice is cooked and pounded with a wooden pestle to make mochi, a sticky, taffy-like rice cake. Because of its consistency and naturally sweet flavor, mochi it is often served at festive occasions. Sweet rice is higher in fat and protein than regular brown rice. For this reason, it is helpful for those who wish to gain weight or increase their strength. Sweet rice and mochi are also good for nursing mothers. The extra fat and protein in sweet rice strengthens mother and baby, and helps a nursing infant gain weight by increasing the amount of fat in mother's milk.

Sweet brown rice can be cooked and eaten plain, mixed with other whole grains, or cooked with beans, nuts, seeds, or dried fruits. It can be used in preparing desserts, breads, pickles, soft cereals, soups, and dumplings. Mochi can be used as a substitute for cheese on pizza. Amazake, or sweet grain milk, is also made from sweet rice. Amazake makes a wonderful milk substitute for use on cereals or as a sweetener in desserts. It is also used in making mirin, a sweet cooking sake, and in sweet rice vinegar.

Pressure-Cooked Sweet Brown Rice

2 cups organic sweet brown rice, washed
3 cups water
pinch of sea salt

Place the rice and water in an uncovered pressure cooker and place over a low flame until the water begins to boil. Add the sea salt, cover, and turn the flame to high. When the pressure is up, place a flame deflector under the cooker, and reduce the flame to medium-low. Cook for 45 to 50 minutes. Remove from the flame and allow the pressure to come down. Remove the cover from the cooker and allow the rice to sit for 4 to 5 minutes before placing in a serving bowl.

Boiled Sweet Brown Rice

2 cups organic sweet brown rice, washed
4 cups water
pinch of sea salt

Place the sweet rice and water in an uncovered heavy pot. Bring to a boil on a low flame. Add the sea salt, cover, and turn the flame up to high. When boiling, place a flame deflector under the pot, cover, and reduce the flame to medium-low. Simmer for 60 minutes. Remove from the flame and allow to sit for 4 to 5 minutes before placing in a serving bowl.

Sweet Brown Rice with Azuki Beans

For a bright colored dish it is best to par-boil the azuki beans before pressure cooking them with the rice. Because the azuki beans are par-boiled rather than soaked, they retain a more firm texture and a very delicious flavor. This dish is referred to as "red rice" in Japan, and is served at many festive occasions.

1 1/2 cups organic sweet brown rice, washed
1/2 cup organic azuki beans, washed
3 to 3 1/2 cups water, including water used to cook beans
pinch of sea salt

Place the azuki beans in a saucepan and cover with water. Bring to a boil. Reduce the flame to medium-low and simmer for 20 minutes. Remove the pan from the burner. Drain the water from the beans and place it in a measuring cup. It can be used in cooking the rice and beans.

Place the azuki beans, rice, and water in an uncovered pressure cooker. Place over a low flame until the water begins to boil. Add the sea salt, cover, and turn the flame to high. When the pressure is up, reduce the flame to medium-low and cook for 45 to 50 minutes. Remove from the burner and allow the pressure to come down. Remove the cover and let the rice and beans sit for 4 to 5 minutes before placing in a serving bowl.

Sweet Brown Rice with Black Soybeans (Roasting Method)

1 1/2 cups organic sweet brown rice, washed
1/2 cup organic black soybeans, washed and drained
3 cups water
pinch of sea salt

After washing and draining the black soybeans, you will notice that the skin of the beans begins to pucker and become slightly wrinkled. Heat a stainless steel skillet and place the soybeans in it. Stirring the soybeans constantly, dry-roast them over a high flame until the water from washing evaporates. Reduce the flame to medium and continue stirring and roasting until the skin of the beans splits, with a whitish streak appearing down the center of each bean. The beans will also release a sweet fragrance.

Immediately remove the beans from the skillet and place in the pressure cooker with the sweet rice and water. Place the uncovered cooker over a low flame until the water begins to boil. Add the sea salt, cover, and turn the flame to high. When the pressure is up, place a flame deflector under the cooker and reduce the flame to medium-low. Cook for 45 to 50 minutes. Remove the cooker from the flame and allow the pressure to come down. Remove the cover and let the rice and beans sit for 4 to 5 minutes before placing in a serving bowl.

Sweet Brown Rice with Dried Chestnuts (Roasting Method)

1 1/2 cups organic sweet brown rice, washed
1/2 cup organic dried chestnuts, washed
3 cups water
pinch of sea salt

Heat a dry skillet and place the chestnuts in it. Dry-roast the chestnuts by stirring constantly until they release a sweet fragrance and start to brown slightly. Remove and place in a pressure cooker.

Place the sweet rice and water in the pressure cooker. Mix the rice and chestnuts. Place the uncovered cooker over a low flame until the water begins to boil. Add the sea salt and cover. Turn the flame to high and bring up to pressure. Place a flame deflector under the cooker and reduce the flame to medium-low. Cook for 45 to 50 minutes. Remove from the burner and allow the pressure to come down. Remove the cover and let the rice and chestnuts sit for 4 to 5 minutes before placing in a serving bowl.

Sweet Brown Rice with Chickpeas

1 1/2 cups organic sweet brown rice, washed
1/2 cup organic chickpeas, washed and soaked 6 to 8 hours
3 cups water
pinch of sea salt

Discard the soaking water from the chickpeas. Place the chickpeas, sweet rice, and water in an uncovered pressure cooker. Place over a low flame until the water begins to boil. Add the sea salt, cover, and turn the flame up to high. When up to pressure, place a flame deflector under the cooker and reduce the flame to medium-low. Cook for 45 to 50 minutes. Remove from the flame and allow the pressure to come down. Remove the cover and let sit for 4 to 5 minutes before placing in a serving bowl.

Sweet Brown Rice with Millet

1 1/2 cups organic sweet brown rice, washed
1/2 cup organic millet, washed
3 cups water
pinch of sea salt

Place the grains in a pressure cooker with the water. Place the uncovered pressure cooker over a low flame until the water begins to boil. Add the sea salt, cover, and turn the flame up to high. When the pressure is up, place a flame deflector under the cooker and reduce the flame to medium-low. Cook for 45 to 50 minutes. Remove from the flame and allow the pressure to come down. Remove the cover and let sit for 4 to 5 minutes before placing in a serving bowl.

Sweet Brown Rice with Sesame Seeds

2 cups organic sweet brown rice, washed
1/4 cup organic tan or black sesame seeds, toasted
3 cups water
pinch of sea salt

Place the sweet rice, water, and sea salt in a pressure cooker. Cover and place over a high flame. When the pressure is up, place a flame deflector under the cooker and reduce the flame to medium-low. Cook for 45 to 50 minutes. Remove from the flame and allow the pressure to come down. Remove the cover and let sit for 4 to 5 minutes. Mix the sesame seeds in the sweet rice before placing in a serving bowl.

Sweet Brown Rice with Walnuts and Raisins

2 cups organic sweet brown rice, washed
1/2 cup organic walnuts, chopped
1/2 cup organic raisins
3 cups water
pinch of sea salt

Place the sweet rice, walnuts, raisins, and water in an uncovered pressure cooker. Place over a low flame until the water begins to boil. Add the sea salt, cover, and bring up to pressure. When the pressure is up, place a flame deflector under the cooker and reduce the flame to medium-low. Cook for 45 to 50 minutes. Remove from the flame and allow the pressure to come down. Remove the cover and let sit for 4 to 5 minutes before placing in a serving bowl.

Sweet Brown Rice with Almonds and Dried Apricots

2 cups organic sweet brown rice, washed
1/2 cup organic Turkish apricots, chopped
1/4 cup organic almonds, blanched 1 minute and skins removed
3 cups water
pinch of sea salt

Place the sweet rice, apricots, almonds, and water in an uncovered pressure cooker. Place over a low flame until the water begins to boil. Add the sea salt, cover, and turn the flame up to high. When the pressure is up, place a flame deflector under the cooker and reduce the flame to medium-low. Cook for 45 to 50 minutes. Remove from the flame and allow the pressure to come down. Remove the cover and let sit for 4 to 5 minutes before placing in a serving bowl.

Mochi

Mochi is a sweet rice dish that is traditionally eaten in Japan. After the sweet rice is cooked, it is pounded with a wooden pestle until all of the grains are crushed. This can take 45 to 60 minutes of vigorous pounding. This pounding action produces a very energizing food.

Traditionally a large tree stump was cut and the center was hollowed out to form a bowl. Hot, cooked sweet rice was placed in the hollowed tree stump and pounded with a heavy wooden mallet. The men in the family would pound while the women would turn the sweet rice and occasionally sprinkle cold water over it to prevent it from sticking to the mallet. It was then spread evenly in wooden boxes or trays that were dusted with rice flour and dried for several days. Mochi was traditionally made in large batches to last throughout the year.

If you make mochi at home, your sweet rice can be cooked with other ingredients or coated with other foods to produce a variety of deliciously flavored mochis. Below are recipes for making mochi at home and suggestions for a variety of mochi dishes. Prepackaged mochi, available at most natural food stores, can be used in any of these recipes.

Basic Homemade Mochi

2 cups organic sweet brown rice, washed
2 cups water
pinch of sea salt

Place the sweet rice, water, and sea salt in a pressure cooker. Cook as for plain sweet rice. When the rice is done, remove from the burner and allow the pressure to come down. Remove the cover. Either leave the rice in the cooker or place it in a heavy wooden bowl.

Moisten a thick wood pestle with cold water to prevent the rice from sticking to it. Pound the rice for about 45 minutes to 1 hour until the grains are completely crushed. From time to time, sprinkle a few drops of water over the rice and moisten the pestle to prevent sticking. Dust a cookie sheet with rice flour. Moisten your hands and spread the sticky mochi evenly over the cookie sheet so that it is about 1/2 inch thick. Cover with cheesecloth to keep out dust and let the mochi sit in a refrigerator or cool place for several days until it becomes dry and hard to the touch. Wrap in paper or wax paper and store in the refrigerator or a cool place.

An alternative way of drying and storing is to spoon the sticky mochi into ziplock sandwich bags. Seal the bags and spread the mochi evenly in the bags by pounding it flat with the palm of your hands so that it is about 1/2 inch thick. Place the bags in a refrigerator or cool place for 1 to 2 days and then freeze to store. Let the mochi thaw before slicing.

To serve mochi, cut it into pieces. You can pan-fry (with or without oil), deep-fry, steam, bake, or make waffles with it. Cooked mochi is also great in miso or tamari broth soups.

Sweet Rice and Millet Mochi

1 1/2 cups organic sweet brown rice, washed
1/2 cup organic millet, washed
2 1/4 cups water
pinch of sea salt

Place the sweet rice, millet, water, and sea salt in a pressure cooker and mix well. Pressure cook the same as for plain mochi. When the grain has finished cooking, bring the pressure down, remove the cover, and pound as suggested above. Dry the mochi using any of the methods explained previously.

Black Soybean Mochi

1/4 cup organic black soybeans, washed
1 strip of kombu, 1 inch square
water, including soaking water used to soak beans
pinch of sea salt
several drops of tamari soy sauce
2 cups organic sweet rice, cooked and pounded into mochi

Place the kombu in the bottom of a pot. Add the soybeans and water to just cover the beans. Do not cover. Bring to a boil over a high flame. Reduce the flame to medium-low and simmer for 2 1/2 to 3 hours or until the beans are 80 percent done. During the first 20 minutes, a gray foam will rise to the surface. Skim this off and discard it. While the beans are cooking, periodically add enough cold water to just cover the beans. This will need to be done several times.

When the beans are 80 percent done, add the sea salt and cook until done.

Turn the flame to high, add several drops of soy sauce, and continue to cook until all remaining liquid has evaporated. Place the cooked soybeans in the bowl or pressure cooker with the freshly pounded mochi. With a heavy spoon, mix the beans in thoroughly and evenly with the mochi. The black soybean mochi is now ready to dry and store before cooking.

Sesame Seed Mochi

1/4 cup tan or black sesame seeds, roasted
2 cups sweet brown rice, freshly cooked

Place the roasted sesame seeds in the bowl or pressure cooker with the freshly cooked sweet rice. Pound until all the grains are completely crushed. The sesame mochi is now ready to dry and store as suggested above.

Raisin-Cinnamon Mochi

1/2 cup organic raisins
water or organic apple juice
1/2 tsp organic cinnamon
2 cups sweet rice, freshly cooked

Place the raisins and cinnamon in a saucepan. Add enough water or apple juice to half-cover the raisins. Stir and bring to a boil. Cover, reduce the flame to medium-low, and simmer for 10 minutes, or until the raisins are soft and tender. Remove the cover, turn the flame to high, and cook off all remaining liquid. Place the cooked raisins in a bowl or pressure cooker with the freshly cooked sweet rice. Pound the rice and raisins until all the grains are completely crushed. The raisin-cinnamon mochi is now ready to dry and store.

Pan-Fried Mochi (Without Oil)

10 pieces of mochi, 3 inches by 2 inches
tamari soy sauce
chopped scallion, for garnish

Place the mochi in a heated cast iron or heavy stainless steel skillet. Reduce the flame to low, cover, and brown one side of the mochi. Remove the cover, turn the mochi pieces over, and brown the other side. As the other side is browning, the mochi will puff up slightly. When puffed up and both sides are browned, remove and place on a serving platter. Before eating, sprinkle 1 to 3 drops of tamari soy sauce over the mochi. Garnish with fresh chopped scallion.

Pan-Fried Mochi (With Oil)

10 pieces of mochi, 3 inches by 2 inches
tamari soy sauce
daikon, freshly grated
light or dark sesame oil

Brush a heavy skillet with a little oil and heat. Place the mochi in the skillet, cover, and reduce the flame to low. Brown one side and remove the cover. Turn the mochi over and brown the other side. When the mochi puffs up and is brown on both sides, place it on a serving platter. Before eating, sprinkle 1 to 3 drops of tamari soy sauce over the mochi and place 1/2 to 1 teaspoon of fresh grated daikon on top. Eat hot.

Mochi with Nori

10 pieces mochi, 3 inches by 2 inches
1 sheet nori, toasted
5 tsp grated daikon
tamari soy sauce

Place the mochi in a heated, heavy skillet. Turn the flame to high, cover, and brown one side. Turn the mochi over, brown the other side, and cook until the mochi puffs up. Cut the nori in several strips about 4 inches long and 3 inches wide. Place 2 drops of soy sauce and 1/2 teaspoon of grated daikon on one side of each piece. Wrap 1 strip of toasted nori around each piece of mochi. Place on a serving platter. Garnish with grated raw daikon.

Deep-Fried Mochi

10 pieces of mochi, 3 inches by 2 inches
sesame or safflower oil, for deep-frying
tamari soy sauce
daikon, freshly grated

Place 2 to 3 inches of oil in a deep-frying pot and heat. Place half of the mochi squares in the hot oil and deep-fry until golden brown and puffed up. Remove and drain on paper towels. Deep-fry the remaining mochi and place on paper towels to drain. Arrange the mochi on a serving platter. Sprinkle 1 to 3 drops of soy sauce on each piece of mochi and garnish with freshly grated daikon.

Sweet Pecan or Walnut Mochi

10 pieces mochi, 3 inches by 2 inches, pan-fried in dry skillet
1 cup pecans or walnuts
tamari soy sauce
1/4 cup brown rice syrup, warmed
lemon or tangerine juice

Heat a skillet and dry-roast the nuts until they turn golden and release a nutty fragrance. Sprinkle several drops of soy sauce over the nuts, mix, and roast 1 more minute. Remove and place on a cutting board. Chop very fine and place in a bowl. Mix the lemon or tangerine juice with the warm syrup. Dip the pan-fried mochi in the hot rice syrup. Roll each piece of mochi in the chopped nuts until completely coated. Remove and arrange on a serving platter. Eat hot.

Mochi Chips

1/2 lb mochi
light sesame or safflower oil, for deep-frying
tamari soy sauce

Slice the mochi in thin rectangles or squares. Set aside to dry for 1 day. Heat 2 to 3 inches of oil in a deep-frying pot. Place the pieces of dried mochi in the hot oil and deep-fry until golden and crisp. Remove and drain. Place in a bowl. Sprinkle a few drops of soy sauce over the chips and mix. Serve.

Baked Mochi with Sweet Azuki Beans

1/2 cup organic azuki beans, washed and soaked 6 to 8 hours
1 strip kombu, 2 inches long, soaked and diced
2 Tbsp organic raisins
1/4 cup dried apples, soaked and chopped
water, including water used to soak beans and dried apples

barley malt or rice syrup
pinch of sea salt
10 pieces plain mochi, 3 inches by 2 inches

Place the kombu in the bottom of a heavy saucepan. Place the raisins, dried apples, and azuki beans in the pot. Add enough water to just cover the azuki beans. Cover the pot and bring to a boil over a high flame. Reduce the flame to medium-low and simmer, adding water from time to time to just cover the beans, for 1 1/2 to 2 hours, or until the beans are 80 percent done. Add the sea salt and barley malt or rice syrup. Cover and cook for another 20 minutes or until the beans are soft and have absorbed most of the liquid. Mash with a wooden pestle or grind in a suribachi until smooth and thick.

Place the pieces of mochi in the bottom of a glass baking dish. Spread the puréed beans over the mochi. Cover the baking dish. Bake at 350 degrees F. for 20 minutes or until the mochi puffs up on the bottom of the dish and the azuki beans are hot. Remove and serve.

Sweet Azuki Beans with Mochi

2 to 3 cups cooked sweet azuki beans (see above recipe)
10 pieces mochi, 3 inches by 2 inches, pan-fried

Cook the azuki beans as in the above recipe but leave a little more water at the end of cooking so that the beans have a slightly thinner consistency. You may need to add a little more barley malt to the beans to compensate for the extra water. Place two pieces of toasted mochi in each serving bowl. Pour the hot, sweet azuki beans over the mochi and serve.

Baked Mochi Croutons

Baked mochi can be used in place of bread croutons in soups and other dishes. Baking makes the mochi a little drier and harder than pan-frying, but when the croutons are placed in hot soup, they hold their shape better.

1/2 lb mochi, cut in 1 inch squares

Place the mochi squares on a dry cookie or baking sheet so that they do not touch each other. Bake at 350 degrees F. for about 20 minutes or until the mochi puffs up. Remove and place several in each bowl of hot soup. Garnish and serve.

Mochi with Creamy Nut Topping

10 pieces mochi, 3 inches by 2 inches
1/4 cup walnuts, pecans, almonds, or peanuts, rinsed
2 to 3 Tbsp water
tamari soy sauce

Heat a skillet and roast the nuts until they turn golden and release a nutty fragrance. Remove and place on a cutting board. Chop very fine. Place the chopped nuts in a suribachi and grind to a smooth paste. Add the water and a few drops of tamari soy sauce for a slightly salty flavor. Grind again until smooth and creamy. Pan-fry the mochi in a dry skillet until it becomes golden brown on both sides and begins to puff up. Spread a thin layer of the nut cream on top of each piece of mochi and serve hot.

Mochi with Sesame Seed Cream Topping

10 pieces mochi, 3 inches by 2 inches
1/4 cup tan or black sesame seeds, washed
2 to 3 Tbsp water
tamari soy sauce

Heat a skillet, add the sesame seeds, and dry-roast until they begin to pop and release a nutty fragrance. Remove and place in a suribachi. Grind until about 80 percent crushed. Add the water and a few drops of soy sauce for a slightly salty flavor. Grind to a smooth paste. Heat a skillet and pan-fry the mochi until it becomes golden brown on both sides and begins to puff up. Spread a thin layer of the sesame cream on each piece of mochi and serve hot.

Broiled Mochi

10 pieces mochi, 3 inches by 2 inches
1 sheet nori, toasted and cut in strips 2 inches wide
tamari soy sauce
daikon, freshly grated, for garnish

Brush the mochi on one side with tamari soy sauce and place on a cookie sheet. Place in the broiler, making sure the mochi is not too close to the flame. Otherwise, it may burn. When golden, turn over and brown the other side. Remove, place a small amount of grated daikon on top, and wrap each piece with a strip of toasted nori. Serve hot.

Steamed Mochi

For a more moist way of preparing mochi, try steaming it. Be careful not to steam the mochi too long or it will completely melt and cover the bottom of the pan.

10 pieces mochi, 3 inches by 2 inches
water
ṭamari soy sauce

Place enough water in a skillet to just cover the bottom. Cover and bring to a boil. Place the mochi in the skillet. Sprinkle 1 to 2 drops of soy sauce on top of each piece. Cover and steam until tender but not completely melted. Remove and serve hot.

Mochi Waffles with Lemon-Walnut Syrup

1 lb mochi
1/2 cup brown rice syrup
2 to 3 Tbsp water
1/4 cup walnuts, roasted and finely chopped
2 to 3 tsp lemon juice, to taste

Slice the mochi in quarters, about 3 1/2 by 2 1/2 by 1/4 inch thick (see diagram). Place 1 piece of mochi in each section of a dry (do not oil) waffle iron. Cook until puffed up and slightly crispy but not hard and dry. Repeat until all mochi has been cooked. Place on a serving platter. While the waffles are cooking, place the rice syrup in a saucepan with the water, roasted walnuts, and a little freshly squeezed lemon juice. When the syrup is hot, pour it over each serving of waffles.

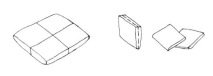

Mochi Pancakes with Vegetable Filling

1/4 cup onion, diced
1/4 cup mushrooms, sliced thin
1/4 cup carrot, sliced in thin matchsticks
1/2 cup cabbage, finely shredded
1/2 cup mung bean sprouts
water
dark sesame oil
1/2 lb plain mochi, coarsely grated
1/2 sheet nori, toasted and cut in thin strips
tamari soy sauce

Brush a small amount of oil in a skillet and heat. Sauté the onion for 1 to 2 minutes. Add the mushrooms and sauté' 1 minute. Add the carrot, cabbage, and mung bean sprouts. Add enough cold water to just coat the bottom of the skillet. Cover, reduce the flame to medium-low, and simmer for 3 to 4 minutes. Remove the cover, sprinkle several drops of soy sauce over the vegetables, and mix in. Cook 1 minute more. Place the cooked vegetables in a bowl.

On a heated, dry pancake griddle, place 1/4 cup coarsely grated mochi, forming a circle or pancake shape. Spread 1 to 2 tablespoonfuls of the sautéed vegetables on top of the mochi. Sprinkle several strips of nori over the vegetables. Next, quickly sprinkle another 1/4 cup grated mochi on top of the vegetables and nori to create a sandwich effect. By now the bottom layer of the mochi should have melted and browned slightly. Flip the pancake over and brown the other side. The mochi will melt completely, encasing the vegetable filling. Remove and arrange on a serving platter. Repeat until all ingredients have been used. Serve hot.

Mochi Pancakes with Fruit Filling

1/2 lb plain mochi, coarsely grated
1 apple, cored, peeled, and sliced
1 pear, cored, peeled, and sliced
2 Tbsp raisins
1 to 1 1/2 cups apple juice or water
1 to 1 1/2 Tbsp kuzu, diluted
pinch of sea salt

Place the apples, pears, raisins, juice, and sea salt in a saucepan. Cover and bring to a boil. Reduce the flame to medium-low and simmer 3 to 4 minutes until the fruit is tender. Add the kuzu, stirring constantly, until it becomes thick and translucent. Remove from the flame.

On a heated, dry pancake griddle, place 1/4 cup of grated mochi, forming it into a circle like a pancake. Spread 1 to 2 tablespoonfuls of the stewed fruit evenly on top of the mochi. Next, sprinkle another 1/4 cup of grated mochi on top of the stewed fruit. The bottom layer of mochi should now be slightly browned and melted. Flip the pancake over and cook on the other side until browned and the mochi melts. The fruit topping should now be sandwiched between the two layers of melted mochi. Repeat until all ingredients are used. Serve hot.

Other variation of fresh or dried fruit may be substituted for the above and used as a filling.

Steamed Cabbage and Mochi

5 cabbage leaves, left whole
5 pieces mochi, 3 inches by 2 inches
water

Place enough water in a skillet to just cover the bottom. Cover and bring to a boil. Place 1 piece of mochi on top of each cabbage leaf (near the bottom portion of the leaf). Fold the leaf over (in half) and cover the mochi, creating a sandwich effect. Place the mochi-stuffed leaves in the skillet. Cover and steam for 3 to 4 minutes until the leaves are tender and the mochi has melted inside. Remove the stuffed leaves, slice in half or thirds, and serve. Chinese cabbage can be substituted for regular cabbage but only requires 2 to 3 minutes cooking time.

Tempeh, Sauerkraut, and Mochi Skillet

1 package tempeh (8 oz), sliced in cubes or rectangular strips
1 cup green cabbage, shredded
1/2 cup sauerkraut
1/2 lb mochi, sliced in strips
sesame oil (optional)
water

Heat a small amount of oil in a skillet. Place the tempeh in the skillet and brown. Add enough water to half-cover. Layer the sauerkraut and cabbage on top of the tempeh. Cover and bring to a boil. Reduce the flame to medium-low and simmer for about 15 minutes. Remove the cover and lay the mochi strips on top of the tempeh and vegetables. Do not mix. Cover and cook until the mochi melts. Remove and serve hot.

Mochi Pizza

5 Tbsp corn oil
1/2 cup onion, diced
1 1/2 cups mushrooms, thinly sliced
1/2 cup green pepper, diced (optional)
2 to 3 tsp tamari soy sauce
1 lb brown rice mochi, coarsely grated (like cheese) on a box
    grater
1/2 cup seitan, sliced in thin strips
1/2 cup black olives, sliced in thin rounds
1/2 lb firm-style tofu, drained
1/4 cup scallion, finely chopped
2 Tbsp umeboshi vinegar
2 Tbsp water

To make the tofu cream, place the tofu, scallion, umeboshi vinegar, and water in a blender and purée until smooth and creamy. Remove and place in a small bowl. Place 1 tablespoonful corn oil in a skillet and heat. Add the onion, green pepper and mushrooms. Sauté 2 to 3 minutes. Season with tamari soy sauce and sauté for another 2 to 3 minutes. Place in a small bowl.

Heat 2 tablespoonfuls corn oil in a 10- to 12-inch cast iron skillet. Cover the bottom with half of the grated mochi. Spread half of the seitan and sautéed vegetables over the mochi. Next, spoon half of the tofu cream over the vegetables and seitan and spread it evenly. Place half of the sliced olives on top of the tofu cream. Turn the flame up slightly to brown the bottom and until the mochi becomes crisp (about 10 minutes). Using a spatula, loosen the mochi from the skillet. It should move very easily. Tip the skillet slightly and let the pizza slide on to a baking sheet. Place the pizza under the broiler and broil for about 5 minutes to thoroughly cook the tofu cream.

Remove the pizza from the broiler, slice in quarters, and place on serving plates. To make another pizza, repeat the above process with the remaining ingredients. Cook, slice, and serve as above.

Vegetable Nabé Pot with Mochi

Nabé is a clay pot from Japan that serves both as a cooking pot and serving dish. Nabé dishes can include a variety of vegetables and foods like tofu, noodles, mochi, seitan, and fu. Nabé is a great one-dish meal that is quick and easy to prepare.

5 to 6 pieces of mochi, pan-fried
2 cups daikon, finely grated
5 to 6 fresh shiitake mushrooms, with the very tip of the stems removed
6 cups water
1 strip kombu, 2 to 3 inches long
1 Tbsp bonito flakes (optional)
1 Tbsp mirin (sweet cooking sake)
2 tsp tamari soy sauce
pinch of sea salt
1 bunch watercress, washed
1 cup Chinese cabbage, sliced in 1 inch thick pieces
1/2 tsp lemon juice

Place the kombu and water in a nabé pot. Cover, place over a medium flame, and bring to a boil. Reduce the flame to medium-low and simmer for 4 to 5 minutes. Remove the kombu and set aside for future use. Add the grated daikon, tamari soy sauce, sea salt, mirin, and shiitake to the stock. Bring to a boil. Reduce the flame to medium-low. Add the lemon juice, watercress, and Chinese cabbage. Cover and simmer for about 1 minute until the greens are tender but still bright green. Remove the cover, add the mochi, and simmer without a cover for 1 minute. Remove and serve hot.

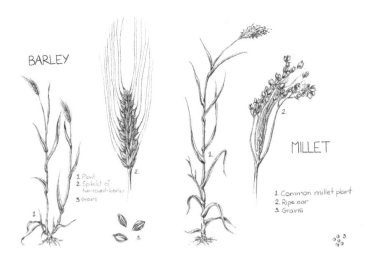

BARLEY

1. Plant
2. Spikelet of
   two-rowed-barley
3. Grains

MILLET

1. Common millet plant
2. Ripe ear
3. Grains

Chapter 3
Barley and Millet

Barley is the oldest known cultivated grain. It has been cultivated for thousands of years in East and West. Many people around the world believed that it not only helped restore health but also contributed to vitality and longevity. By itself, barley has a rather neutral taste. It has a chewy texture, is easy to digest, and very nourishing. Barley helps offset the effects caused by eating too much animal food, and is delicious when prepared in soups, stews, casseroles, and salads, or when combined with brown rice. Because it has more light, upward energy, it can be used often in the spring and summer. Barley can also be ground into flour and used to make breads and pastries.

Several types of whole barley are available in natural food stores. The most natural and vitamin-rich barley is called hulled or hulless barley, which means that it has the protective outer shell removed but not the vitamin-rich endosperm and germ layers. It is similar to brown rice but a little more fat or round. It is the most chewy of the various types of barley. There is also a partially refined barley that has had part of the endosperm layer removed through a process called pearling. This type of barley is referred to as pearled or partially pearled barley. This type of barley is more off-white in color. It is slightly less nutritious than hulled or hulless barley and less chewy.

The barley you find in most supermarkets is also called "pearled" barley. However, the endosperm and germ layers have been removed. It is basically carbohydrate and starch with all the other nutrients removed. It is very white in color, smaller in size than other types of barley, and cooks very quickly.

There is another food that should not be confused with pearled barley. In

Japanese it is called *hato mugi*, and in English, is referred to as *pearl barley*. It is also called Job's tears. This food is actually a wild grass, and is thought to be a relative of millet and sorghum. Hato mugi has properties that are similar to barley. It is round in shape and off-white in color, with a light tan streak running down one side. If you stretch your imagination slightly, it does resemble a pearl. It has a slightly stronger flavor than barley and is grown in China, Taiwan, Japan, Indonesia, and the Philippines. Like barley, hato mugi has strong upward energy and is eaten to help dissolve excess protein and fat in the body resulting from the consumption of animal food.

Roasted barley makes a delicious tea, known in Japanese as *mugi-cha*. In the West, barley hops are used in making beer, and barley malt is used as a natural sweetening in place of sugar and other more refined products in a wide assortment of desserts and baked goods.

Pressure-Cooked Barley

2 cups organic hulled or unhulled barley, washed
3 cups water
pinch of sea salt

Place the barley and water in a pressure cooker. Set aside and soak for 4 to 6 hours. Add the sea salt to the pressure cooker, cover, and place over a high flame. When the pressure is up, reduce the flame to medium-low, and place a flame deflector under the cooker. Pressure cook for 50 minutes. Remove from the flame, allow the pressure to come down, and remove the cover. Let the barley sit in the cooker for 4 to 5 minutes before placing in a serving bowl.

Boiled Barley

2 cups organic hulled or unhulled barley, washed
4 cups water
pinch of sea salt

Place the barley, water, and sea salt in a heavy pot. Cover and bring to a boil over a high flame. Reduce the flame to medium-low, place a flame deflector under the pot, and simmer for 1 hour and 15 minutes. Remove from the flame and place in a serving bowl.

Barley with Whole Oats

1 1/2 cups organic barley, washed and soaked
1/2 cup organic whole oats, washed and soaked
3 cups water, including water used to soak grains
pinch of sea salt

Place the barley, whole oats, water, and sea salt in a pressure cooker. Cover and bring up to pressure over a high flame. Reduce the flame to medium-low, place a flame deflector under the cooker, and cook for 50 minutes. Remove from the flame and allow the pressure to come down. Remove the cover and let the grains sit for 4 to 5 minutes before placing in a serving bowl.

Barley with Sweet Corn

2 cups organic barley, washed and soaked
2 ears sweet corn, removed from the cob
3 cups water, including water used to soak barley
pinch of sea salt

Place the barley, sweet corn, water, and sea salt in a pressure cooker. Cover and bring up to pressure over a high flame. Reduce the flame to medium-low and place a flame deflector under the cooker. Cook for 50 minutes. Remove from the flame and allow the pressure to come down. Remove the cover and let the grains sit for 4 to 5 minutes before placing in a serving bowl.

Barley with Wild Rice

1 1/2 cups organic barley, washed and soaked
1/2 cup organic wild rice, washed
3 cups water, including water used to soak barley
pinch of sea salt

Place the barley, wild rice, water, and sea salt in a pressure cooker. Cover and bring up to pressure over a high flame. Reduce the flame to medium-low, place a flame deflector under the cooker, and cook for 50 minutes. Remove from the flame and allow the pressure to come down. Remove the cover and let the grains sit for 4 to 5 minutes before placing in a serving bowl.

Barley with Lentils

1 1/2 cups organic pearled barley, washed
1/2 cup organic brown or green lentils, washed
4 cups water
pinch of sea salt

Place barley, lentils, water, and sea salt in a heavy pot. Cover and bring to a boil over a high flame. Reduce the flame to medium-low and simmer for 1 hour and 15 minutes. Remove from the flame and place in a serving bowl.

Barley with Chickpeas

1 1/2 cups organic barley, washed and soaked
1/2 cup organic chickpeas, washed and soaked, discard water
3 cups water
pinch of sea salt

Place the barley, chickpeas, water, and sea salt in a pressure cooker. Cover and bring up to pressure over a high flame. Reduce the flame to medium-low and place a flame deflector under the cooker. Cook for 60 minutes. Remove from the flame and allow the pressure to come down. Remove the cover and let the barley and chickpeas sit for 4 to 5 minutes before placing in a serving bowl.

Baked Barley with Beans

1 cup organic pearled barley, washed
1/2 cup organic navy, lima, or northern beans, washed and
    soaked, discard soaking water
4 to 5 shiitake mushrooms, soaked and sliced
1 strip kombu, 2 to 3 inches long, soaked and diced
1 cup onion, diced
1 cup sweet corn, removed from the cob
1/2 cup carrot, diced
1/4 cup celery, diced
2 Tbsp bonito flakes (optional)
6 to 7 cups water, including water used to soak shiitake and kombu
tamari soy sauce

Place all the ingredients in a heavy baking dish. Sprinkle a few drops of soy sauce on top and mix thoroughly. Cover the dish and bake at 325 to 350 degrees F. for 2 to 2 1/2 hours or until the beans are tender. Remove and serve.

Barley, Mushroom, and Bean Casserole

1 cup organic pearled barley, washed
1/2 cup organic lima beans, washed and soaked
1 cup onion, diced
1 cup mushrooms, washed and diced
2 Tbsp bonito flakes (optional)
1 Tbsp parsley, minced
4 1/2 to 5 cups water
2 tsp corn oil
2 cloves garlic, minced (optional)
1 tsp tamari soy sauce

Place the oil in a heavy pot and heat. Add the onions and optional garlic. Sauté for 2 to 3 minutes. Add the mushrooms and sauté for another 2 to 3 minutes. Add all remaining ingredients, cover, and bring to a boil over a high flame. Reduce the flame to low and simmer for 1 1/2 to 2 hours until the beans are tender and the water has been absorbed. Remove and serve.

Barley Gomoku

1 cup organic pearled barley, washed
1 strip kombu, 1 to 2 inches long, soaked and diced
3 shiitake mushrooms, soaked and diced
1/4 cup cooked seitan, diced
2 pieces dried tofu, soaked and diced
1/4 cup carrot, diced
2 Tbsp celery, diced
1 ear sweet corn, removed from the cob
1 Tbsp dried lotus root, soaked and diced
1 1/2 cups water

Place all ingredients in a pressure cooker, cover, and bring up to pressure over a high flame. Reduce the flame to medium-low and place a flame deflector under the cooker. Cook for 45 minutes. Remove from the flame and allow the pressure to come down. Remove the cover and let the gomoku sit for 4 to 5 minutes before placing in a serving bowl.

Barley Stuffed Cabbage Leaves

2 cups cooked barley
6 to 8 green cabbage leaves, washed
1 cup onion, diced
1/2 cup mushrooms, washed and diced
1/2 cup cooked seitan (optional), ground in a hand food mill
1/4 cup sunflower seeds, toasted
1/4 cup parsley, minced
1 Tbsp fresh lemon juice
2 cups water
2 to 3 Tbsp unbleached white flour
2 tsp corn oil
tamari soy sauce

Heat the oil in a skillet. Sauté the onion for 2 to 3 minutes. Add the mushrooms and sauté for another 2 to 3 minutes. Remove and place in a mixing bowl. Add the seitan, sunflower seeds, parsley, and lemon juice and mix thoroughly. Boil the cabbage leaves with a pinch of sea salt for 1 to 2 minutes until slightly limp. Remove and drain. Cut out the very bottom part of the tough stem or rib of each leaf. Place about 1/4 to 1/3 cup of the barley stuffing on each leaf and roll up, folding the edges in toward the center. Fasten the leaves together securely with toothpicks.

Place the stuffed cabbage leaves in a heavy pot. Add the water, cover, and bring to a boil. Reduce the flame to low and simmer for 35 to 40 minutes until the leaves are very soft. Remove the cabbage rolls and place in a serving dish. Dilute the flour in a little cold water and gradually add it to the cooking water from the cabbage. Stir constantly until thick, creamy, and smooth. Season to taste with a little tamari soy sauce. Simmer for about 5 minutes. Pour the sauce over the stuffed cabbage and serve hot.

Barley Stuffed Squash

1 acorn or buttercup squash, washed, halved, seeds removed
1 cup cooked barley
1 cup whole wheat bread crumbs
2 tsp corn oil
1 cup onion, diced
1/4 cup celery, diced
2 tsp parsley, minced
1/2 cup mushrooms, washed and diced

1 tsp tamari soy sauce
water

Place the oil in a skillet and heat. Sauté the onion for 1 to 2 minutes. Add the mushrooms and celery and sauté for another 2 to 3 minutes. Add the soy sauce and mix. Add the barley and sauté for 1 to 2 minutes. Place in a mixing bowl. Add the bread crumbs and enough water to just moisten the crumbs. Fill the squash halves with equal amounts of stuffing. Cover with foil wrap and bake at 400 degrees F. for about 40 to 45 minutes until the squash is tender. Remove the foil and brown the stuffing slightly. Remove and place in a serving dish.

Barley with Mixed Vegetables

1 cups organic barley, washed
1 1/2 cups water
pinch of sea salt
1/2 cup fresh green peas, shelled
1/2 cup sweet corn, removed from cob
1/2 cup carrot, diced
1/4 cup sunflower seeds, roasted
water

Pressure cook the barley for 50 minutes as described previously. Place 1/2 inch of water in a saucepan, cover, and bring to a boil. Place the sweet corn in the pan and boil for 1 1/2 to 2 minutes. Remove, drain, and place in a mixing bowl. Next, boil the green peas for 2 to 2 1/2 minutes. Remove, drain, and place in the mixing bowl. Boil the carrot for 1 1/2 minutes, remove, and drain. Place in the mixing bowl. Remove the cooked barley from the pressure cooker and place in the mixing bowl. Place the sunflower seeds in the bowl. Thoroughly mix all the ingredients and place in a serving bowl.

Fried Barley with Vegetables

2 cups cooked barley
1/2 cup mushrooms, diced
1/4 cup celery, diced
1/2 cup scallion, finely chopped
1 to 2 tsp sesame oil
tamari soy sauce

Place the oil in a skillet and heat. Add the mushrooms and celery. Sauté for 2 to 3 minutes. Add the barley and sprinkle a few drops of soy sauce over it. Cover and reduce the flame to low. Cook until the barley is hot. Remove the cover and sprinkle the chopped scallion on top. Add a few more drops of soy sauce, cover, and cook for 2 to 3 minutes. Remove the cover and mix the barley and vegetables. Place in a serving bowl.

Fried Barley with Tempeh and Summer Vegetables

2 cups cooked barley
1 cup tempeh, diced
1/2 cup sweet corn, removed from the cob
1/4 cup green beans, sliced
1/4 cup green peas, shelled
1/4 cup chives or parsley, minced
1 to 2 tsp sesame oil
tamari soy sauce

Place the oil in a skillet and heat. Add the tempeh and sauté until slightly browned. Add the corn, beans, and peas. Place the barley on top of the vegetables. Sprinkle with a few drops of tamari soy sauce. Cover, reduce the flame to low, and cook until the barley is hot. Remove the cover, add the chives or parsley, and sprinkle a few more drops of soy sauce over the barley. Cover and cook for 2 to 3 minutes. Remove the cover and mix the vegetables, tempeh, and barley. Cook for another minute or so. Remove and place in a serving bowl.

Barley-Vegetable Salad with Tamari-Ginger Sauce

3 cups cooked barley
1/2 cup carrots, diced
1/4 cup celery, diced
1/4 cup red onion, diced
1/4 cup red radish, halved and thinly sliced
1/4 cup sweet corn, removed from the cob
1/4 cup green peas or green beans
5 shiitake mushrooms, soaked and diced
1/2 cup cooked chickpeas
1/4 cup seitan, diced
water

Tamari-Ginger Sauce

1 Tbsp tamari soy sauce
1/4 to 1/3 tsp ginger juice
1/2 to 2/3 cup water

Place the cooked barley, chickpeas, red onion, red radish, celery, and chick-peas in a mixing bowl. Place a small amount of water in a saucepan and bring to a boil. Boil the sweet corn for 1 1/2 minutes, the carrot for 1 1/2 minutes, and the green peas or green beans for 2 to 3 minutes. Place in the mixing bowl. Place 1/2 inch water in a saucepan and season with tamari soy sauce for a slightly salty flavor. Place the shiitake mushrooms in the saucepan, cover, and bring to a boil. Reduce the flame to medium-low and simmer for about 10 minutes until tender. Remove and drain. Place the shiitake in the mixing bowl. Set the cooking water aside and use for soup stock.

To prepare the dressing, place the tamari soy sauce and water in a saucepan and heat. Turn off the flame, and add the ginger juice, and mix. Mix the barley and vegetables in the mixing bowl. Pour the tamari-ginger dressing over the barley salad just before serving. Place in a serving dish.

Barley-Lentil Salad with Umeboshi Dressing

2 cups cooked barley
1 cup cooked green or brown lentils
1/2 cup carrot, diced
1/4 cup celery, diced
1 cup snow peas, sliced in half
1/4 cup parsley, minced
1/2 cup red radish, halved and sliced thin
1/4 cup sunflower seeds, roasted

Umeboshi Dressing

1/4 cup scallion or chives, chopped
2 umeboshi plums, pits removed
3/4 cup water

Place the barley, lentils, celery, red radish, parsley, and sunflower seeds in a mixing bowl. Place 1/2 inch water in a saucepan and bring to a boil. Boil the carrots for 1 1/2 minutes, remove, and drain. Place in the mixing bowl. Boil the snow peas for 1 minute, remove, and drain. Place in the mixing bowl.

Grind the umeboshi plums in a suribachi until they are a smooth paste. Add the scallion and grind 1 minute. Add the water and purée until smooth. Mix the salad ingredients and pour the dressing on the salad just before serving. Mix well and place in a serving bowl.

Summer Barley Salad

2 cups leftover barley
2 ears sweet corn, removed from cob
1/4 cup celery, diced
1/4 cup carrot, finely grated
1/2 cup snow peas, sliced in half
1/2 cup cucumber, thinly sliced
1/4 cup Macintosh apple, thinly sliced
red leafy, Boston, or bibb lettuce leaves
2 Tbsp umeboshi vinegar
1 tsp brown rice or sweet brown rice vinegar
1 tsp mirin (sweet cooking sake)
1 Tbsp parsley, scallion, or chives, minced
1/2 to 3/4 cup water

Place the cooked barley, celery, carrot, cucumber, and apple in a mixing bowl. Blanch the snow peas in a small amount of boiling water for 1 minute, remove, and drain. Place them in the mixing bowl with the other ingredients. Place the umeboshi vinegar, rice vinegar, mirin, and parsley in a suribachi. Grind for 1 minute. Add water and mix well. Pour the dressing over the salad ingredients and mix thoroughly. Line a bowl or platter with the lettuce leaves. Place the barley salad on top of the leaves and serve.

Barley-Seitan Burgers

1 cup cooked barley
1 cup cooked seitan, chopped
1/4 cup tan sesame seeds, toasted
2 Tbsp onion, minced
2 Tbsp celery, minced
2 Tbsp carrot, minced
1 Tbsp parsley, minced
whole wheat pastry flour
tamari soy sauce
sesame or corn oil

Mix the barley, onion, celery, carrot, and parsley. Grind the seitan in a hand food mill and place in the mixing bowl. Mix in a small amount of whole wheat pastry flour and water (just enough to hold the mixture together). Season with a few drops of soy sauce and mix again. Form the mixture into patties or burgers. Place the oil in a skillet or on a pancake griddle and heat. Fry the burgers on one side until browned. Flip over and fry the other side until browned. Remove and place on a serving platter.

Millet

Millet, a small round grain thought to have originated in Asia and Africa, is a staple food in macrobiotic cooking. In China it was considered one of the five sacred crops, along with rice, barley, wheat, and soybeans. Millet has been used as a food since Neolithic times, and was a staple in China, India, Japan, Korea, Africa, and Europe. There are temperate, semi-tropical, and tropical varieties of millet. It is usually yellow in color but there are some red varieties also. There are both non-glutinous and glutinous varieties, although the glutinous variety, called *kibi awa*, is hard to find outside of Japan. Glutinous millet is sweet and sticky, much like sweet brown rice. It makes wonderful porridge and desserts, and can be used to make millet mochi.

Millet is high in protein, iron, and B vitamins, especially niacin. These small, compact grains have an incredible capacity to absorb water. Thus a little goes a long way. When cooked, millet becomes light and fluffy, but if you do not add enough water to it, it can be somewhat dry and bland. Because of its dry, fluffy consistency, it is usually served as a soft gruel, in soups, cooked with beans and vegetables, or served with a gravy or sauce. It can be used in breads, stuffings, burgers, puddings, and cakes. In Japan it is mixed with sweet brown rice to make millet mochi. It can also be fermented to produce a sweet drink called millet amazake.

Millet can occasionally be dry-roasted prior to cooking to bring out its deliciously sweet, nutty flavor. Millet can be quite warming to the body, and can be used more frequently in late summer, autumn, and winter. When washing millet, make sure to drain it in a very fine wire mesh strainer. Millet will fall through most colanders or large mesh strainers

Millet cooks quickly, usually in 25 to 30 minutes. It is most often boiled. Some varieties may require up to 35 minutes cooking time. Boiling produces a more moist dish. Millet can be pressure cooked in about 15 minutes but will turn out dry if not enough water is used.

Basic Boiled Millet

2 cups organic millet, washed
6 cups boiling water
pinch of sea salt

Place the water and sea salt in a pot, cover, and bring to a boil. Remove the cover and stir in the millet. Cover, reduce the flame to medium-low, and boil for 30 to 35 minutes. Remove the cover and place in a serving bowl.

Basic Boiled Millet Number 2

2 cups organic millet, washed
6 cups boiling water
1 strip kombu, 2 inches square, soaked and diced

Place the millet and kombu in the pot of boiling water. Cover and reduce the flame to medium-low. Simmer for 30 to 35 minutes. Remove from the flame and place in a serving bowl.

Basic Boiled Millet (Roasted)

2 cups organic millet, washed
6 cups boiling water
pinch of sea salt

After washing the millet, place in a strainer and drain. Heat a stainless steel skillet. Place the damp millet in the skillet and dry-roast, constantly stirring to evenly roast, for several minutes until a strong nutty fragrance is released and the millet turns slightly golden. Remove and place in a pot of boiling water with a pinch of sea salt. Cover and reduce the flame to medium-low. Simmer for 30 to 35 minutes. Remove from the flame and place in a serving bowl.

Basic Pressure-Cooked Millet

2 cups organic millet, washed
4 cups water
pinch of sea salt

Place the millet, water, and sea salt in a pressure cooker. Cover and bring up to pressure over a high flame. Reduce the flame to medium-low and place a flame deflector under the cooker. Cook for 12 to 15 minutes. Remove from the flame and allow the pressure to come down. Remove the cover and place the millet in a serving bowl.

Pressure-Cooked Millet with Sweet Brown Rice

1 cup organic millet, washed
1 cup sweet brown rice, washed and soaked 6 to 8 hours
3 1/2 to 4 cups water, including water used to soak rice
pinch of sea salt

Place the millet, sweet brown rice, water, and sea salt in a pressure cooker. Cover and bring up to pressure over a high flame. Reduce the flame to medium-low and place a flame deflector under the cooker. Cook for 45 minutes. Remove and allow the pressure to come down. Remove the cover and let the grains sit for 4 to 5 minutes before placing in a serving bowl.

Millet with Squash

2 cups organic millet, washed
1 cup buttercup or butternut squash, cubed
6 cups boiling water
pinch of sea salt

Place the millet, squash, and sea salt in the pot of boiling water. Cover and reduce the flame to medium-low. Simmer for 30 to 35 minutes. Remove from the flame and place in a serving dish.

Millet with Sweet Vegetables

2 cups organic millet, washed and dry-roasted
1/2 cup winter squash, cubed
1/2 cup cabbage, sliced in 1 inch chunks
1/4 cup onion, diced
1/4 cup carrot, diced
6 cups boiling water
pinch of sea salt

Place all of the above ingredients in a pot of boiling water. Mix and cover. Bring to a boil again. Reduce the flame to medium-low and simmer for 30 to 35 minutes. Remove the cover and place the millet and sweet vegetables in a serving bowl.

Millet with Sautéed Vegetables

2 cups organic millet, washed
1/4 cup onion, diced
3 shiitake mushrooms, soaked, stems removed, and diced
1/2 cup carrot, diced
1/2 cup green string beans, sliced in half
sesame oil
6 cups boiling water
pinch of sea salt

Place a small amount of sesame oil in a skillet and heat. Sauté the onions for 1 to 2 minutes. Add the shiitake, carrot, and string beans. Sauté for 2 to 3 minutes. Place the sautéed vegetables, millet, and sea salt in the pot of boiling water. Mix, cover, and bring to a boil again. Reduce the flame to medium-low and simmer for 30 to 35 minutes. Remove from the flame and place in a serving bowl.

Millet with Cauliflower

2 cups organic millet, washed
6 cups boiling water
2 cups cauliflower, cut in florets
pinch of sea salt

Place the millet, cauliflower, and sea salt in the pot of boiling water. Cover and bring to a boil again. Reduce the flame to medium-low and simmer for 30 to 35 minutes. Remove the cover and place in a serving bowl.

Millet with Almonds

2 cups organic millet, washed
1/2 cup organic almonds, washed
6 cups boiling water
pinch of sea salt

90

water, for blanching almonds

Place 1/2 inch water in a small saucepan, cover, and bring to a boil. Add the almonds, cover, and simmer for 1 minute. Pour the almonds into a strainer and drain. Squeeze each almond between your thumb and index finger to remove the skin. Discard the skins. Add the millet, almonds, and sea salt to the pot of boiling water. Mix, cover, and bring to a boil again. Reduce the flame to medium-low and simmer for 30 to 35 minutes. Remove from the flame and place the millet and almonds in a serving bowl.

Millet with Pumpkin Seeds and Shiso

2 cups organic millet, washed
6 cups boiling water
pinch of sea salt
1/2 cup pumpkin seeds, washed and dry-roasted
2 Tbsp shiso condiment

Boil the millet (as in the basic boiled millet recipe) for 30 to 35 minutes. Remove from the flame. Remove the cover and mix in the roasted pumpkin seeds and shiso condiment so they are evenly distributed throughout the millet. Place in a serving bowl.

Millet with Sesame Seeds and Chives

2 cups organic millet, washed
6 cups boiling water
pinch of sea salt
1/4 cup tan or black sesame seeds, washed and dry-roasted
1/4 cup chives, finely chopped

Boil the millet as instructed for 30 to 35 minutes. Remove from the flame. Remove the cover and thoroughly mix in the roasted sesame seeds and chives so they are evenly distributed throughout the grain. Serve.

Millet with Sweet Corn

2 cups organic millet, washed
3 ears sweet corn, removed from cob
6 cups boiling water

pinch of sea salt
parsley, minced, for garnish

Place the millet, sweet corn, and sea salt in the pot of boiling water. Mix, cover, and bring to a boil again. Reduce the flame to medium-low and simmer for 30 to 35 minutes. Remove from the flame. Place the millet and sweet corn in a serving bowl, mixing in the minced parsley as a garnish.

Millet with Seitan and Vegetables

2 cups organic millet, washed
1 cup cooked seitan, diced
1 cup green peas, shelled
1 ear sweet corn, removed from cob
6 cups boiling water

Place the millet, seitan, and vegetables in the pot of boiling water. Do not add sea salt as the seitan is cooked in soy sauce and is already salty. Mix the ingredients, cover, and bring to a boil again. Reduce the flame to medium-low and simmer for 30 to 35 minutes. Remove from the flame and place in a serving bowl.

Pressure-Cooked Millet Mashed Potatoes

2 cups organic millet, washed
1 medium-sized cauliflower, sliced in florets
1/2 cup organic red lentils, washed
6 1/2 cups water
pinch of sea salt

Place the millet, cauliflower, lentils, water, and sea salt in a pressure cooker. Mix thoroughly. Place the cover on the cooker and bring up to pressure over a high flame. Reduce the flame to medium-low and place a flame deflector under the cooker. Cook for 20 minutes. Remove from the flame and allow the pressure to come down. Remove the cover. With a potato masher or wooden pestle, mash the millet and cauliflower until they are the consistency of mashed potatoes. Place in a serving bowl.

Boiled Millet Mashed Potatoes

2 cups organic millet, washed
1 medium-sized cauliflower, sliced in florets
6 cups boiling water
pinch of sea salt

Place the millet, cauliflower, and sea salt in the pot of boiling water. Mix, cover, and bring to a boil again. Reduce the flame to medium-low and simmer for 30 to 35 minutes. Remove from the flame and take the cover off. Mash the millet and cauliflower with a potato masher or wooden pestle until they are the consistency of mashed potatoes. Place in a serving bowl.

Millet Mashed Potatoes with Red Pepper-Miso Sauce

5 to 6 cups cooked millet mashed potatoes
2 cups sweet red pepper, sliced thin
1 cup onion, sliced in thin half-moons
1 Tbsp mellow barley miso, puréed
1/2 cup plain soymilk
olive oil or rice bran oil
parsley, minced, for garnish

Place a small amount of oil in a skillet and heat. Add the onion and sauté for 1 to 2 minutes. Add the sliced pepper and sauté for another 3 to 4 minutes. Add the soymilk and puréed miso. Mix well. Cover the skillet, reduce the flame to low, and simmer for about 5 to 7 minutes. Remove from the flame and place in a serving bowl. Spoon the sauce over the millet mashed potatoes when serving. Garnish with chopped parsley and serve.

Millet Mashed Potatoes with Bechamel Sauce

5 to 6 cups cooked millet mashed potatoes
1 cup mushrooms, diced
1/2 cup onion, diced
4 to 5 Tbsp unbleached white flour
4 cups water
tamari soy sauce or sea salt, to taste
1 Tbsp corn oil
2 Tbsp parsley, minced

Place the corn oil in a skillet and heat. Sauté the onion for 1 to 2 minutes. Sauté the mushrooms for 3 to 4 minutes. Add the flour, gradually, mixing constantly. Sauté for another minute. Gradually add the water, stirring constantly to prevent lumping. Bring to a boil, stirring constantly, until smooth and creamy. Season to taste with soy sauce and simmer, covered, for 5 minutes. If seasoning with sea salt, cover and simmer for 10 minutes. Place the sauce in a serving bowl. Ladle the sauce over each serving of millet mashed potatoes when served and garnish with a little minced parsley.

Millet Gomoku (Millet with Mixed Vegetables)

2 cups organic millet, washed and dry-roasted
1/2 cup cooked seitan, fried tempeh, or deep-fried tofu, diced
1/2 cup carrot, diced
1/4 cup burdock, diced
1/4 cup celery, diced
1 cup sweet corn, removed from cob
1/4 cup daikon, diced
1/4 cup rutabaga, diced
4 cups water

Place all ingredients in a pressure cooker, mix, and cover. Bring up to pressure over a high flame. Reduce the flame to medium-low and place a flame deflector under the cooker. Cook for 15 minutes. Remove from the flame and allow the pressure to come down. Remove the cover and place the gomoku in a serving bowl.

Millet Burgers with Tamari-Ginger Sauce

4 cups leftover cooked millet
1/4 cup onion, minced
1/4 cup carrot, finely diced
1/4 cup celery, finely diced
2 Tbsp parsley, minced
1/4 cup pumpkin seeds, roasted and half-ground or crushed
1/2 cup water
whole wheat pastry flour
tamari soy sauce
light or dark sesame oil

Place the millet, onion, carrot, celery, parsley, and pumpkin seeds in a mix-

94

ing bowl. If the millet is dry, add the above amount of water. If the millet is soft and wet, add enough whole wheat pastry flour to hold the millet together well enough to form burgers. Season with a little tamari soy sauce. Form the millet mixture into balls and flatten out to form burgers or patty shapes. Heat oil on a pancake griddle. Place 4 to 5 burgers on the griddle and fry over a medium flame until golden. Flip the burgers over and fry the other side until golden. Remove and place on a serving platter.

Tamari-Ginger Sauce

1/4 cup tamari soy sauce
3/4 cup water
1 tsp ginger juice

Place the soy sauce and water in a saucepan. Heat over a high flame until almost boiling. Reduce the flame to low and simmer 1 to 2 minutes. Turn the flame off and add the ginger juice. Mix and spoon the sauce over each burger. Serve hot.

Millet and Lentil Burgers

2 cups leftover cooked millet
2 cup cooked lentils
1/2 cup onion, minced
1/4 cup celery, minced
2 Tbsp parsley, minced
2 Tbsp garlic, minced (optional)
tamari soy sauce
sesame or corn oil

Mix the millet, lentils, and vegetables. Season with a little tamari soy sauce and mix again. Form into burgers. Heat an oiled skillet and place 4 to 5 burgers on it. Fry until golden. Flip over and fry the other side until golden. Repeat until all burgers have been fried. Place on a serving platter. Serve with your favorite sauce, gravy, or natural mustard and sauerkraut.

Millet Croquettes with Vegetable-Kuzu Sauce

3 cups leftover cooked millet
sesame or safflower oil, for deep-frying
1/2 cup onion, sliced in thin half-moons

1/2 cup celery, sliced on a thin diagonal
1/4 cup carrot, sliced in thin half-diagonals
1 cup broccoli florets
2 cups water
3 tsp kuzu, diluted
tamari soy sauce
1 tsp ginger juice

Take 1/3 cup of cooked millet in your hands and form into a ball or triangle as in making a rice ball. Repeat until all the millet has been formed into balls or triangles. Heat 2 to 3 inches of oil in a deep-frying pot. Deep-fry several croquettes until golden. Remove and drain on paper towels. Repeat until all croquettes have been deep-fried.

While frying the croquettes, place the onion, celery, and carrot in a saucepan with the water. Cover and bring to a boil. Reduce the flame to medium-low and cook for 1 minute. Add the broccoli florets, cover, and simmer for 1 minute. Reduce the flame to low and add the kuzu, stirring constantly until thick and translucent. Season to taste with tamari soy sauce. Simmer 1 more minute. Turn the flame off, add the ginger juice, and mix. Place 2 to 3 croquettes in each serving bowl and pour the vegetable-kuzu sauce over them. Serve hot.

Millet Loaf with Mushroom Sauce

1 cup organic millet, washed
1/2 cup carrot, diced
1/2 cup leek, sliced
1/4 cup celery, diced
1/4 cup burdock, diced
3 cups boiling water
pinch of sea salt
1/4 cup whole wheat pastry flour
1 1/2 cups water or vegetable stock
1/2 cup onion, minced
1/4 lb mushrooms, sliced
1 1/2 Tbsp tamari soy sauce
sesame oil or corn oil
parsley, minced, for garnish

Place the millet, carrot, leek, celery, and sea salt in the pot of boiling water. Mix, cover, and bring to a boil again. Reduce the flame to medium-low and simmer for 30 to 35 minutes. Remove from the flame. Very lightly oil a loaf pan or casserole dish and place the cooked millet and vegetables in it. Press the millet down firmly in the pan so that the surface is even.

Brush a skillet with oil and heat. Sauté the onion and mushrooms for several minutes until the onions are translucent. Sprinkle the flour over the vegetables and mix it in with the vegetables to evenly coat them. Slowly add the water, stirring constantly to prevent lumping. Bring to a boil. Reduce the flame to low, cover, and simmer for 5 to 7 minutes, stirring occasionally to prevent sticking and burning.

With a chopstick, poke several small holes in the millet so that it can absorb the sauce. Pour the mushroom sauce over the millet. Bake at 350 degrees F. for 30 to 35 minutes. Remove from the oven. Slice and serve or scoop out with a spoon and serve. Garnish with chopped parsley.

Stuffed Chinese Cabbage Rolls with Kuzu Sauce

5 to 6 Chinese cabbage leaves, washed
2 cups water
2 cups leftover cooked millet and vegetables
1/2 cup onion, diced
1/2 cup mushrooms, sliced
1/4 cup carrot, sliced in matchsticks
2 to 3 tsp kuzu, diluted
1 to 1 1/2 Tbsp tamari soy sauce

Place the water in a pot, cover, and bring to a boil. Place the cabbage leaves in the boiling water, cover, and cook for 1 minute. Remove and drain the cabbage leaves. Take 1/3 to 1/2 cup of the cooked millet and vegetables in your hands and form into oblong cylinders. Repeat, using all of the millet. Stuff each cabbage leaf with millet and roll up. Place the stuffed cabbage leaves in a skillet with 1/4 inch of water. Cover and bring to a boil. Reduce the flame to low and simmer for 3 to 5 minutes. Remove the stuffed cabbage leaves and place in a serving dish.

Take the cooking water from the cabbage leaves and add the onion, mushrooms, and carrot. Cover and bring to a boil. Reduce the flame to low and simmer for 1 to 2 minutes. Remove the cover, add the kuzu sauce, stirring constantly until thick and translucent. Season with tamari soy sauce and simmer another 2 to 3 minutes. Pour the sauce over the cabbage rolls and serve hot.

Stuffed Squash

1 medium-sized acorn or buttercup squash, washed, cut in half, and seeds removed

2 cups leftover cooked millet, plain
1/4 cup leek, chopped
1/4 cup mushrooms, diced
2 Tbsp parsley, minced
1/4 cup sunflower seeds, roasted
tamari soy sauce
sesame oil

Place the millet, leeks, mushrooms, parsley, and sunflower seeds in a mixing bowl. Mix thoroughly. Add a few drops of tamari soy sauce and mix again. Very lightly oil the outside skin of each squash half to prevent cracking while baking. Place the stuffing mixture in each half of the squash and press down. Cover the squash and bake at 350 to 375 degrees F for about 40 to 45 minutes until the squash is tender. Remove the cover and place the squash on a serving platter. Spoon out the squash and stuffing on to serving plates. Serve as is or with your favorite gravy or sauce.

Millet and Chickpea Salad

3 cups cooked millet
1 cup cooked chickpeas
1/2 cup red onion, diced
1/2 cup green peas, shelled
1/4 cup carrot, diced
1 Tbsp burdock, diced
1/2 cup sweet corn, removed from cob
1 Tbsp chives, scallion, or parsley, chopped
3 umeboshi plums, pits removed
3 Tbsp organic roasted tahini
1 Tbsp onion, finely grated
3/4 cup water

Place the millet, chickpeas, and red onion in a mixing bowl. Blanch the green peas for 2 minutes in boiling water. Remove, drain, and place in the mixing bowl. Blanch the carrot for 1 minute, the burdock for 2 minutes, and the sweet corn for 1 1/2 minutes. Place in the mixing bowl.

Grind the umeboshi plums in a suribachi until it becomes a smooth paste. Add the tahini and grind again until evenly mixed with the umeboshi. Add the onion and grind. Slowly add the water, puréeing constantly until the dressing is smooth and creamy. Pour the dressing over the millet salad ingredients and mix thoroughly. Place in a serving bowl. Garnish with chopped chives.

Fried Millet with Vegetables

3 cups leftover cooked millet
1/4 cup onion, diced
1/4 cup carrot, diced
1/2 cup cabbage, sliced in 1 inch pieces
1/4 cup water
1/4 cup scallion, finely chopped
tamari soy sauce
sesame oil

Oil a skillet and heat. Sauté the onion for 1 to 2 minutes. Layer the carrot, cabbage, and millet on top of the onion. Add water, cover, and reduce the flame to low. When the millet is hot and the vegetables are cooked, season with several drops of tamari soy sauce and mix. Cover and cook for another 3 to 4 minutes. Sprinkle the scallion on top, cover, and cook for another minute or so. Place in a serving bowl.

Chapter 4
Wheat, Rye, and Oats

Wheat is native to ancient Europe and Asia. Today it is cultivated worldwide and has become the world's chief cereal crop. In whole form, whole wheat berries are rather hard to digest and require thorough chewing. As a result, wheat is traditionally consumed in flour form as bread, pasta, or noodles or processed into forms that are more digestible and easier to prepare. These include bulgur, wheat that has been partially boiled, dried, and ground; cracked wheat, wheat berries that have been steel cut; and couscous, wheat that has been partially refined and cracked but not bleached.

Wheat is divided into several classifications. Hard wheat contains more gluten than soft wheat and is used mainly for flour. Soft wheat contains proportionately more carbohydrate and is used for mixing with harder flours or making pastries. Durum wheat is used in making pasta and noodles. Spring wheat refers to wheat that is planted in the spring and harvested in the autumn. Winter wheat is sown in the fall, sprouts beneath the snow, and is reaped in the spring. Pastry wheat, a type of spring wheat, is low in gluten and used as flour for making pastry and crackers. Wheat is also classified by color such as red, white, golden, or silver. These categories are not mutually exclusive; for example, a popular grain for baking bread is called hard red winter wheat.

There are many ways to prepare whole wheat and whole wheat products. Whole wheat berries, retaining the whole energy and nutrients of the grain, may be pressured-cooked or boiled. However, they are rather hard to eat by themselves and require thorough chewing. As a result, they are customarily combined with other grains, such as brown rice, in a proportion of about 10 to 30 percent wheat to 70 to 90 percent other grain. Soaking for several hours or overnight before cooking contributes to further softening of the wheat berries. Wheat berries that have been mechanically cut may be enjoyed from time to time for variety, though their energy and nutrients are reduced. Cracked wheat can be prepared as a morning cereal or small side dish. Bulgur makes a light, appetizing summer dish or salad, as does couscous which fluffs up even more. However, because of its partially refined quality, couscous is best served only on occasion. In macrobiotic cooking it is often served as couscous cake, a dessert that can be prepared with a fruit topping. Whole wheat flakes, wheat germ, and wheat bran are also available for use as cold breakfast cereals or supplemental foods. However, such products are usually highly refined and processed and retain little of the wheat's original energy and nutrients, and are not recommended for regular use.

The recipes in this chapter explain how to use whole wheat berries and partially refined wheat products such as bulgur and couscous. Recipes for wheat products such as bread, noodles, seitan, and fu are presented in a subsequent chapter.

Boiled Whole Wheat

2 cups organic whole wheat berries, soaked 6 to 8 hours
3 1/2 to 4 cups water, including water used to soak wheat
pinch of sea salt

Place the wheat, water, and sea salt in a heavy pot. Cover and bring to a boil. Reduce the flame to medium-low and simmer for 2 1/2 to 3 hours or until tender and all water has been absorbed. It may be necessary to occasionally add more water during cooking if it becomes too dry. Place in a serving bowl.

Pressure-Cooked Whole Wheat

2 cups organic whole wheat berries, soaked 6 to 8 hours
3 1/2 cups water, including water used to soak wheat
pinch of sea salt

Place the wheat and water in an uncovered pressure cooker. Bring to a boil. Add the sea salt, cover, and turn the flame up to high. When the pressure is up, place a flame deflector under the cooker and reduce the flame to medium-low. Cook for 1 hour. Remove from the flame and allow the pressure to come down. Remove the lid and place in a serving bowl.

Whole Wheat with Barley

1 cup organic barley, washed
1 cup organic whole wheat berries, washed
4 cups water
pinch of sea salt

Place all ingredients in a pressure cooker, cover, and bring up to pressure over a high flame. Reduce the flame to medium-low and place a flame deflector under the cooker. Cook for 50 minutes. Remove from the flame and allow the pressure to come down. Remove the cover and allow the grain to sit for 4 to 5 minutes before placing in a serving bowl.

Wheat Berries with Azuki Beans

1 1/2 cups organic azuki beans, washed and soaked 6 to 8 hours
1/2 cup organic whole wheat berries, washed and soaked 6 to 8 hours
1 strip kombu, 2 to 3 inches long, soaked 3 to 5 minutes, diced
2 1/2 to 3 cups water, including water used to soak kombu, azuki beans, and wheat
1/8 to 1/4 tsp sea salt

Place the kombu on the bottom of a heavy pot. Place the wheat berries and then the azuki beans on top of the kombu. Add enough water to just cover the azuki beans. Cover and bring to a boil over a high flame. Reduce the flame to medium-low and simmer for 1 1/2 to 2 hours or until the beans and wheat are about 70 to 80 percent done. Occasionally add water to the beans and wheat while cooking. Each time add only enough to just cover the azuki beans. When the beans are about 70 to 80 percent done, add the sea salt. Cover and cook for another 30 minutes or so until the grains and beans are soft and tender. The wheat will still be chewy even when done. Place in a serving bowl.

Whole Wheat with Chickpeas

1 1/2 cup organic chickpeas, washed and soaked, discard water
1/2 cup organic whole wheat berries, washed, soaked 6 to 8 hours
2 1/2 to 3 cups water, including water used to soak kombu and wheat
1 strip kombu, 2 to 3 inches long, soaked and diced
1/8 to 1/4 tsp sea salt

Place the kombu, whole wheat berries, chickpeas, and water in a pressure cooker. Cover and bring up to pressure over a high flame. Reduce the flame to medium-low and cook for 1 hour to 1 hour and 15 minutes. Remove from the flame and allow the pressure to come down. Remove the cover, add the sea salt, and place the uncovered cooker over a medium-low flame. Cook for another 10 to 15 minutes. Place in a serving bowl.

Whole Wheat with Lentils

1 1/2 cups organic lentils, washed
1 cup cooked whole wheat berries
1/2 cup onion, diced
1/4 cup carrot, diced
1/4 cup celery, diced
water, including water used to soak kombu
1 strip kombu, 2 inches long, soaked and diced
1 to 2 tsp mellow barley miso, puréed
2 Tbsp parsley, minced

Place the kombu, onion, celery, carrot, wheat, and lentils in a heavy pot. Add enough water to just cover the lentils. Bring to a boil over a high flame. Reduce the flame to medium-low, cover, and simmer for 45 to 50 minutes, adding water as needed to just cover the lentils. When the lentils are soft, reduce the flame to low and add the puréed miso. Simmer for another 2 to 3 minutes. Mix in the parsley and place in a serving bowl.

Baked Beans and Wheat Berries

2 cups organic northern or navy beans, washed and soaked
1/2 cup organic soft, spring wheat berries, washed and soaked
1 cup onion, diced
1 pkg. bonito flakes, optional
1 cup round fu, soaked 10 minutes, sliced in chunks
1 to 1 1/2 Tbsp miso mustard or any natural mustard
1 strip kombu, 2 to 3 inches long, soaked and diced
1/4 cup barley malt or 1/3 cup rice syrup
1/4 tsp sea salt
water

Place the kombu in a heavy pot. Place the wheat and beans on top. Add water to just cover the beans. Bring to a boil without a cover. Reduce the flame to medium and simmer for 10 to 15 minutes. Cover the beans, reduce the flame to medium-low, and simmer for 1 1/2 to 2 hours. During this time it will be necessary to add small amounts of cold water (3 to 4 times approximately) as the beans cook, each time adding only enough water to just cover the beans. After 1 1/2 to 2 hours, the beans should be about 70 to 80 percent done. Remove the cover, add the bonito flakes, fu, onion, barley malt, and sea salt. Mix thoroughly.

Place the beans in a heavy pot, cover, and bake for another hour or so until the beans and wheat are tender. Add small amounts of water if needed while baking. Remove the cover and brown the beans slightly for several more minutes. For those wishing to avoid baked foods, after adding the seasonings and other ingredients, simply boil the beans for another hour or so until tender.

Whole Wheat Salad with Green Goddess Dressing

1 cup cooked whole wheat berries
3 cups green cabbage, very finely shredded
1/4 cup carrot, coarsely grated
1/2 cup walnuts, roasted and chopped
1/4 cup celery, diced
1 cup red apple, cut in 1/4 inch thick chunks
1/4 cup raisins, soaked 10 to 15 minutes
1/4 cup seedless red grapes

Place all ingredients in a mixing bowl and prepare the green goddess dressing below.

Green Goddess Dressing

2 to 3 umeboshi plums, pits removed
3/4 cup cooked brown rice
1 cup water
1 to 2 tsp sweet brown rice vinegar
2 Tbsp onion, grated or minced
1/2 cup parsley, finely chopped
2 Tbsp organic roasted tahini
1 Tbsp tamari soy sauce

Place the umeboshi, water, sweet brown rice vinegar, rice, and onion in a blender. Purée until smooth. Add the tahini, tamari soy sauce, and parsley. Purée again until smooth and creamy. Pour the dressing over the salad ingredients and mix thoroughly. Place in a serving bowl.

Boiled Bulgur

1 cups organic bulgur
2 to 2 1/2 cups boiling water
pinch of sea salt
1/2 cup scallion, chives, or parsley, for garnish, finely chopped

Place the bulgur in the pot of boiling water together with the sea salt. Cover and bring to a boil again. Reduce the flame to low and simmer about 15 to 20 minutes. Turn off the flame and allow to sit for 5 minutes. Remove the cover, mix lightly, and serve with a garnish, natural sauce, or condiment.

Fried Bulgur with Vegetables

2 cups cooked bulgur
1/2 cup scallion, finely chopped
1/2 cup onion, diced
1/4 cup carrot, diced
1/4 cup celery, diced
tamari soy sauce
sesame oil

Place a small amount of oil in a skillet and heat. Add the onions and sauté for 1 to 2 minutes. Add the celery, carrot, and bulgur. Sprinkle a few drops of soy sauce over the mixture, cover, and reduce the flame to low. Cook until the vegetables are tender and the bulgur is hot. Add the scallion, cover, and cook for another 1 to 2 minutes. Remove the cover and mix the bulgur and vegetables. Sauté for another minute or so. Place in a serving bowl.

Cracked Wheat

1 cup organic cracked wheat
3 cups boiling water
pinch of sea salt

Place the sea salt and cracked wheat in the boiling water. Cover and bring to a boil again. Reduce the flame to low and simmer for 40 minutes. Turn off the flame and let sit for 10 minutes. Remove the cover, mix, and place in a serving bowl.

Bulgur with Vegetables

1 cup organic bulgur
2 to 2 1/2 cups boiling water
1 cup onion, diced
1/2 cup carrot, diced
1/4 cup celery, diced
1 Tbsp parsley, minced
pinch of sea salt

Place the onion, carrot, celery, bulgur and sea salt in the pot of boiling water. Cover and bring to a boil again. Reduce the flame to low and simmer for 15 to 20 minutes. Remove from the flame and allow to sit for 5 minutes. Remove the cover and mix the chopped parsley in. Place in a serving bowl.

Bulgur with Sautéed Vegetables

2 cups cooked bulgur
1/2 cup onion, diced
1 cup mushrooms, diced
1/2 cup red cabbage, diced
1/4 cup parsley, minced
2 to 2 1/2 cups water
tamari soy sauce
sesame or corn oil

Place the oil in a skillet and heat. Add the onion and sauté for 1 to 2 minutes. Add the mushrooms and sauté for 1 to 2 minutes. Add several drops of soy sauce. Add the cabbage and bulgur. Cover and bring to a boil. Reduce the flame to low and simmer for 10 to 15 minutes. Remove from the flame and allow to sit for 10 minutes. Remove the cover and mix in the parsley. Place in a serving bowl.

Bulgur Salad with Umeboshi-Parsley Dressing

4 cups cooked bulgur
1/4 cup red cabbage, sliced in 1 inch squares
1/2 cup green string beans, sliced in 1 to 2 inch long pieces
1/2 cup carrot, diced
1/4 cup yellow summer squash, sliced in thin quarter-moons

1/2 cup cooked chickpeas
1 Tbsp tamari-roasted sunflower seeds
water
several lettuce leaves

Place 1 to 2 inches of water in a saucepan, cover, and bring to a boil. Boil the vegetables in the following order, then remove and drain. Boil the yellow squash for 1 minute; string beans for 1 1/2 to 2 minutes; carrot for 1 1/2 minutes; and the red cabbage for 1 1/2 to 2 minutes. Place the bulgur, vegetables, chickpeas, and roasted sunflower seeds in a mixing bowl. Prepare the umeboshi-parsley dressing below.

Umeboshi-Parsley Dressing

2 umeboshi plums, pits removed
1 Tbsp parsley, minced
1 Tbsp onion, minced
3/4 to 1 cup water

Place the umeboshi plums in a suribachi and grind until smooth. Add the onion and parsley. Grind again for 1 to 2 minutes. Add the water and purée all ingredients. Pour the dressing over the salad just before serving and mix thoroughly. Arrange the lettuce leaves in a bowl or serving platter and place the salad over them. Serve at room temperature or slightly chilled.

Tabuli

1 cup organic bulgur
2 to 2 1/2 cups boiling water
pinch of sea salt
1 cup onion, minced
1/4 cup sweet red pepper, diced
1 cup parsley, finely minced
1/4 cup fresh mint, finely chopped
2 to 3 Tbsp extra virgin olive oil or rice bran oil
3 to 4 Tbsp fresh lemon juice
1/4 cup fresh black olives (optional)
1/2 lb firm style tofu, for making tofu cheese
mellow barley miso, for making tofu cheese
1 Tbsp shiso leaves, chopped
1/4 cup sunflower seeds or pine nuts, toasted
several lettuce leaves, washed

Prepare the tofu cheese in advance for this recipe. Cut 1/2 pound of firm style tofu in half. Completely coat the top, bottom, and all sides of the tofu with 1/4 inch thick layer of mellow barley miso. Place in a bowl and cover with a piece of cotton cheesecloth. Let sit (do not refrigerate) for 1 to 3 days. If the temperature in the kitchen is warm, the tofu will ferment in 1 day. If cool, it may take 2 to 3 days. After the tofu has fermented, scrape off the miso (it may be used in other dishes) and rinse the tofu under cold water to remove all remaining miso. Grind the tofu cheese in a hand food mill and set aside.
Cook the bulgur as described previously. Remove and place in a mixing bowl.

Mix to fluff up and to cool the bulgur to room temperature. Place the following ingredients in the mixing bowl with the bulgur: pepper, onion, parsley, olives, tofu cheese, shiso, mint, and sunflower seeds or pine nuts. Add the olive oil and lemon juice. Mix thoroughly with your hands. Place in the refrigerator or a cool place and let sit for about 2 hours. Line a platter or shallow bowl with several lettuce leaves and place the salad on top. Serve.

Kidney Beans and Bulgur

1 cup organic kidney beans, washed and soaked 6 to 8 hours
water
1 strip kombu, 2 inches long, soaked and diced
1/2 cup organic bulgur
1/2 cup onion, diced
1 Tbsp brown rice or barley miso, puréed
1 Tbsp parsley, finely chopped, for garnish

Place the kombu in the bottom of a heavy pot. Place the beans on top. Add enough cold water to just cover the beans. Bring to a boil, reduce the flame to medium-low, and simmer for 10 minutes. Cover the beans and simmer for another 1 1/2 to 2 hours until 70 to 80 percent done. Add water several times during cooking to prevent burning, each time adding only enough to cover the beans. When the beans are 70 to 80 percent done, mix in the bulgur and onion. Add enough water to cover. Bring to a boil again over a high flame. Reduce the flame to medium-low and simmer for another 20 to 30 minutes until the beans are tender and the bulgur is soft. Reduce the flame to low and add the miso. Simmer for another 3 to 4 minutes. Place in a serving bowl and garnish with chopped parsley.

Bulgur with Lentils

1 cup organic lentils, washed
1 strip kombu, 2 inches long, soaked and diced
water, for cooking lentils
1 cup organic bulgur
1 Tbsp corn oil
1 cup onion, diced
1 to 2 cloves garlic, minced (optional)
1/4 cup celery
1/4 cup sweet corn
1/4 cup parsley
2 cups water
1 Tbsp lemon juice or brown rice vinegar
1/8 tsp sea salt

Place the kombu and lentils in a heavy pot. Add enough water to just cover the lentils. Cover and bring to a boil. Reduce the flame to medium-low and simmer for about 25 to 30 minutes, adding water occasionally just to cover the lentils. Place the oil in a skillet and heat. Sauté the onion and garlic for 2 to 3 minutes. Add the celery and sweet corn. Sauté for another 1 to 2 minutes. Place the sautéed vegetables in the pot with the lentils.

Add the bulgur and 2 cups of water to the pot with the partially cooked lentils and vegetables. Add the sea salt. Cover and bring to a boil. Reduce the flame to medium-low and simmer for another 20 to 25 minutes until the lentils and bulgur are tender and most of the water has been absorbed. Turn the flame off and let sit for 10 minutes. Remove the cover, mix in the lemon juice or vinegar and parsley. Place in a serving dish.

Lentil and Bulgur Burgers

3 to 4 cups leftover cooked lentils and bulgur
1/4 cup whole wheat pastry flour
1/4 cup scallion, finely minced
corn oil
tamari soy sauce

Place the leftover lentils and bulgur in a mixing bowl with the flour and scallion. Sprinkle a few drops of tamari soy sauce over and mix thoroughly. Form the mixture into patties or burgers. Oil a skillet or pancake griddle and heat. Place several burgers in the skillet and fry until golden. Flip over and fry the other side until golden. Serve as is or with a little natural mustard and sauerkraut garnish.

Baked Squash with Bulgur Stuffing

1 acorn or buttercup squash, halved and seeds removed
1 cup leftover cooked bulgur
1 cup whole wheat bread crumbs
1/2 cup onion, diced
1/4 cup celery, diced
1/2 tsp dried sage (optional)
1/4 cup water
corn oil
tamari soy sauce

Place a small amount of corn oil in a skillet and heat. Sauté the onion and celery for 1 to 2 minutes. Place in a mixing bowl. Add the bulgur and bread crumbs. Mix in the sage. Season with a few drops of soy sauce. Add water and mix again. Place half of the stuffing in each squash half. Cover and bake at 375 degrees F. for 40 to 45 minutes. Remove cover and bake for an additional 5 minutes. Place on a serving platter. Slice and serve or scoop out the squash and stuffing and serve.

Vegetarian Chili

2 cups organic kidney beans, washed and soaked 6 to 8 hours
1 strip kombu, 2 inches long, soaked and diced
1/2 cup organic bulgur
1 cup onion, diced
1/4 cup sweet red pepper, diced (optional)
1 to 2 tsp corn oil
1/2 to 1 tsp natural chili powder, to taste (optional)
water
1/4 tsp sea salt or 2 tsp puréed mellow barley miso
scallion or parsley, finely chopped for garnish

Place the kombu and kidney beans in a heavy soup pot. Bring to a boil over a high flame. Reduce the flame to medium and simmer for 10 to 15 minutes. Cover and reduce the flame to medium-low. Simmer for an additional 1 1/2 hours until the beans are 70 to 80 percent done. Add water several times during cooking; each time add just enough to cover the beans.

Sauté the onion and pepper for 2 to 3 minutes. When the beans are 70 to 80 percent done mix in the sautéed vegetables, bulgur, chili powder, and sea salt. Add water to cover about 2 inches above the beans. Cover and bring to a boil. Reduce the flame to medium-low and simmer another 30 minutes until the beans are fully done. Add water, if needed, for desired consistency during cooking. Serve with chopped scallion or parsley garnish. Chili is great when served with homemade corn bread.

Basic French or Moroccan Couscous

1 cup couscous
1 cup water
pinch of sea salt

Place the water and sea salt in a sauce pan. Cover and bring to a boil over a high flame. Mix in the couscous. Cover and bring to a boil again. Turn off the flame and let the couscous sit for 5 minutes. Remove the cover and place in a serving bowl.

Basic Whole Wheat Couscous

1 cup whole wheat couscous
1 1/2 to 1 3/4 cups water
pinch of sea salt

Place the water and sea salt in a sauce pan. Cover and bring to a boil over a high flame. Mix in the couscous. Cover and bring to a boil again. Turn the flame to low and simmer for 20 minutes. Remove from the flame and let sit for 5 minutes. Remove and place in a serving bowl.

Fried Couscous with Vegetables

2 to 3 cups leftover cooked couscous
1/2 cup onion, diced
1/2 cup mushrooms, diced
1/4 cup carrot, diced
1/4 cup leek, chopped
2 Tbsp scallion, finely chopped
sesame oil
tamari soy sauce

Heat a small amount of oil in a skillet. Sauté the onion for 1 minute. Add the mushrooms and sauté for 1 to 2 minutes. Add the carrot, leek, and couscous. Sprinkle a few drops of tamari soy sauce over and cover. Reduce the flame to low. Cook for 2 to 3 minutes. Mix all ingredients. Mix in the scallion and sauté, stirring occasionally, for 3 to 4 minutes longer until all vegetables are tender and the couscous is hot. Place in a serving bowl.

Couscous Salad with Umeboshi-Tahini Dressing

3 cups cooked French or Moroccan couscous
1 cup cooked chickpeas, drained
1/2 cup green peas, shelled
1/4 cup red radish, sliced in thin rounds or half-moons
1/4 cup celery, diced
water
several lettuce leaves, washed and drained
2 to 3 umeboshi plums, pits removed
3 Tbsp organic roasted tahini
2 tsp onion, grated
1 to 2 Tbsp parsley, finely chopped
3/4 cup water

Place 1/2 inch water in a saucepan, cover, and bring to a boil. Boil the green peas for 1 1/2 to 2 minutes. Remove, drain, and place in a mixing bowl. Place the couscous, chickpeas, radish, and celery in a mixing bowl and mix. Place the umeboshi plum in a suribachi and grind until smooth. Add the tahini and grind until smooth. Add the parsley and onion. Grind 1 minute. Slowly add the water and purée until smooth and creamy.

Place the lettuce leaves in a serving bowl or on a serving platter. Mix the dressing with the couscous and vegetables just before serving and place on top of the lettuce leaves. Serve at room temperature or slightly chilled.

Couscous with Vegetables

2 cups whole wheat couscous
3 1/2 cups water
1/2 cup green beans, sliced in 1 inch lengths
1/4 cup onion, diced
1/4 cup carrot, diced
1/4 cup scallion, finely chopped
pinch of sea salt

Place the water and sea salt in a pot and bring to a boil. Add the couscous, green beans, onion, and carrot. Mix and cover. Reduce the flame to low and simmer for 15 to 20 minutes. Remove from the flame. Remove the cover and mix in the scallion. Place in a serving bowl.

Baked Couscous and Cod

1 1/2 lbs fresh cod, washed
water, for soaking fish
pinch of sea salt, for soaking fish
2 cups French or Moroccan couscous
2 cups water
1/2 cup onion, diced
1/4 cup celery, diced
1/4 cup mushrooms, diced
1/2 cup green peas, shelled
sesame oil
tamari soy sauce or a pinch of sea salt
1 to 2 tsp parsley, finely minced, for garnish
juice from half a lemon

Place the fish in a bowl and cover with cold water. Add a pinch of sea salt. Soak the fish for 30 to 60 minutes. Remove and discard the soaking water. Set aside. Place water in a pot, cover, and bring to a boil. Add the couscous, mix, and cover. Bring to a boil again. Turn the flame off and let sit, covered, for 5 minutes.

Lightly oil a skillet and heat. Sauté the onion, celery, mushrooms, and green peas for 1 to 2 minutes. Mix the vegetables with the couscous and add a pinch of sea salt or a few drops of tamari soy sauce. Lightly oil a baking dish. Place the couscous and vegetables in the baking dish. Place the fish on top of the couscous. Cover the baking dish and bake at 375 degrees F for about 20 minutes or so until the fish is tender. Remove the cover and brown for another 10 minutes. Sprinkle with chopped parsley for garnish and squeeze lemon juice over. Serve.

Baked Sole with Couscous Stuffing

4 to 5 fresh sole fillets, washed and soaked as above

1 cup cooked couscous
1/2 cup green beans, sliced French style or julienne
1/4 cup slivered almonds
2 tsp parsley, chopped
1/4 cup carrot, sliced in matchsticks
tamari soy sauce
sesame oil
5 lemon wedges, for garnish

Mix the couscous, green beans, almonds, and carrot with several drops of soy sauce. Take 1/4 to 1/5 of this stuffing mixture and roll it up inside each fillet. Place the fillets on an oiled baking dish and bake at 375 degrees F for 20 to 25 minutes until the fish is tender. Garnish each piece with chopped parsley. Place on a serving platter with several lemon wedges for garnish.

Baked Squash with Couscous Stuffing

1 buttercup or acorn squash, halved and seeds removed
1 cup cooked couscous
1/2 cup mushrooms, diced
1/4 cup onion, diced
1/4 cup carrot, diced
2 Tbsp sunflower seeds, roasted
2 tsp parsley, chopped
l clove garlic, minced (optional)
corn oil
tamari soy sauce

Lightly oil a skillet and sauté the garlic, onion, mushrooms, and carrot for 2 to 3 minutes. Mix with the couscous, sunflower seeds, parsley, and several drops of soy sauce. Stuff each half of the squash. Cover and bake at 375 degrees F for 40 to 45 minutes until the squash is tender. Remove cover and bake for another 5 minutes or so. Place on a serving platter. Slice to serve or scoop out the squash and stuffing with a spoon.

Rye

Rye is a traditional staple in Scandinavia and other northern areas of Europe and Asia. Like wheat berries, whole rye is on the hard side and requires thorough chewing to digest. It is used principally as flour to make rye bread, crackers, or other baked products. It is also processed into flakes and used in producing some strong alcoholic beverages.

Whole rye can be prepared plain as a small side dish, either pressure-cooked or boiled as in making brown rice or barley. One of the harder grains, rye may be softened by soaking for several hours or overnight, or it may be dry-roasted prior to cooking.Rye is often prepared in small volume combined with brown rice, and this makes an especially chewy dish. It is also cooked with carrots, onions, and other vegetables. Rye flour is traditionally combined with whole wheat flour to make rye bread, crackers, and other baked goods.

Boiled Rye

1 cup organic rye, washed and soaked 6 to 8 hours
3 cups water, including water used to soak rye
pinch of sea salt

Place the rye, water, and sea salt in a heavy pot. Cover and bring to a boil. Reduce the flame to medium to low and simmer for 2 to 2 1/2 hours.

Pressure-Cooked Rye

1 cup organic rye, washed and soaked 6 to 8 hours
2 cups water, including water used to soak rye
pinch of sea salt

Place all ingredients in a pressure cooker. Cover and bring up to pressure over a high flame. Reduce the flame to medium-low and place a flame deflector under the cooker. Cook for 1 hour. Remove from the flame and let the pressure come down. Remove the cover and place in a serving bowl.

Pressure-Cooked Rye (Roasting Method)

1 cup organic rye, washed and dry-roasted
2 cups water
pinch of sea salt or 1 square inch of kombu, soaked and diced

Place all ingredients in a pressure cooker, cover, and bring up to pressure over a high flame. Reduce the flame to medium-low and cook for 45 to 50 minutes. Remove from the flame and allow the pressure to come down. Remove the cover and place in a serving bowl.

Rye and Vegetable Salad

1 cup organic rye, washed and dry-roasted
2 1/2 cups water
pinch of sea salt
1/2 cup carrot, diced
1 cup onion, diced
4 shiitake mushrooms, soaked and diced
1/4 cup cabbage, finely chopped
1/2 umeboshi plum, pit removed and finely chopped
1/4 cup parsley or watercress
1 to 2 tsp fresh ginger juice
water

Place the rye, water, and sea salt in a pressure cooker and cook as above for 45 to 50 minutes. Remove from the burner and let the pressure come down. Remove the cover. Place 1/2 inch water in a saucepan, cover, and bring to a boil. Remove the cover. Boil the carrot, onion, cabbage, and mushrooms for 1 minute. Remove and place in the pressure cooker with the rye. Boil the parsley or watercress separately for 1 minute. Remove, drain, and chop. Place in the pressure cooker with the rye. Mix in the umeboshi plum and ginger juice. Place in a serving bowl.

Rye with Sautéed Vegetables

1 cup organic rye, washed and soaked 6 to 8 hours
2 cups water, including water used to soak rye
pinch of sea salt
1/2 cup leek, sliced
1 cup mushrooms, diced
1/4 cup carrot, diced
corn or sesame oil
tamari soy sauce

Place the rye, water, and sea salt in a pressure cooker. Bring up to pressure and reduce the flame to medium-low. Cook for 45 to 50 minutes. Remove from the flame and let the pressure come down. Remove the cover. Sauté the mushrooms, carrot, and leek in a small amount of oil for 4 to 5 minutes, stirring occasionally. Season with a few drops of tamari soy sauce and sauté for another minute or so. Mix the vegetables and rye and place in a serving bowl.

Oats

In ancient times, oats spread across Northern Europe and became the principal food in Scotland, Ireland, and parts of England. Oats are now grown in many other parts of the world. Three forms are commonly available. Whole oats, from which only the outer husks have been removed, provide the most energy and vitality. They are preferred for everyday use, even though they take longer to prepare than the other two types. Scotch oats have been steamed and steel-cut in small pieces. They make for a very chewy dish. Rolled oats have been steamed and passed through rollers. Although the most common form of oat-meal eaten today, rolled oats retain less energy and nutrients than whole oats. Still, they may be prepared from time to time and are often the best quality grain available when traveling or eating out. Oats are also processed into flakes, puffed oats, and into flour for baking.

Oats have more fat than other grains, give a warm energy, and provide stamina and endurance. Whole oats make the best quality oatmeal and can be prepared by boiling over a low fire for several hours or, ideally, overnight. Oats may also be mixed in small proportions with brown rice and other grains. Rolled oats and Scotch oats may be prepared from time to time, especially when cooking time is short or while traveling. Rolled oats or oat flour are often added to breads, cookies, and puddings to produce tasty desserts and baked goods. Basic oat recipes are presented in this chapter. Please refer to the chapter on breakfast cereals for guidelines for making oatmeal and oat porridges.

Basic Boiled Whole Oats

1 cup organic whole oats, washed and dry-roasted
3 to 4 cups water
pinch of sea salt

Place the water and sea salt in a heavy pot, cover, and bring to a boil. Re-move the cover, add the oats, and bring to a boil again. Reduce the flame to me-dium-low and simmer for 2 to 3 hours until soft. Place in a serving bowl and add your favorite garnish or condiment.

Basic Pressure-Cooked Whole Oats

1 cup organic whole oats, washed and dry-roasted
2 cups water

pinch of sea salt
chopped parsley, scallion, or chives, finely chopped

Place all ingredients in a pressure cooker, cover, and bring up to pressure. Reduce the flame to medium-low and cook for 45 to 50 minutes. Remove from the flame and let the pressure come down. Remove the cover and mix in chopped parsley, scallion, or chives for garnish. Place in a serving bowl.

Scotch or Steel Cut Oats

1 cup Scotch or steel cut oats, washed and drained
3 cups water
pinch of sea salt
1 sheet nori, toasted and cut in thin strips, for garnish
1/4 cup sunflower seeds, toasted, for garnish
2 tsp parsley or scallion, finely chopped for garnish
1 to 2 tsp packaged shiso leaf condiment, for garnish

Place the water and sea salt in a heavy pot, cover, and bring to a boil. Remove the cover. Add the oats, cover, and bring to a boil again. Reduce the flame to medium-low and simmer for 25 to 30 minutes. Place in individual serving bowls and garnish each with several strips of toasted nori, toasted sunflower seeds, chopped parsley or scallion, and a little shiso leaf condiment.

Whole Oats, Barley, and Whole Wheat

1/2 cup organic whole oats, washed
1 1/2 cup organic barley, washed
1/2 cup organic whole wheat berries, washed
4 cups water
pinch of sea salt

Place oats, barley, wheat, and water in a pressure cooker. Set aside to soak for 6 to 8 hours. Add sea salt, cover, and bring up to pressure over a high flame. Reduce the flame to medium-low and place a flame deflector under the cooker. Cook for 50 minutes. Remove from the flame and let the pressure come down. Remove the cover and let the grain sit for 4 to 5 minutes before placing in a serving bowl.

Brown Rice and Oat Burgers

2 cups leftover brown rice and whole oats
1/2 cup onion, minced
1/4 cup celery, minced
1/4 cup carrot, minced
2 Tbsp parsley, minced
tamari soy sauce
whole wheat pastry flour (if needed)
sesame or corn oil, for frying

Mix the rice and oats, onion, celery, carrot, and parsley. Sprinkle a few drops of soy sauce over the mixture. If the grain is very moist, add a little whole wheat pastry flour. If dry, add a little water and pastry flour. Mix thoroughly and form into burger shapes. Oil a skillet and heat. Place several burgers in the skillet and fry until golden brown. Flip over and fry the other side until golden brown. Place on a serving platter. Repeat until all burgers have been fried. Serve as is or with your favorite garnish, sauce, or gravy.

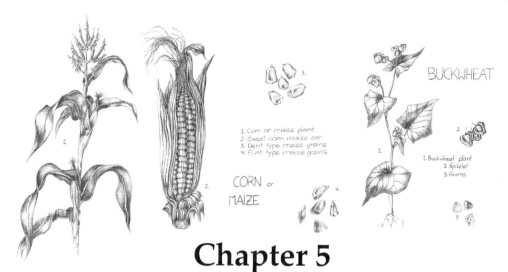

1. Corn or maize plant
2. Sweet corn maize ear
3. Dent type maize grains
4. Flint type maize grains

CORN or MAIZE

BUCKWHEAT

1. Buckwheat plant
2. Spikelet
3. Grains

Chapter 5
Corn and Buckwheat

Native Indian corn or maize has been grown for thousands of years in South, Central, and North America. The original varieties of corn were smaller, more compact, and hardier than the large hybrid varieties grown today. In recent years, there has been a movement to preserve traditional strains of corn, and seeds from these original strains are available to home gardeners from selected organic seed companies. Native corn is called open-pollinated or standard to distinguish it from hybrid corn. Organically grown hybrid corn is preferred over corn grown with chemical methods.

Corn itself is divided into five basic types: 1) sweet corn, the variety most commonly eaten today; 2) dent corn, a whole dried yellow corn with indented crowns available in most natural food stores and the corn from which most cornmeal is made; 3) flour corn, a starchy variety favored in Latin American cuisine; 4) flint corn, another field corn high in starch used in Latin cooking; and 5) popcorn, the most ancient and earliest domesticated variety of corn, whose modern descendent has become a staple in movie theaters around the world.

Native American and Latin American corn cuisine were based primarily on the use of masa, or whole corn dough. Masa is made from corn kernels taken from the cob, dried, cooked with wood ashes and water, and used as the basis for making tacos, tostadas, arepas, empanadas, and other traditional corn dishes. These whole grain preparations retain the basic energy and vitality of the whole corn. However, many of the dishes in modern Mexican restaurants or available in the supermarket today are made with refined cornmeal and other artificial ingredients rather than whole corn dough and other natural foods.

Most modern corn dishes are prepared with cornmeal, the flour made from whole corn. Though retaining lesser energy and nutrients than corn dough, good quality organic unrefined cornmeal that does not have any chemicals, sugar, or other refined or artificial ingredients may be used from time to time to make corn bread, corn muffins, or other dishes. A coarsely ground form of cornmeal is corn grits, a popular warm breakfast food in the American South. A crispy, flaky form of cornmeal, popular as a cold breakfast food in the United States, is corn flakes. Instead of cornstarch, a highly refined corn-based thickener, macrobiotic cooking uses kuzu root powder or arrowroot flour in preparing sauces, gravies, and other dishes requiring thickening.

There are hundreds of ways to prepare corn and corn products. Corn on the cob, for example, may be boiled, steamed, or baked, and each method produces a slightly different taste, texture, and energy. Whole corn kernels, freshly removed from the cob before cooking or dried and thoroughly soaked before using, may be added in small volume to a pot of brown rice and pressure cooked or boiled to give rice dishes a light, upward quality of energy. Fresh or dried corn kernels may also be used in a wide variety of soups, stews, salads, vegetable dishes, puddings, and other dishes.

In Italy and Southern Europe, a popular corn dish is polenta, made from ground fresh corn kernels baked with cooked kidney beans, carrots, onions, and a variety of seasonings. Masa can be used to make arepas, small oval-shaped corn balls served plain or stuffed with a variety of ingredients; bollos polones, boiled stuffed corn balls; and tortillas, the thin flat corn shells that are deep-fried and filled with a variety of beans and vegetables. Cornmeal may be used from time to time as a breakfast cereal or used to make corn bread, muffins, and other baked products and desserts.

Whole Corn

2 cups organic whole dried dent, flint, or blue corn, soaked
   6 to 8 hours or overnight
4 cups water
1 cup sifted, pure wood ash
pinch of sea salt

Place the soaked corn, wood ash, and 2 cups of water in a pressure cooker. Cover and bring up to pressure over a high flame. Reduce the flame to medium-low and place a flame deflector under the cooker. Pressure cook for 1 hour. Remove from the flame and allow the pressure to come down. Remove the cover and place the corn in a colander or strainer. Rinse out all of the wood ash from the corn under cold water. The loosened skins from the corn should float off during the rinsing. If this does not happen, place the corn back in the pressure cooker with water and more wood ash and pressure cook for 10 more minutes.

Place the rinsed corn in a clean pressure cooker and add the sea salt and remaining 2 cups of water. Pressure cook again for another 1 hour. Remove from the flame and allow the pressure to come down. Remove the cover and place the corn in a serving bowl. The corn is now ready to eat as is, use in soups, stews, bean and vegetables dishes, and salads, or grind into masa corn dough.

Homemade Corn Masa (Corn Dough) - Method 1

2 cups organic whole dried dent or flint corn, washed and
    soaked 6 to 8 hours or overnight
4 cups water
1 cup pure wood ash
pinch of sea salt

Place the soaked corn, 2 cups water, and the wood ash in a pressure cooker. Cover and bring to pressure over a high flame. Reduce the flame to medium-low and cook for 1 hour. Remove from the flame and allow the pressure to come down. Remove the cover. Pour the corn in a strainer or colander and rinse under cold water until all wood ash is removed. The skins of the corn should become loose and float off when rinsing. If this does not happen, place back in the pressure cooker with water and more wood ash and cook 10 minutes longer.

Place the washed corn in a clean pressure cooker with the remaining 2 cups of water and the sea salt. Cover and bring up to pressure over a high flame. Reduce the flame to medium-low and cook for 1 hour. Remove from the flame and allow the pressure to come down. Remove the cover. Place the corn in a bowl and allow to cool completely. Grind the corn in a hand grinder such as a steel flour mill (do not use a blender or hand food mill). Knead the dough for 10 to 15 minutes. The corn masa (dough) is now ready to use in the arepa and tortilla recipes presented below.

Homemade Corn Masa - Method 2

This method of making corn masa uses corn flour instead of freshly cooked whole, dried corn. It is not as delicious or nutritious as masa made from whole corn, but is quick and easy to prepare.

4 cups finely ground corn flour
2 cups boiling water

1/4 tsp sea salt

Place the flour and sea salt in a mixing bowl. Mix thoroughly. Pour the boiling water in the bowl and mix quickly with a fork. Knead the dough for 10 to 15 minutes with your hands. It is now ready to use in the recipes that follow.

Arepa

Arepa are delicious corn cakes that are a traditional staple in many parts of Latin America. They can eaten simply as is or stuffed with a variety of ingredients such as seeds or sautéed vegetables.

1 1/2 to 2 lbs corn masa (dough)
1/4 tsp sea salt
water
light or dark sesame oil

Crumble the dough in a bowl and add the sea salt, mixing it in thoroughly. Knead the dough, adding a small amount of water, until the dough is soft and the consistency of bread dough. Form the dough into 8 to 10 balls about the size of a fist or slightly smaller. Flatten the balls into a circular-shaped patty or cake. Brush a cast iron skillet with oil and heat. Place several arepas in the skillet and cook for 2 to 3 minutes on each side or until a slightly browned crust forms.
Bake the arepas in a pre-heated 350 degree F oven for about 20 minutes or until they puff up slightly. They are done when they make a hollow, popping sound when tapped with your fingers. Place on a serving platter. Serve as is or with a sauce.

Sesame Arepas

1 1/2 to 2 lbs corn masa
1/4 tsp sea salt
1/2 cup tan or black sesame seeds, toasted
water
light or dark sesame oil

Crumble the corn dough in a bowl. Add the sea salt and sesame seeds, mixing them thoroughly throughout the dough. Knead the dough with a small amount of water until soft and the consistency of bread dough. Form the dough into cakes as above and pan-fry for 2 to 3 minutes on each side until a crust forms. Bake the arepas in a pre-heated 350 degree F oven for about 20 minutes or until they make a hollow, popping sound when tapped with your fingers. Remove and place on a serving platter.

Vegetable Arepas

1 1/2 to 2 lbs corn masa
1/4 tsp sea salt
water
1/4 cup onion, minced
1/4 cup mushrooms, minced
1/4 cup green or sweet red pepper, minced
corn oil, for sautéing vegetables
light or dark sesame oil, for frying arepas

Place a small amount of corn oil in a skillet and sauté the onion and mushrooms for 3 to 4 minutes. Place the vegetables in a mixing bowl. Crumble the corn dough in the mixing bowl and add the sea salt. Mix the vegetables and sea salt with the corn dough. Knead the dough, adding a small amount of water, until it becomes soft with the consistency of bread dough. Form the dough into several balls as above and flatten into cakes. Pan-fry the arepas for 2 to 3 minutes in a cast iron skillet until a crust forms on the arepas.

Pre-heat the oven at 350 degrees F and bake the arepas for 20 minutes or until they make a hollow, popping sound when tapped with your fingers. Place on a serving platter.

Bollos Polones (Boiled Corn Dumplings)

2 lbs corn masa
1/4 tsp sea salt
small amount of water, for kneading dough
10 cups water, for boiling dumplings
1 cup cooked kidney, pinto, or black beans
1/2 cup cooked seitan, minced
1/4 cup onion, minced
parsley or scallion, chopped, for garnish

Crumble the corn dough in a mixing bowl. Add the sea salt and mix thoroughly with the corn dough. Knead the dough, adding a small amount of water until it becomes soft with the consistency of bread dough. Form the dough into 10 to 12 balls. Mix the cooked beans, seitan, and onion. Make a hole in the middle of each ball with your thumb and insert the bean stuffing. Close the hole, using more dough if necessary, or by turning the balls in your hands, pressing gently until the hole closes.

Place the water in a pot, cover, and bring to a boil. Place the balls in the water and cook for about 20 minutes until done. Remove and place in a serving bowl. Garnish with chopped parsley or scallion. The balls may be served as is or with a miso, miso-tahini, carrot sauce, or another natural topping.

Homemade Tortillas

2 lbs corn masa
1/4 tsp sea salt
water
corn oil, for frying

Crumble the corn dough in a mixing bowl. Add the sea salt and mix thoroughly. Knead the dough, adding a small amount of water until it becomes the consistency of bread dough. Form the dough into 10 to 12 balls. Flatten each ball with the palm of your hand, pressing down, and then roll into thin circles about 5 inches across. Tortilla presses are available in kitchen supply stores and some natural food stores, which make this process easier. Simply place the balls of dough, one at a time, on the press, and press the lever down. The pressure causes the balls to flatten into thin, circular shapes.

Oil a cast iron pancake griddle or skillet with corn oil and heat. Fry the tortillas until dry and speckled with little brown spots. Flip over and fry the other side. Place the fried tortillas on paper towels to drain. Repeat the above process until all torillas have been fried, adding oil as needed. Keep warm in a low oven until ready to serve.

Tacos

10 to 12 tortilla shells (see above recipe)
2 cups organic kidney, pinto, or black turtle beans, washed
and soaked 6 to 8 hours, discard soaking water
water, for cooking beans
1 strip kombu, 2 to 3 inches long, soaked and diced
1 Tbsp barley miso, puréed, or 1/2 tsp sea salt
1 cup cooked seitan, sliced in thin strips
1 cup onion, finely diced
2 cups lettuce, shredded

Place the kombu and beans in a heavy pot. Add enough water to just cover the beans. Bring to a boil. Reduce the flame to medium and boil for 10 minutes without a cover. Cover the beans and reduce the flame to medium-low. Simmer for 1 1/2 to 2 hours until 70 to 80 percent done, adding small amounts of water occasionally while cooking, each time to just cover the beans. When the beans are 70 to 80 percent done, season with the puréed miso or sea salt and simmer for another 1/2 hour until done. Remove, place in a hand food mill, and purée. Place in a bowl.

Take the freshly made, warm tortillas, one at a time, in your hand and place 3 to 4 tablespoonfuls of beans, several strips of seitan, a tablespoonful of onion, and a little shredded lettuce on one-half of the tortilla. Fold the tortilla in half, covering the filling. Place on a serving platter. Repeat until all tortillas have been stuffed and folded. Serve warm.

Tostadas with Tofu Sour Cream and Vegetables

10 to 12 fresh tortillas (see above recipe)
1/2 cup onion, sliced in half-moons
1/2 cup summer squash, sliced in thin half-moons
1/2 cup mushrooms, sliced thin
1 cup leek, sliced thin
1 cup broccoli, sliced in small florets
1/2 cup sweet corn, removed from the cob
sesame or corn oil, for sautéing vegetables
tamari soy sauce, to taste, for seasoning vegetables

Tofu Sour Cream

1 lb firm style tofu, drained
1/2 cup water
1/4 cup umeboshi vinegar
2 to 3 tsp sweet brown rice vinegar
1/4 cup scallion or chives, finely chopped

Place a small amount of oil in a skillet and heat. Add the onion and sauté for 1 to 2 minutes. Add the mushrooms, corn, broccoli, and leek, and sauté until the broccoli is tender. Season to taste with a few drops of tamari soy sauce. Place an equal amount of sautéed vegetables on top of each tortilla.

To make the tofu sour cream, place the tofu, water, umeboshi, and sweet rice vinegar in a blender. Purée until smooth and creamy. Pour in a bowl. Mix in the chopped scallion or chives. Spoon the tofu sour cream over the vegetables on each tortilla and serve warm. If the tortillas are cold, warm in the oven or on a hot skillet before placing the vegetables and tofu sour cream on them.

Empanadas

10 to 12 freshly made tortilla shells (see above recipe)
3 to 4 cups cooked kidney, pinto, or black turtle beans, puréed
1 cup onion, diced
1 cup sweet corn, removed from the cob
light sesame or safflower oil, for deep-frying

Place the cooked beans, onion, and corn in a mixing bowl and mix. Place about 1/4 cup of the bean mixture on a fresh tortilla shell. Fold the tortilla over, covering the bean stuffing, and press the edges together with a fork or your fingers to hold the stuffing inside. Repeat until all tortillas have been stuffed and folded and the edges have been sealed.

Heat 2 to 3 inches of oil in a deep-frying pot. Deep-fry 2 to 3 empanadas on each side for 4 to 5 minutes until golden. Remove and drain on paper towels. Repeat until all empanadas have been deep-fried and drained. Place on a serving platter and serve hot.

Tamales

1 1/2 to 2 lbs corn masa
1/4 tsp sea salt
water
24 clean corn husks
2 cups cooked seitan, chopped
1 to 2 cloves garlic, minced
2 tsp organic chili powder (optional)
2 tsp dark sesame oil

Soak the corn husks in cold water for several minutes. If using dried corn husks, soak for several hours until soft. Crumble the corn dough in a mixing bowl and add the sea salt. Mix thoroughly. Knead the dough, adding a small amount of water, until it becomes soft with the consistency of bread dough. Cover with a damp towel. Place the seitan in a hand food mill and grind to a coarse consistency.

Place the oil in a skillet and heat. Sauté the garlic for 1 minute. Add the ground seitan. Sauté for 3 to 4 minutes. Remove and place in a bowl. Place 2 to 3 corn husks on a cutting board so that they overlap. Place 2 to 3 tablespoonfuls of the corn dough in your hands and form it into a rectangular shape. Place 2 tablespoonfuls of the seitan-vegetable mixture in the center of the dough and form again. Place the stuffed dough in the center of the corn husks. Roll the corn husks, first folding the sides in toward the center, around the stuffing and then fold both ends over the dough to completely encase the filling. Tie the roll with a piece of string or a strip of corn husk to fasten securely, to prevent the filling from falling out. Place on a plate. Repeat until all corn husks have been stuffed and tied.

Place 2 inches of water in a pot, cover, and bring to a boil. Place the stuffed corn husks in a bamboo steamer. These steamers usually have two or three levels or layers so that you can place all of the stuffed corn husks in them. Place the steamer on top of the pot of boiling water and steam for about 45 minutes to 1 hour. Remove the tamales from the steamer. Remove the tie from the corn husks and allow to cool slightly. Open the husks. The tamales inside should now be firm and come away from the husks easily. Serve the tamales in the unfolded husks on a serving platter.

Enchiladas

10 to 12 tortillas
light sesame or safflower oil, for frying tortillas
1/2 cup onion, diced
1 to 2 cloves garlic, minced (optional)
2 cups cooked seitan, chopped and ground in hand food mill
1/4 cup sweet red pepper, diced
1 to 2 tsp parsley, chopped
1/2 cup sweet corn, removed from cob
corn oil, for sautéing vegetables
1 cup mochi, coarsely grated
1 cup tofu sour cream (see previous recipe)
1 cup lettuce, shredded
1/2 cup black olives, pitted and sliced

Heat the corn oil in a skillet. Add the garlic, pepper, and onion. Sauté for 1 to 2 minutes. Add the seitan and sweet corn. Sauté for another 2 to 3 minutes. Mix in the parsley. Place in a bowl. Pre-heat the oven to 350 degrees F. Place 1 inch of oil in a deep-frying pot and heat. Dip the tortillas, one at a time, in the hot oil for a few seconds. Remove and place in layers of paper towels.

Fill each tortilla with the seitan-vegetable mixture. Sprinkle equal amounts of the grated mochi over the seitan. Roll up the stuffed tortillas and place them in a lightly oiled baking dish. Bake for 10 to 15 minutes. Remove and serve with the tofu sour cream spooned on top and garnish with the shredded lettuce and black olives.

Kidney Beans and Whole Corn

2 cups organic kidney beans, washed and soaked 6 to 8 hours,
   discard soaking water
1 strip kombu, 2 to 3 inches long, soaked and diced
2 cups whole dried corn, cooked (see previous recipes)
1 cup onion, diced
1/2 cup carrot, diced
1 Tbsp barley miso, puréed

    Place the kombu and beans in a heavy pot. Add enough water to just cover. Bring to a boil without a cover. Reduce the flame and simmer about 10 minutes. Cover the pot and reduce the flame to medium-low. Cook for 1 1/2 to 2 hours until about 70 to 80 percent done, adding water occasionally as needed while the beans are cooking. When the beans are 70 to 80 percent done, add the corn, onion, carrot, and miso. Cover and continue to cook for another 30 minutes or until tender. Remove and place in a serving bowl.

Homemade Hominy

1 cup organic whole dried white flint or yellow dent corn, soaked 6 to 8 hours
   or overnight
2 cups water
1/2 cup pure wood ash
pinch of sea salt

    Place the soaked corn, wood ash, and 1 cup water in a pressure cooker. Cover and bring up to pressure over a high flame. Reduce the flame to medium-low and place a flame deflector under the cooker. Cook for 1 hour. Remove from the flame and allow the pressure to come down. Remove the cover and pour the corn in a colander or strainer. Rinse out all wood ash under cold water.
    Place the rinsed corn in a clean pressure cooker. Add the remaining 1 cup of water and a pinch of sea salt. Bring up to pressure and cook for 1 more hour. Remove from the flame and allow the pressure to come down. Remove the cover and place the corn in a colander. Rub off all of the skins, rinse the corn well, and discard the skins. Place in a serving bowl. The hominy is now ready to eat. It can also be sautéd with vegetables, used to make fried cakes, or used in salads.

Sautéed Hominy and Vegetables

4 cups cooked hominy
1 cup onion, diced
1/2 cup carrot, diced
1 cup green string beans, sliced in 1 inch lengths
1/2 cup mushrooms, sliced
scallion, chopped, for garnish
sesame oil
tamari soy sauce

Heat an oiled skillet. Add the hominy and brown slightly. Add the onion and mushrooms and sauté for 2 to 3 minutes. Add the carrot and string beans. Sauté for another 4 to 5 minutes. Season with a little tamari soy sauce to taste and sauté for another 2 to 3 minutes. Remove and place in a serving bowl. Garnish with chopped scallion.

Boiled Sweet Corn

4 to 5 ears fresh sweet corn, husks removed
water
pinch of sea salt
umeboshi plum or paste

Place 2 inches of water in a pot with the sea salt, cover, and bring to a boil. Remove the cover and place the ears of corn in the water. Cover and boil for 3 to 5 minutes until tender. Remove and place on a serving platter. When served, spread a little umeboshi plum or paste on the corn for a delicious flavor.

Baked Sweet Corn

4 to 5 ears fresh sweet corn, husks left on
umeboshi plum or paste

Remove only the silk and 1 layer of husk from each ear of corn. Soak the ears in cold water for 30 minutes. Bake the corn in a 350 degree F oven for 30 to 35 minutes. Remove and place on a serving platter. Remove the husks just before eating. Spread a little umeboshi plum or paste on the corn before eating.

Roasted Sweet Corn

4 to 5 ears fresh sweet corn, husks left on
umeboshi plum or paste

Remove the corn silk and soak each ear of corn in cold water for 30 minutes or so. Remove and shake off excess water. Place the corn on a grill above hot coals or right on the hot coals of an open fire. Roast for about 20 to 25 minutes until tender. Remove from the coals and place on a platter. Just before eating, remove the husks and rub a little umeboshi plum or paste on each ear.

Succotash

1 cup organic lima beans, washed and soaked 6 to 8 hours,
**   discard soaking water**
1 strip kombu, 1 to 2 inches long, soaked and diced
2 cups fresh sweet corn, removed from the cob
1 cup onion, diced
water
1/8 tsp sea salt

Place the kombu and soaked lima beans in a heavy pot. Bring to a boil and simmer, uncovered, for 10 minutes. Cover and reduce the flame to medium-low. Simmer for 1 1/2 to 2 hours until 70 to 80 percent done, adding water occasionally during cooking, each time adding only enough to just cover the beans. When the beans are about 70 to 80 percent done, add the sweet corn, onion, and sea salt. Cover and simmer for 30 minutes longer until tender and creamy. Remove and place in a serving bowl.

Creamed Corn

4 to 5 ears sweet corn, husks removed
water
pinch of sea salt

Remove the corn from the cob by grating it off with a corn scraper or a box grater. Scrape any remaining corn and juice from the cob with the back or dull side of a knife blade. Place the corn in a saucepan with a small amount of water and a pinch of sea salt. Cover and bring to a boil. Reduce the flame to low and simmer about 10 minutes. Remove and place in a serving bowl.

Corn Salad with Creamy Tofu-Dill Dressing

2 cups fresh sweet corn, removed from the cob
1/4 cup red onion, diced
1/2 cup fresh green beans, sliced in 1 inch lengths
1/2 cup red radish, sliced in thin half-moons
1/4 cup carrot, coarsely grated
1 cup lettuce, finely shredded
water, for boiling vegetables

Creamy Tofu-Dill Dressing

1/2 lb firm style tofu, drained
1/4 cup water
2 Tbsp umeboshi vinegar
1 to 2 tsp sweet brown rice vinegar
1/2 tsp tamari soy sauce
1/4 cup fresh dill, chopped

Place a small amount of water in a saucepan, cover, and bring to a boil. Blanch the corn for 2 to 3 minutes, then remove and drain. Place in a mixing bowl. Blanch the green beans for 3 minutes, remove and drain. Place in the mixing bowl. Place the red onion, carrot, red radish, and lettuce in the mixing bowl. Mix and place in a serving bowl. To prepare the dressing, place the tofu, water, umeboshi vinegar, sweet rice vinegar, soy sauce, and dill in a blender. Purée until smooth and creamy. Spoon the dressing over each serving of salad just before serving.

Corn and Hijiki Salad with Umeboshi-Parsley Dressing

3 cups sweet corn, removed from the cob
1/2 cup hijiki, washed and soaked 3 to 5 minutes, drained and chopped
1/2 cup broccoli, florets
1/2 cup cauliflower, florets
1/4 cup red radish, sliced in thin rounds
1/4 cup pumpkin or sunflower seeds, roasted
water

Umeboshi-Parsley Dressing

2 umeboshi plums, pits removed

1 tsp parsley, minced
1 tsp onion, grated
3/4 cup water

Place 1 inch of water in a saucepan, cover, and bring to a boil. Blanch the sweet corn for 2 to 3 minutes. Remove, drain, and place in a mixing bowl. Blanch the broccoli for 2 to 3 minutes, then remove and drain. Place in the mixing bowl. Blanch the cauliflower for 3 minutes, remove and drain. Place in the mixing bowl. Place the hijiki in the water, cover, and simmer for 10 to 15 minutes. Remove, drain, and place in the mixing bowl. Add the red radishes and seeds to the bowl and mix well.

To prepare the dressing, place the umeboshi plums in a suribachi and grind to a smooth paste. Add the parsley and onion and grind again. Add the water and grind again until all ingredients are thoroughly mixed. Mix the dressing in with the salad just before placing in a serving bowl.

Arame and Corn

1 cup arame, rinsed, drained, and sliced
2 cups sweet corn, removed from the cob
1/2 cup onion, sliced in half-moons
1/2 cup snow peas, sliced in half
dark sesame oil
tamari soy sauce
water

Heat a small amount of oil in a skillet. Sauté the onion for 1 to 2 minutes. Place the arame on top of the onion and add enough water to half cover the arame. Place the sweet corn on top of the arame. Cover and bring to a boil. Reduce the flame to medium-low and simmer for 25 minutes. Season with a little soy sauce. Simmer for another 2 to 3 minutes. Place the snow peas on top of the corn, cover, and simmer for another 1 to 2 minutes. Remove the cover, turn the flame to high, and cook off most of the remaining liquid. Mix and place in a serving bowl.

Corn and Vegetable Aspic with Miso-Lemon Dressing

1/4 cup onion, diced
1/4 cup carrot, diced
1 cup sweet corn, removed from cob
1/4 cup green peas, shelled

1/4 cup celery, diced
1/4 cup fresh shiitake mushrooms, sliced
4 cups water, including water used to boil vegetables
5 Tbsp agar flakes (read directions on package)
tamari soy sauce
1 tsp fresh ginger juice
1 Tbsp mellow barley miso
1 1/2 tsp lemon juice
1 Tbsp parsley,
1/2 cup water

Place 2 cups of water in a saucepan, cover, and bring to a boil. Boil the vegetables separately in the following order: onion for 1 minute, corn for 2 minutes, carrot for 2 minutes, green peas for 2 to 3 minutes, shiitake mushrooms for 1 1/2 to 2 minutes, and celery for 1 minute. Place the cooked vegetables in a shallow casserole dish. Spread them evenly.

Add the remaining water to the vegetable cooking water to equal 4 cups. Add the agar flakes to the water in the saucepan. Bring to a boil, stirring constantly. After coming to a boil, reduce the flame to low and simmer for 2 to 3 minutes. Season the water mildly with a few drops of soy sauce and add the ginger juice. Stir and pour the hot liquid over the vegetables in the casserole dish. Set the dish aside and allow the mixture to gel. If you are in a hurry place the dish in the refrigerator to speed the process.

To prepare the dressing, place the parsley in a suribachi and grind for several seconds. Add the miso and lemon juice. Purée to a smooth paste. Gradually add the water, stirring constantly with the pestle until the dressing is smooth and creamy. When the aspic has gelled, slice and place on individual serving plates. Place a teaspoonful or so of dressing on top of each serving.

Soybean and Corn Relish

1 cup organic yellow soybeans, washed and soaked 6 to 8 hours, discard
   soaking water
1 strip kombu, 1 to 2 inches long, soaked and diced
3 cups water
2 cups sweet corn, removed from cob
1/2 cup carrot, diced
1/4 cup burdock, diced
1/4 cup lotus root, diced
dark sesame oil
2 tsp barley miso, puréed
1 tsp fresh ginger juice

1 Tbsp chives or scallion, chopped

Place the kombu, soybeans, and water in a pressure cooker. Place the uncovered cooker over a high flame and bring to a boil. Boil for 10 minutes. Cover and bring up to pressure. Reduce the flame to medium-low and simmer for 35 to 40 minutes. Remove from the flame and allow the pressure to come down. Remove the cover.

Heat a small amount of oil in a cast iron skillet and sauté the burdock for 1 to 2 minutes. Layer the lotus and carrot on top of the burdock. Add the soybeans and remaining cooking water. Cover and bring to a boil. Reduce the flame to medium-low and simmer for 30 minutes. Add the miso, cover, and simmer for another 2 to 3 minutes. Turn the flame to high, remove the cover, and cook off most of the remaining liquid. Mix in the ginger juice and chives or scallion. Place in a serving bowl.

Corn Grits

1 cup yellow or white corn grits
3 to 3 1/2 cups water
pinch of sea salt

Place the water and sea salt in a pot, cover, and bring to a boil. Place the corn grits in the pot, stirring constantly. Cover, bring to a boil again, and reduce the flame to medium-low. Simmer for 30 to 35 minutes. Place in individual serving dishes and garnish with your favorite condiment. Serve hot.

Polenta (Cornmeal)

1 cup yellow cornmeal
3 cups water
pinch of sea salt

Place the water and sea salt in a pot, cover, and bring to a boil. Place the cornmeal in the pot, stirring constantly to prevent lumping. Bring to a boil again, cover, and reduce the flame to medium-low. Simmer for 20 to 25 minutes. Place in individual serving bowls and garnish with your favorite condiment or sauce. Serve hot.

Fried Polenta with Mushroom Sauce

1 cup yellow cornmeal
3 cups water
pinch of sea salt
corn oil, for frying the polenta

Mushroom Sauce

2 cups mushrooms, sliced thin
1 Tbsp corn oil
1/2 cup onion, minced
2 cups water
1 cup plain soymilk (optional; water may be substituted)
4 Tbsp unbleached white flour
2 Tbsp parsley, minced
tamari soy sauce, to taste

Place 3 cups of water in a pot with a pinch of sea salt, cover, and bring to a boil. Add the cornmeal, stirring constantly to prevent lumping and bring to a boil again. Cover, reduce the flame to medium-low, and simmer for 20 to 25 minutes. Remove from the flame and pour the polenta in a glass cake pan or shallow casserole dish. Set aside and allow to cool until firm to the touch. Slice the polenta into 1/2 inch thick slices.

Place a small amount of corn oil on a pancake griddle and heat. Place several pieces of the sliced polenta on the griddle and fry until golden. Flip over and fry the other side until golden. Remove and place on a platter. Repeat until all polenta has been fried. You may keep warm in a slow oven until the sauce is ready.

To prepare the mushroom sauce, place the corn oil in a skillet and heat. Sauté the onion for 1 to 2 minutes. Add the mushrooms and sauté for another 2 to 3 minutes. Add the flour, stirring constantly, until the onion and mushrooms are coated with it. Combine the water and soymilk and slowly pour it in the skillet, stirring constantly to prevent lumping, until the sauce becomes smooth and thick. Bring to a boil. Reduce the flame to medium-low and season to taste with a little tamari soy sauce. Cover and simmer for 5 to 7 minutes. Remove from the flame and stir in the chopped parsley. Place the sauce in a serving bowl. To serve, place 2 to 3 slices of polenta on each plate and spoon the mushroom sauce over it. Serve hot.

Polenta with Red Pepper-Miso Sauce

1 cup yellow cornmeal
3 cups water
pinch of sea salt

Red Pepper-Miso Sauce

2 cups sweet red pepper, sliced thin
1 cup onion, sliced in half-moons
1 to 1 1/2 Tbsp mellow barley miso, puréed
1/2 to 3/4 cup plain soymilk
corn or extra virgin olive oil

Place the water and sea salt in a pot, cover, and bring to a boil. Add the cornmeal, stirring constantly and bring to a boil again. Cover, reduce the flame, and simmer for 20 to 25 minutes. Pour the polenta in a glass cake dish or casserole. Set aside to cool until firm to the touch. Slice the polenta and place 2 to 3 pieces on each serving plate.

To prepare the sauce, heat a small amount of oil in a skillet and sauté the onion for 1 to 2 minutes. Add the pepper and sauté for another 2 to 3 minutes. Add the soymilk and puréed miso. Cover and reduce the flame to low. Simmer for 4 to 5 minutes until the onion and pepper are tender. Remove from the flame and place in a serving dish. Spoon the hot sauce over each serving of polenta.

Winter Baked Polenta and Vegetables

1 cup yellow cornmeal
3 1/2 cups water
pinch of sea salt
2 cups kale, chopped
1 cup onion, diced
1 cup winter squash, sliced in thin pieces
1 cup mushrooms, sliced thin
3 cloves garlic, minced
corn oil
tamari soy sauce

Prepare the polenta as described in the previous recipes. Pour half of the polenta in an oiled casserole dish. Heat a small amount of corn oil and sauté the garlic and onion for 1 to 2 minutes. Add the mushrooms, sprinkle with several drops of tamari soy sauce, and sauté for 2 to 3 minutes longer. Add the squash and kale. Sauté another minute or so. Spread the vegetables evenly over the polenta in the casserole dish. Pour the remaining polenta over the vegetables and spread evenly. Place the polenta in a 375 degree F oven and bake for 25 to 30 minutes. Remove and slice or spoon onto individual serving plates.

Summer Polenta and Vegetables

1 cup yellow cornmeal
3 cups water
pinch of sea salt
1 cup cooked chickpeas
1 cup cooked seitan, sliced in thin strips
1 cup sweet corn, removed from the cob
1/2 cup green beans, sliced in 2 inch lengths
1/2 cup cucumber, sliced in julienne strips
1/4 cup red radish, sliced in thin quarter-moons
1 Tbsp tamari soy sauce
1 tsp natural mustard
1 Tbsp parsley, minced
1/2 to 2/3 cup water

Prepare the basic polenta as described previously, and pour in a glass cake dish and allow to cool until firm to the touch. Slice the polenta into squares, rectangles, or triangles and place 2 to 3 pieces on each serving plate. Blanch the corn for 2 minutes and the green beans for 3 minutes in a little boiling water. Drain and place in a mixing bowl. Add the chickpeas, seitan, cucumber, and radish.

Place the mustard, soy sauce, and parsley in a suribachi and grind for 1 minute. Add the water and purée until smooth. Pour over the vegetables and mix well. Spoon the vegetables over each serving of polenta. Serve at room temperature or slightly chilled.

Deep-Fried Polenta Croutons

1 cup yellow cornmeal
3 cups water
pinch of sea salt
light sesame or safflower oil, for deep-frying

Prepare the polenta as described in the previous recipes. Pour in a glass cake dish and allow to cool until firm to the touch. Slice into 2 inch squares. Heat 2 to 3 inches of oil in a heavy deep-frying pot. Place several pieces of polenta in the hot oil and deep-fry until golden. Remove and drain. Repeat until all polenta has been fried. Serve on top of cooked kidney beans, homemade chili, or black bean soup.

Deep-Fried Macaroni and Corn Fritters

1 cup whole grain elbow macaroni, cooked
1 cup sweet corn, removed from cob
1/2 cup corn flour
1/4 cup whole wheat pastry flour
1/2 cup brown rice mochi, coarsely grated
1/2 cup mushrooms, diced
1/4 cup onion, diced
1/4 cup parsley, minced
pinch of sea salt
3/4 cup water
1 tsp kuzu, diluted in 2 tsp water
1/2 tsp tamari soy sauce
light sesame or safflower oil, for deep-frying

Tamari Soy Sauce-Ginger Dip Sauce

1 cup water
1/4 cup tamari soy sauce
1 tsp ginger, grated

Place flours, grated mochi, vegetables, and sea salt in a mixing bowl and mix well. Add the water, cooked macaroni, kuzu, and soy sauce. Mix thoroughly. Heat 3 inches of oil in a heavy deep-frying pot. Drop the batter, 1 tablespoonful at a time in the hot oil. You may deep-fry 5 to 6 tablespoonfuls at a time. Deep-fry until golden brown. Remove and place on paper towels to drain. Repeat until all batter has been fried.

To prepare the dip sauce, place the water and soy sauce in a saucepan and heat. Turn the flame off and add the grated ginger. Place in small, individual dipping bowls. Place the fritters on individual serving plates and dip in the sauce before eating.

Pan-Fried Corn Fritters

2 cups corn flour
1 to 1 1/2 cups water
1 cup sweet corn, removed from cob
1/2 cup cooked brown rice
pinch of sea salt
corn oil

Mix all ingredients in a mixing bowl. Heat an oiled skillet. Spoon 2 table-spoonfuls of the mixture for each fritter on the hot skillet. Press down slightly with a spoon or fork. Fry until golden. Flip the fritters over and fry the other side until golden. Remove and place on a serving platter. Repeat until all batter has been fried. Serve with the tamari soy sauce-ginger dip sauce above.

Corn Bread Oyster Stuffing

4 cups homemade corn bread, cubed
2 cups whole wheat bread, cubed
1 lb fresh shucked oysters, chopped
1/2 lb mushrooms, diced
1 cup onion, diced
1/4 cup sweet red pepper, diced
1/2 cup parsley, minced
1/2 cup celery, diced
2 cups oyster juice, clam juice, or water
1 tsp organic sage
tamari soy sauce
2 tsp corn oil

Heat the oil in a skillet and sauté the onion for 1 to 2 minutes. Add the mushrooms and pepper. Sauté for another 3 to 4 minutes. Place in a mixing bowl. Add the corn bread, whole wheat bread, oysters, parsley, and seasonings. Sprinkle several drops of soy sauce over. Add the oyster or clam juice and mix. Oil a baking pan and place the stuffing in it, spreading it evenly in the pan. Cover and bake at 350 degrees F for 25 to 30 minutes. Serve with fish, seitan, or squash. Instead of baking the stuffing separately, stuff a winter squash, fish fillets, or seitan roast with it and bake as you would regular whole wheat or grain stuffings.

Buckwheat

The traditional staple of Russia, Eastern Europe, and parts of central and northern Asia, buckwheat is the hardiest of the cereal plants because of the cold weather it endures. Its kernels are called groats, and it is usually roasted and eaten in whole form or in coarse or fine granules. All these forms of buckwheat are known as kasha. Whenever available, the whole groats should be used, as they retain more energy and nutrients than the granules.

In the Far East, buckwheat has also been eaten for centuries in the form of noodles, especially in Japan, called soba. Soba comes in several varieties and is classified according to its percentage of buckwheat flour. Buckwheat noodles traditionally include whole wheat flour, and are discussed in the noodle chapter.

Kasha has a deep rich taste and may be prepared in many styles. The most basic method is dry-roasting for a few minutes and then boiling with a pinch of sea salt. Because of its soft, fluffy nature, it does not require soaking beforehand. For a creamy morning cereal, about twice the usual volume of water can be added. Buckwheat is also delicious gomoku-style with five or more vegetables such as celery, burdock, green peas, and onions. In the summer, it is delicious served cool in a salad, especially along with sauerkraut. Buckwheat can be milled into flour for making hearty pancakes, waffles, and muffins. Buckwheat flour is also used for dumplings, called *sobagaki*, that puff up quickly.

Basic Boiled Buckwheat

2 cups organic buckwheat, washed
4 cups boiling water
pinch of sea salt
scallion, chives, or parsley, finely chopped, for garnish

Heat a stainless steel skillet and dry-roast the buckwheat over a high flame, stirring constantly. Roast until it becomes dry and releases a nutty fragrance. Be careful not to burn the buckwheat. Place the sea salt and buckwheat in the pot of boiling water, cover, and reduce the flame to medium-low. Simmer for 20 minutes. Remove and place in serving dishes. Garnish and serve hot.

Buckwheat and Sautéed Vegetables

2 cups organic buckwheat, washed
4 cups boiling water

1/2 cup onion, diced
1/2 cup cabbage, shredded
1/2 cup carrot, diced
light or dark sesame oil
pinch of sea salt
chives, scallion, or parsley, finely chopped, for garnish

Place a small amount of oil in a skillet and heat. Sauté the onion for 1 to 2 minutes. Add the carrot and cabbage and sauté for another 2 to 3 minutes. Add the buckwheat and sauté for 1 to 2 minutes. Place the buckwheat, sautéed vegetables, and sea salt in the pot of boiling water, cover, and bring to a boil again. Reduce the flame to medium-low and simmer for 20 minutes. Mix in the chopped chives, scallion, or parsley and place in a serving bowl.

Buckwheat, Tempeh, and Sauerkraut

2 cups organic buckwheat, washed
1 cup tempeh, diced
1/2 cup sauerkraut, chopped
1/4 cup parsley, chopped
4 cups boiling water
light sesame oil, for pan-frying tempeh

Place a small amount of oil in a skillet and heat. Place the tempeh in the skillet and fry until golden, stirring to prevent burning. Place the tempeh, buckwheat, and sauerkraut in the pot of boiling water, cover, and bring to a boil again. Reduce the flame to medium-low and simmer for 20 minutes. Add the parsley, cover, and simmer for 1 minute. Remove the cover, mix, and place in a serving bowl.

Fried Kasha and Vegetables

3 to 4 cups cooked buckwheat
1/2 cup onion, diced
1 cup leek, chopped
1/2 cup mushrooms, sliced
1/2 cup carrots, sliced in matchsticks
1 tsp fresh ginger juice
light sesame oil
tamari soy sauce
scallion, finely chopped, for garnish

Heat a small amount of oil in a skillet. Sauté the onion for 1 to 2 minutes. Add the mushrooms and sauté for 1 to 2 minutes. Add the carrot and leek. Place the cooked buckwheat on top of the vegetables. Reduce the flame to low, sprinkle with a few drops of tamari soy sauce, and cover. Fry until the vegetables are tender and the buckwheat is hot. Add the chopped scallion and a few more drops of soy sauce, cover, and cook for 1 to 2 more minutes. Remove the cover and mix the vegetables and buckwheat. Place in a serving bowl.

Kasha Varnitshkes

2 cups cooked buckwheat
2 cups cooked elbow or bow tie noodles
1/2 cup onion, diced
1 cup mushrooms, diced
2 cloves garlic, minced (optional)
1 to 2 Tbsp light sesame oil
tamari soy sauce
parsley, finely chopped, for garnish

Heat the oil in a skillet. Add the garlic and onion and sauté for 1 minute. Add the mushrooms and sauté for 1 to 2 minutes. Add the noodles and buckwheat, sprinkle with a little tamari soy sauce, and mix. Cover and reduce the flame to low. Cook until the noodles and buckwheat are hot. If necessary, add a few drops of water to the skillet to generate steam. Remove the cover and sauté for another 2 to 3 minutes. Mix in the parsley and place in a serving bowl.

Buckwheat Salad with Tamari-Ginger Dressing

2 cups cooked buckwheat
1/2 cup deep-fried tempeh cubes
1/4 cup red onion, sliced in very thin half-moon rings
1/4 cup snow peas, sliced in half
1/2 cup kale, chopped
1/4 cup sweet corn, removed from cob
1/4 cup red radish, quartered and sliced
1/4 cup sauerkraut, chopped
1/4 cup sauerkraut juice
3/4 cup water, for boiling tempeh
1/4 cup tamari soy sauce, for boiling tempeh
water, for blanching vegetables

Place the cooked buckwheat in a mixing bowl and fluff up with a fork until room temperature. Place water in a saucepan with soy sauce and add the tempeh cubes. Cover and bring to a boil. Reduce the flame to medium-low and simmer for 20 minutes. Remove, drain, and place in the mixing bowl.

Place about 1 inch of plain water in a saucepan, cover, and bring to a boil. Blanch the vegetables in the following order: snow peas for 1 minute, sweet corn for 1 1/2 minutes, and kale for 1 1/2 minutes. Drain and place in the mixing bowl. Place the red onion, red radish, sauerkraut, and sauerkraut juice in the mixing bowl and mix well.

Tamari-Ginger Dressing

1 Tbsp tamari soy sauce
1/4 to 1/3 tsp ginger juice
1/2 to 2/3 cup water
1/4 cup parsley, finely chopped

Place the soy sauce and water in a saucepan and bring to a boil. Reduce the flame to low and simmer for 1 to 2 minutes. Turn the flame off and let cool to room temperature. Add the parsley. Pour the dressing over the salad and mix well. Place in a serving bowl.

Stuffed Cabbage

1 cup organic buckwheat, washed
2 cups boiling water, for buckwheat
pinch of sea salt
5 to 6 cabbage leaves, whole
water, for boiling cabbage
1/4 cup onion, diced
1/4 cup carrot, diced
1/4 cup mushrooms, diced
1/4 cup celery, diced
1/4 cup sauerkraut, chopped
1/2 cup tempeh, diced
light sesame oil
1 strip kombu, 2 to 3 inches long, soaked
2 tsp tamari soy sauce

Place the buckwheat and sea salt in the boiling water, stir, cover, and bring to a boil again. Reduce the flame to medium-low and simmer for 20 minutes. Remove and place in a mixing bowl, fluffing with a fork to cool. Place a small amount of sesame oil in a skillet and heat. Sauté the onion for 1 to 2 minutes. Add the tempeh and sauté 2 to 3 minutes. Add the mushrooms, carrot, and celery. Sauté for another 2 to 3 minutes. Place the sautéed vegetables in the mixing bowl with the buckwheat.

Add the sauerkraut to the mixing bowl and mix. Place 1 to 2 inches of water in a saucepan, cover, and bring to a boil. Place the cabbage leaves in the water, cover, and cook for 1 1/2 to 2 minutes. Remove and drain. Cut out the thick stem portion of the cabbage as shown in the illustration. Take about 1/4 cup of the buckwheat mixture and form, by hand, into a croquette or cylindrical shape. Place the mixture on a cabbage leaf. Fold the sides of the cabbage leaf in toward the center and roll into a croquette. Fasten the leaf with a toothpick to hold together. Repeat until all leaves are stuffed.

Place the kombu in a skillet or pot and place the stuffed cabbage leaves in the skillet. Add enough water to half-cover the stuffed cabbage. Season with tamari soy sauce. Cover and bring to a boil. Reduce the flame to low and simmer for 25 to 30 minutes until the cabbage is tender. Remove and place in a serving dish. The remaining liquid in the skillet can be thickened with a little diluted kuzu to make a sauce for the stuffed cabbage leaves.

Buckwheat Casserole

2 cups, organic buckwheat, washed and dry-roasted
4 cups boiling water
pinch of sea salt
1/2 cup onion, diced
1 cup cabbage, sliced in 1 inch squares
1/2 cup carrot, quartered and sliced thin

Mushroom Sauce

1/2 cup whole wheat pastry flour
3 cups water
1 cup onion, diced
1/4 lb mushrooms, diced
2 to 2 1/2 Tbsp tamari soy sauce
corn oil
parsley, chives, or scallion, finely chopped, for garnish

Place the buckwheat, sea salt, onion, cabbage, and carrot in the saucepan with the boiling water. Mix, cover, and bring to a boil again. Reduce the flame to medium-low and simmer for 20 minutes. Place the buckwheat in a lightly oiled casserole dish and cover. Bake at 350 degrees F for 10 to 15 minutes.

To prepare the sauce, brush a skillet with corn oil and heat. Sauté the onion and mushrooms for 3 to 4 minutes. Add the flour and mix thoroughly, coating the vegetables. Slowly pour in the water, stirring constantly to prevent lumping. Bring to a boil. Reduce the flame to low, cover, and simmer for 5 to 7 minutes. Add the soy sauce, cover, and simmer an additional 5 to 10 minutes. Stir occasionally to prevent sticking and burning. Poke several small holes in the casserole with a chopstick. Pour the sauce over the casserole. Bake, uncovered, for another 20 to 25 minutes. Remove and garnish with chopped parsley, chives, or scallion.

Buckwheat Croquettes

4 to 5 cups cooked buckwheat
1 cup onion, diced
1/2 cup carrot, diced
1/2 cup celery, diced
1/2 cup water
1 Tbsp parsley, chopped
tamari soy sauce
light sesame oil or safflower oil
2 Tbsp tamari soy sauce
1/2 cup water
1/2 tsp fresh ginger juice

Place the buckwheat, onion, carrot, and celery in a mixing bowl. If the buckwheat is dry, add water and mix thoroughly. If the buckwheat is very wet, add a little whole wheat pastry flour just to hold the mixture together. Form the mixture into croquettes, taking 1/3 to 1/2 cup for each croquette. Repeat until all the mixture has been used. Heat 2 inches of oil in a heavy deep-frying pot. Place 4 to 5 croquettes in the hot oil and deep-fry each side until golden brown. Remove and place on paper towels to drain. Deep-fry the remaining croquettes, and drain. Place on a serving platter.

To prepare the dip sauce, place the tamari soy sauce and water in a saucepan and heat. Reduce the flame to low and simmer for 2 to 3 minutes. Turn flame off and add the ginger juice. Place the sauce in dipping bowls. Dip the croquettes in the sauce before eating.

Buckwheat and Rice Burgers

2 cups cooked buckwheat
2 cups cooked brown rice

1/2 cup onion, minced
1/4 cup celery, minced
1/4 cup carrot, minced
2 Tbsp parsley, minced
1/4 cup sunflower or pumpkin seeds, roasted
1/2 cup water
2 to 3 Tbsp whole wheat pastry flour
2 to 3 tsp tamari soy sauce
1/2 tsp ginger juice
light or dark sesame oil

Place the buckwheat, rice, and all ingredients except the oil in a mixing bowl. Mix thoroughly and form the mixture into several burgers. Heat enough oil to lightly cover the bottom of a skillet. Fry the burgers on one side until golden brown. Flip over and fry the other side until golden brown. Remove and place on a serving platter. Serve as is or with a dip sauce or gravy.

Kasha Knishes

Kasha knishes are buckwheat and vegetables wrapped in a pastry dough and baked. They are a nice treat, especially on a cold winter day.

3 to 4 cups cooked buckwheat
1 cup onion, diced
1 cup leek, chopped
1/2 cup mushrooms, sliced
1/2 cup tempeh, sliced in small cubes and deep-fried
1/4 cup parsley, minced
3 Tbsp miso mustard or other natural mustard
1/4 cup sauerkraut juice

Place all of the above ingredients in a mixing bowl and mix thoroughly. To prepare the pastry dough, see below.

Pastry Dough

2 cups whole wheat pastry flour
2 cups unbleached white flour
1/4 to 1/2 cup corn oil
1/4 tsp sea salt
1 cup cold water

Mix the flours and sea salt. Add the oil and mix in evenly with the flour by sifting it between the palms of your hands. Pour in the water and mix well, forming a ball of dough. Place the dough in the refrigerator for 1/2 hour. Remove the dough from the refrigerator and divide it into 8 equal balls. Roll the balls out one at a time on a lightly floured board or table. Form the balls into circular shapes about 5 to 6 inches across. Place enough buckwheat mixture on each circle of dough to cover half of each circle.

Dip your fingers in water and moisten the edges of each of the circles. Fold the uncovered half of the circles over the buckwheat mixture, covering it. Each circle should now have a half-moon shape. To seal the dough, press the edges together with a fork or your fingers. Take a fork and poke holes in the top of each knish. Place the knishes on an oiled baking dish and bake in a pre-heated 350 degree oven for about 40 minutes until the crust is golden brown. Remove and place on a serving platter.

Chapter 6
Whole Grain Soups and Stews

Whole grains and their products can be used as the foundation for soups and stews or added in small volume to mixed soups. Whole grain soups and stews are nourishing and delicious. Popular varieties include barley soup, brown rice soup, fresh corn soup, and buckwheat soup. Noodles, seitan, fu, and other grain products can also be added to soups and stews. Grain soups are often cooked with vegetables and sea vegetables.

As the usual first course, soup sets the tone for the entire meal and creates an appetite for everything that is to follow. The taste, aroma, color, and texture of the soup should complement the other courses. If the meal on the whole is light, the soup may be on the thick or hearty side, and in some cases, constituting almost a meal in itself. If there are many courses to the meal and much rich, nourishing fare, a simpler and lighter soup would be more appropriate.

Similarly, the ingredients may be adjusted to take into account seasonal and climatic changes. In hot weather, more cooling soups are appealing, containing lighter ingredients, such as corn, barley, and leafy green vegetables, and requiring slightly less miso, tamari soy sauce, sea salt, or other seasoning. In cold weather, more thick, warming soups can be prepared, that include more root and sweet-tasting round vegetables and slightly more seasoning.

Brown Rice and Vegetable Soup

1/2 cup organic brown rice, washed
1/2 cup onion, diced
4 shiitake mushrooms, soaked, stems removed, and diced
1/4 cup celery, diced
1/4 cup carrot, diced
2 Tbsp burdock, diced
1/2 cup leeks, sliced
5 to 6 cups water
1 1/2 to 2 1/2 Tbsp tamari soy sauce
scallion or parsley, finely chopped, for garnish
pinch of sea salt

Layer the onion, shiitake, celery, carrot, and burdock in a soup pot. Place the rice on top. Add the water and a pinch of sea salt. Cover and bring to a boil. Reduce the flame to medium-low and simmer for about 50 minutes. Add the leek and soy sauce, cover, and simmer again for another 10 minute. Place in serving bowls and garnish with chopped scallion or parsley.

Brown Rice and Pumpkin Soup

2 cups leftover cooked brown rice
1 cup Hokkaido pumpkin or buttercup squash, cut in 1/4 to 1/2 inch cubes
1/2 cup onion, diced
5 to 6 cups water
1/4 to 1/2 tsp sea salt
1 sheet nori, toasted and cut in thin strips or squares, for garnish
2 Tbsp scallion, finely chopped, for garnish

Place the onion on the bottom of a pot. Add the pumpkin. Place the cooked rice on top of the pumpkin. Add water and a pinch of sea salt. Cover and bring to a boil. Reduce the flame to medium-low and simmer for about 30 minutes. Add the remaining sea salt, cover, and simmer for another 10 minutes or so. Place in individual serving bowls and garnish with nori and scallion.

Brown Rice and Azuki Bean Soup

2 cups leftover cooked brown rice with azuki beans

1 cup daikon, quartered and sliced thin or diced
3 shiitake mushrooms, soaked, stems removed, and diced
1 strip kombu, 2 inches square, soaked and diced
1/4 cup scallion, chopped
5 to 6 cups water
1/4 to 1/2 tsp sea salt

Place the kombu, shiitake, daikon, and azuki bean rice in a pot. Add water, cover, and bring to a boil. Reduce the flame to medium-low and simmer about 30 minutes until creamy. Add the sea salt and cook for 10 minutes longer. Add the chopped scallion and simmer, uncovered, for 1 minute. Place in serving bowls.

Brown Rice Miso Soup

2 cups leftover cooked brown rice
1/2 cup onion, sliced in thin half-moons
1/2 cup carrot, sliced in matchsticks
1/4 cup cabbage, sliced or diced
3 to 4 Tbsp wakame, soaked and chopped
4 to 5 cups water
4 to 5 tsp barley miso, diluted
scallion, finely chopped, for garnish

Place the water in a pot, cover, and bring to a boil. Add the rice and wakame. Reduce the flame to medium and simmer for about 5 to 7 minutes. Add the onion, carrot, and cabbage. Cover and simmer for another 3 to 5 minutes. Reduce the flame to low and wait for the water to stop boiling. Add the diluted miso and simmer for another 2 to 4 minutes. Place in serving bowls and garnish with chopped scallion.

Quick Shoyu Broth and Rice

2 cups leftover cooked brown rice
4 to 5 cups water, including water used to soak shiitake and kombu
4 to 5 shiitake mushrooms, soaked, stems removed, and sliced
1 strip kombu, 2 inches square, soaked
2 to 3 Tbsp tamari soy sauce
1/4 cup scallion, finely chopped

Place the shiitake and water in a pot. Roll the kombu up in a log shape and slice in very thin matchsticks and place in the pot. Cover and bring to a boil. Reduce the flame to medium-low and simmer for 10 to 12 minutes. Add the rice and soy sauce, cover, and simmer for another 5 minutes. Add the chopped scallion, mix, and place in individual serving dishes.

Rice and Green Tea Soup

2 cups leftover cooked brown or white rice
4 to 5 cups hot green tea
1 medium umeboshi plum
1/2 sheet nori, toasted and cut in thin strips
1 Tbsp scallion, finely chopped

Place equal amounts of rice in 4 to 5 individual soup bowls. Pull the plum apart into small pieces and place 2 to 3 pieces in each bowl with the rice. Place 1 tablespoonful of green tea in 4 cups boiling water. Turn off the flame and let steep for 1 minute. Pour the hot green tea over each bowl of rice. Garnish with several strips of nori and chopped scallion and serve hot.

Clear Soup with Rice Dumplings

1/2 lb firm style tofu, cubed
light sesame or safflower oil, for deep-frying
1 cup leek, sliced in 1 inch pieces
1 cup carrot, sliced in match sticks
1/2 cup green beans, sliced in 2 inch lengths
1/2 cup turnip, cubed
5 cups water
1 strip kombu 2 to 3 inches long, soaked and minced
1 cup brown rice flour
1/2 cup boiling water
1/2 tsp sea salt
1 1/2 Tbsp tamari soy sauce
1 sheet nori, toasted and cut in thin strips

Heat 2 to 3 inches of oil in a heavy deep-frying pot. Deep-fry the tofu cubes until golden brown. Remove and place on paper towels to drain. Place the kombu and water in a pot, cover, and bring to a boil. Reduce the flame to medium-low and simmer for 10 minutes. Add the carrot, green beans, and turnip. Cover and simmer 2 to 3 minutes.

Place the rice flour in a mixing bowl with a pinch of sea salt. Mix and add the boiling water. Stir the mixture vigorously with a fork for 1 to 2 minutes. Knead the dough for 2 to 4 minutes. Roll the dough into balls the size of golf balls. Press your thumb in the center of each dumpling to make a slight indentation. This will help them cook better.

Season the soup stock with sea salt and soy sauce and drop the dumplings in. They will sink to the bottom. Add the leek. When the dumplings rise to the surface they are done. Simmer the soup for another 2 to 3 minutes. Place in individual serving bowls and garnish with strips of toasted nori.

Creamy Rice and Vegetable Soup

1 cup leftover cooked brown rice
1/2 cup rolled oats
1/2 cup onion, diced
1/4 cup celery, diced
1/2 cup carrot, diced
1 cup broccoli, sliced in small florets
4 to 5 cups water
1/4 to 1/2 tsp sea salt
scallion, finely chopped, for garnish

Place the rice, oats, and water in a pot. Cover and bring to a boil. Reduce the flame to medium-low and simmer for 10 to 15 minutes. Remove from the flame and purée the rice, oats, and liquid in a hand food mill. Place the creamy purée back in the pot and add the onion, celery, and carrot. Cover and bring to a boil. Reduce the flame to medium-low and simmer for about 5 to 7 minutes. Add the sea salt, cover, and simmer for another 7 minutes. Add the broccoli, cover, and simmer another 2 minutes until bright green and tender. Place in serving bowls and garnish with chopped scallion.

Daikon and Greens Miso Soup with Sweet Rice Dumplings

1 cup daikon, sliced in thin rectangles
1/2 to 1 cup daikon greens, sliced in 1 inch long pieces
4 to 5 cups water
2 Tbsp wakame, soaked and chopped
1/2 cup celery, sliced on a thin diagonal
1 1/2 to 2 Tbsp mellow barley miso, puréed
scallion, finely chopped, for garnish

Sweet Rice Dumplings

1/2 cup sweet brown rice flour
1/4 cup boiling water
pinch of sea salt

Place the water in a pot, cover, and bring to a boil. Add the wakame, cover, and boil 2 to 3 minutes. Add the daikon and celery. Simmer for another 2 to 3 minutes. Place the sweet brown rice flour and sea salt in a bowl and mix. Add the boiling water, mix vigorously with a fork, and form into a ball of dough.
Knead 1 to 2 minutes. Roll dough into several balls slightly smaller than golf balls. Make a light thumb-print in the center of each dumpling.

Drop the dumplings in the boiling water with the vegetables. They will sink to the bottom. They are done when they float to the surface. Add the daikon greens. Reduce the flame to low and add the puréed miso. Simmer, without boiling, for 2 to 4 minutes. Place in serving bowls and garnish with chopped scallion.

Hearty Miso Soup and Mochi

1/2 cup onion, sliced in thin half-moons
1/4 cup carrot, sliced in matchsticks
1/4 cup Hokkaido pumpkin or buttercup squash, cubed
4 fresh shiitake mushrooms, sliced thin
1/4 cup burdock, shaved
1 cup kale, finely chopped
4 to 5 cups water
2 Tbsp wakame, soaked and chopped
1 1/2 to 2 Tbsp miso, puréed
8 to 10 pieces of mochi, pan-fried without oil
2 Tbsp scallion, finely chopped
1 tsp dark or light sesame oil

Place oil in a pot and heat. Sauté the onions for 1 to 2 minutes. Add burdock and sauté 2 to 3 minutes. Add the carrot, pumpkin or squash, and shiitake and sauté 1 to 2 minutes. Add the water and wakame. Cover and bring to a boil. Reduce the flame to medium-low and simmer for about 3 to 5 minutes. Reduce the flame to very low and add the puréed miso and the kale. Simmer for 2 to 4 minutes without boiling. Place 2 pieces of mochi in each serving bowl and pour the hot soup over it. Garnish each bowl with chopped scallion.

154

Ozoni

Ozoni is a type of miso soup traditionally served on New Years Day in Japan. The ingredients vary depending on the area of Japan. In Kyoto, ozoni includes fresh greens, mochi, taro potato, daikon, and white miso. You may use other ingredients if you wish. If you do not have white miso, yellow or a sweet mellow barley miso may be used instead.

6 cups water
6 small rounds of daikon, about 1/4 inch thick
3 small taro potatoes (albi), peeled and quartered
12 pieces brown rice mochi, about 2 inches long, pan-fried
3 to 4 Tbsp white (shiro) miso, diluted
6 sprigs watercress, boiled separately for 1 minute
1/2 sheet nori, toasted and cut in thin strips, for garnish

Place the daikon, taro, and water in a pot. Add a pinch of sea salt, cover, and bring to a boil. Reduce the flame to medium-low and simmer several minutes until the vegetables are soft. Reduce the flame to low and add the miso. Simmer, without boiling, for 2 to 4 minutes. Place 2 pieces of pan-fried mochi, 1 piece of daikon and taro, and 1 sprig watercress in each serving bowl and pour hot soup broth over them. Garnish with toasted nori strips.

Sweet Rice Soup

5 to 6 cups water
1 cup sweet brown rice, washed
3 shiitake mushrooms, soaked, stems removed, and diced
1/2 cup carrot, cut in matchsticks
1 cup onion, diced
1/4 cup celery, diced
1/4 to 1/2 tsp sea salt
1 strip kombu, 2 inches square, soaked
1/8 cup burdock, quartered and sliced thin
scallion or parsley, finely chopped, for garnish

Place the kombu, water, and rice in a pot. Cover and bring to a boil. Reduce the flame to medium-low and simmer for 3 to 5 minutes. Remove the kombu and set aside for use in other dishes. Simmer the sweet rice for 35 to 40 minutes. Purée sweet rice and liquid in a hand food mill until creamy. Place in a pot. Add the onion, carrot, shiitake, celery, and burdock. Cover and bring to a boil. Reduce the flame to medium-low and simmer for about 15 to 20 minutes. Season with sea salt and cook another 10 minutes. Place in serving bowls and garnish.

French Onion Soup

2 to 3 cups onion, sliced in thin half-moons
6 cups water
1 strip kombu, 2 to 3 inches long, soaked and sliced in thin strips
5 to 6 shiitake mushrooms, soaked, stems removed, and sliced thin
1 Tbsp bonito flakes
1/2 lb mochi, cut in 1 inch cubes and pan-fried
1 cup whole wheat bread cubes, deep-fried or pan-roasted
1 tsp sesame oil
1 1/2 to 2 1/2 Tbsp tamari soy sauce
2 Tbsp parsley, minced, for garnish

Place oil in a pot and heat. Ssauté onion for 3 to 4 minutes. Add the water, shiitake, kombu, and bonito flakes. Cover and bring to a boil. Reduce the flame to medium-low and simmer for 30 minutes or so until the onion is very soft. Add the soy sauce, cover, and simmer another 5 minutes. Place several pieces of cubed mochi in individual serving dishes and ladle the soup over them. Garnish each bowl with several bread cubes and a little parsley.

Mochi with Green Tea

5 to 6 cups green tea, hot
10 to 12 small pieces mochi, pan-fried
pinch of sea salt per bowl of soup

Place 2 pieces of fried mochi in each serving bowl. Add a very small pinch of sea salt to each bowl. Pour the hot green tea over the mochi, and let sit for 1 minute. Eat the mochi while hot and drink the tea.

Azuki Bean Soup with Sweet Rice Dumplings

1 cup azuki beans, washed
1 strip kombu, 2 inches long, soaked and diced
1 cup onion, diced

1 cup Hokkaido pumpkin or buttercup squash, cubed
1/2 cup carrot, sliced thin
5 to 6 cups water
1/2 tsp sea salt
3 to 4 drops tamari soy sauce

Sweet Rice Dumplings

1/2 cup sweet brown rice flour
1/4 cup boiling water
pinch of sea salt

Place the kombu, onion, squash, carrot, and beans in a pot. Add water, cover, and bring to a boil. Reduce the flame to medium-low and simmer for 1 1/2 hours or until the beans are about 80 percent done. Season with sea salt and soy sauce. Continue to cook another 5 minutes. Place the sweet rice flour in a bowl, add the sea salt, and pour the boiling water over it. Mix vigorously with a fork for 2 to 3 minutes. Form into a ball of dough. Roll the dough into several balls a little smaller than golf balls. With your thumb, make a shallow imprint in the center of each dumpling. Place the dumplings in the soup. They will sink to the bottom. Simmer until the dumplings rise to the surface. Place in serving bowls and garnish.

Barley-Lentil Soup

1/2 cup barley, washed and soaked
1/4 cup lentils, washed
1 strip kombu, 2 inches long, soaked and diced
1/2 cup onion, diced
1/4 cup celery, diced
1/3 cup mushrooms, diced
1/4 cup carrot, diced
5 to 6 cups water
1/4 to 1/2 tsp sea salt
scallion, finely chopped, for garnish

Place the kombu in the pot. Add the barley and lentils. Add water, cover, and bring to a boil. Reduce the flame to medium-low and simmer until the barley is almost done. The cooking time will vary depending on the type of barley used. Add the onios, celery, mushrooms, carrot, and sea salt. Cover and simmer another 15 to 20 minutes. Place in serving bowls and garnish with chopped scallion.

Barley-Kidney Bean Soup

1/2 cup barley, soaked
1/4 cup kidney beans, soaked, discard soaking water
1 cup onion, diced
1/4 cup celery, diced
1/2 cup leek, sliced
3 to 4 shiitake mushrooms, soaked, stems removed, and diced
5 to 6 cups water
1/4 to 1/2 tsp sea salt

Place the onion, shiitake, beans, and barley in a pot. Add water, cover, and bring to a boil. Reduce the flame to medium-low and simmer until the barley and beans are soft. Add the celery and sea salt. Cook another 15 to 20 minutes. Add the leeks, cover, and cook another 2 to 3 minutes. Place in serving bowls.

Seitan-Barley Soup

1/2 cup barley, soaked
1 cup cooked seitan, diced or cubed
5 to 6 cups water
1 cup onion, diced
1 cup mushrooms, diced
1/4 cup celery, diced
1/4 cup rutabaga or turnip, diced
1/2 cup carrot, diced
tamari soy sauce
scallion, finely chopped, for garnish

Place the barley and water in a pot, cover, and bring to a boil. Reduce the flame to medium-low and simmer until the barley is tender. Add the seitan and vegetables. Cover and simmer for another 10 minutes. Season to taste with soy sauce and simmer another 4 to 5 minutes. Place in serving bowls and garnish.

Hato Mugi (Pearl Barley) Stew

1 cup hato mugi, washed
1 strip kombu, 2 inches long, soaked and diced
3 to 4 shiitake mushrooms, soaked, stems removed, and diced

1/4 cup dried daikon, rinsed, soaked, and diced
1/2 cup sweet corn, removed from cob
1/4 cup celery, diced
1/4 cup carrot, diced
1 Tbsp burdock, diced
5 to 6 cups water
1/4 to 1/2 tsp sea salt
scallion, finely chopped, for garnish

Place hato mugi, kombu, shiitake, vegetables, and water in a pot. Cover and bring to a boil. Reduce the flame to medium-low and simmer for about 35 to 40 minutes. Season with sea salt and cook for another 10 minutes. Place in serving bowls and garnish.

Millet and Sweet Vegetable Soup

1 cup millet, washed
1 cup onion, diced
1/2 cup buttercup squash, cubed
1/4 cup celery, diced
1/4 cup carrot, diced
1/2 cup cabbage, diced
1 strip kombu, 2 inches long, soaked and diced
5 to 6 cups water
1/4 to 1/2 tsp sea salt
parsley, finely chooped, for garnish
1/2 sheet toasted nori, cut in strips, for garnish

Place the kombu in the pot and layer the vegetables and millet on top in the following order: onion, celery, cabbage, squash, carrot, and millet. Add water, cover, and bring to a boil. Reduce the flame to medium-low and simmer for 30 minutes. Season with sea salt and simmer another 10 minutes. Place in serving bowls and garnish with parsley and nori strips.

Lentil-Millet Soup with Smoked Tofu

1/2 cup onion, diced
1/4 cup celery, diced
1/2 cup lentils, washed
1 cup leftover millet
1/2 cup smoked tofu, minced or ground in a hand food mill

1/4 cup carrot, diced
2 Tbsp parsley
1 clove garlic, minced
1/4 to 1/2 tsp sea salt
4 to 5 cups water
sesame or corn oil

Place a small amount of oil in a pot and heat. Sauté the garlic and onion for 2 to 3 minutes. Add the lentils and water. Cover and bring to a boil. Reduce the flame to medium-low and simmer for 35 to 40 minutes. Add the millet and vegetables. Cover and cook 5 minutes. Season with sea salt, cover, and cook another 10 minutes. Reduce the flame to low and add the smoked tofu and parsley. Simmer, without a cover, for 2 to 3 minutes. Place in serving bowls.

Corn Chowder

2 ears sweet corn, removed from cob
4 cups water
1 cup onion, diced
1/4 cup celery, diced
1/4 to 1/2 cup yellow corn grits
1/4 to 1/2 tsp sea salt
sesame oil
scallion, parsley, chives, or watercress, finely chopped, for garnish

Boil the corn cobs in the water for 4 to 5 minutes. Remove the cobs and discard. Brush a pot with a little oil and heat. Sauté the onion for 2 to 3 minutes. Add the sweet corn, celery, and water. Bring to a boil and mix in the corn grits, stirring constantly with a wire whisk to prevent lumping. Cover, bring to a boil, and reduce the flame to medium-low. Simmer for 20 minutes. Add the sea salt, cover, and simmer for another 10 minutes. Place in serving bowls and garnish.

Corn Soup

1 cup sweet corn, removed from cob
1/4 cup onion, diced
1/4 cup fresh green peas, removed from pod
1/2 cup green string beans, sliced in 1 inch lengths
1/4 cup carrot, diced
1/4 cup yellow wax beans, sliced in 1 inch lengths

4 to 5 cups water
2 to 2 1/2 Tbsp umeboshi vinegar
chives, scallion, or parsley, finely chopped, for garnish

Place the water and vegetables in a pot, cover, and bring to a boil. Reduce the flame to medium-low and simmer for 5 to 7 minutes. Add the umeboshi vinegar, cover, and simmer another 3 to 4 minutes. Serve and garnish.

Navy Bean and Corn Soup

4 ears fresh sweet corn, removed from cob
1/4 cup celery, diced
1/2 cup onion, diced
5 to 6 cups water
1/4 to 1/2 cup navy beans, washed and soaked, discard soaking water
1/4 tsp sea salt
1 tsp brown rice vinegar
tamari soy sauce, for extra seasoning if desired
scallion or parsley, finely chopped, for garnish

Place the beans and water in a pressure cooker, cover, and bring up to pressure. Reduce the flame to medium-low and cook for 50 minutes. Remove from the flame and allow the pressure to come down. Remove the cover. Add the sweet corn, celery, onion, and sea salt. Place on a high flame and bring to a boil. Reduce the flame to medium-low, cover, and simmer for 10 minutes. Reduce the flame to low, and add the vinegar and soy sauce. Simmer 1 to 2 minutes. Place in serving bowls and garnish.

Creamy Kasha (Buckwheat) Soup

1 cup buckwheat groats, roasted
5 to 6 cups boiling water
1 cup onion, diced
1/4 cup celery root, diced
1/4 cup cabbage, diced
1/4 cup sauerkraut, chopped
1/4 cup carrot, diced
1/4 cup parsley, minced
pinch sea salt
tamari soy sauce, to taste
sesame oil

Heat a small amount of sesame oil in a pot. Sauté the onion for 2 to 3 minutes. Add the buckwheat and sauté 2 to 3 minutes. Add the boiling water and sea salt. Cover and reduce the flame to medium-low. Simmer for 15 minutes. Add the celery root, cabbage, and carrot. Cover and simmer 3 to 4 minutes. Remove the cover, season with a little soy sauce, and add the sauerkraut and parsley. Simmer, uncovered, for another 2 to 3 minutes. Place in serving bowls.

Oatmeal Dulse Soup

1 cup rolled oats
1/4 cup dulse, rinsed, soaked, and finely sliced
1 cup onion, diced
1/2 cup celery, diced
5 to 6 cups water
1/4 to 1/2 tsp sea salt
parsley, finely chopped, for garnish

Place the oats, dulse, onions, celery, and water in a pot. Cover and bring to a boil. Reduce the flame to medium-low and simmer for 10 to 15 minutes. Add the sea salt, cover, and simmer another 10 to 15 minutes. Serve and garnish.

Cream of Mushroom Soup

l/2 cup rolled oats
1 cup leftover cooked brown rice
5 to 6 cups water
2 cups mushrooms, diced
1/2 cup onion, diced
2 tsp corn oil
1/4 to 1/2 tsp sea salt
tamari soy sauce
scallion or parsley, finely chopped, for garnish

Place the oats, rice, and water in a pot. Cover and bring to a boil. Reduce the flame to medium-low and simmer for 15 to 20 minutes until creamy. Place the ingredients in a hand food mill and purée until smooth and creamy. Heat the oil in a skillet and sauté the onion for 2 to 3 minutes. Add the mushrooms and several drops of soy sauce. Sauté for 4 to 5 minutes. Place the sautéed vegetables in a pot with the oat-rice purée. Cover and bring to a boil. Reduce the flame to medium-low and simmer 15 to 20 minutes. Add the sea salt and simmer another 10 minutes. Place in serving bowls and garnish.

Cream of Celery Soup

1/2 cup rolled oats
1 cup leftover cooked brown rice
5 to 6 cups water
2 cups celery and celery leaves, diced
1/2 cup onion, diced
1/2 cup mushrooms, diced
2 to 3 tsp corn oil
tamari soy sauce
1/4 to 1/2 tsp sea salt
parsley, scallion, or chives, finely chopped, for garnish

Place the oats, rice, and water in a pot. Cover and bring to a boil. Reduce the flame to medium-low and simmer for 15 to 20 minutes. Heat oil in a skillet and sauté the onion for 2 to 3 minutes. Add the celery and mushrooms, along with several drops of soy sauce. Sauté for another 3 to 5 minutes. Place the vegetables in a pot with the oat-rice purée. Cover and bring to a boil. Reduce the flame to medium-low and simmer for 20 minutes. Season with sea salt, cover, and simmer another 10 minutes. Place in serving bowls and garnish.

Minestrone

1/4 cup kidney beans, soaked 6 to 8 hours, discard soaking water
1/4 cup navy beans, soaked 6 to 8 hours, discard soaking water
1/4 cup lentils, washed
1 strip kombu, 2 to 3 inches long, soaked and diced
6 cups water
1/4 cup onion, diced
1/4 cup green string beans, sliced in 1 inch long pieces
1/4 cup yellow wax beans, sliced in 1 inch long pieces
1/4 cup celery, diced
1/4 cup carrot, diced
1/4 cup leek, finely chopped
2 cups whole grain elbows, shells, or other small pasta, cooked
3 Tbsp umeboshi vinegar
2 tsp tamari soy sauce
scallion, parsley, or chives, finely chopped, for garnish

Place the kombu, beans, lentils, and water in a pressure cooker. Leave uncovered and bring to a boil. Reduce the flame to medium and simmer for 10 minutes. Cover the cooker and bring up to pressure. Reduce the flame to medium-low and cook for 45 minutes. Remove from the flame and allow the pressure to come down. Remove cover. Add the vegetables and bring to a boil. Cover with a regular lid (not the pressure cooker lid) and simmer for 5 minutes. Add the pasta, umeboshi vinegar, and soy sauce. Simmer for another 5 minutes. Place in serving bowls and garnish.

Noodles in Broth

1/2 lb udon, soba, or somen, cooked
4 to 5 shiitake mushrooms, soaked, stems removed, and sliced thin, save
  soaking water
1 strip kombu, 2 to 3 inches long, soaked, sliced in very thin matchsticks,
  save soaking water
5 to 6 cups water, including water used to soak shiitake and kombu
tamari soy sauce, to taste (about 1 1/2 to 2 tsp per cup of water)
scallion, finely chopped, for garnish

Place the shiitake, kombu, and water in a pot. Cover and bring to a boil. Reduce the flame to medium-low and simmer for 15 to 20 minutes. Reduce the flame to low and add the soy sauce. Simmer for another 5 minutes. Place the cooked noodles in serving bowls and pour hot broth over them. Garnish and serve.

Winter Udon in Kuzu Broth

1/2 lb udon, cooked
4 shiitake mushrooms, soaked, stems removed, and sliced thin
4 to 5 slices deep-fried tofu (2 x 3 inches) sliced in thin strips
1 strip kombu, 2 to 3 inches long, soaked, sliced in very thin matchsticks
1/2 cup onion, diced
1 pkg bonito flakes, (optional)
1/4 to 1/2 Tbsp ginger, grated, for garnish
5 cups water
4 to 5 Tbsp kuzu, diluted
tamari soy sauce, to taste
scallion, finely chopped, for garnish

Place the shiitake, kombu, tofu, and water in a pot. Cover and bring to a boil. Reduce the flame to medium-low. Add the onion and bonito flakes. Cover and simmer for 15 to 20 minutes. Add the diluted kuzu, stirring constantly to prevent lumping. Reduce the flame to low and add soy sauce to taste. Simmer for 5 minutes. Place cooked udon in serving bowls and pour the thick broth over them. Garnish with a dab of ginger and chopped scallion and serve hot.

Seitan Stew

2 cups cooked seitan, cubed
1 cup onion, cut in thick wedges
1 cup carrot, cut in chunks
1/4 cup burdock, sliced on a thin diagonal
1 cup Brussels sprouts, cut in half
1/4 cup celery, cut on a diagonal
1 cup taro potato, cubed
5 to 6 cups water
tamari soy sauce
1 cup seitan starch water or 4 Tbsp diluted kuzu
scallion, finely chopped, for garnish

Place the first eight ingredients in a pot, cover, and bring to a boil. Reduce the flame to medium-low and simmer for 7 to 10 minutes. Season with soy sauce to taste. Add the starch water or kuzu, stirring constantly to prevent lumping. When thick, simmer 4 to 5 minutes. Place in serving bowls and garnish.

Seitan-Barley Soup

1 cup cooked seitan, cubed
1/2 cup barley, soaked 6 to 8 hours in 6 cups water, save water
1 cup onion, diced
1/2 cup carrot, diced
1/4 cup celery, diced
1/4 cup mushrooms, diced
1/4 cup sweet corn, removed from cob
1/4 cup leeks, sliced thin
tamari soy sauce, to taste
scallion, chives, or parsley, finely chopped, for garnish

Place the barley in a pressure cooker with soaking water. Cover and bring up to pressure. Reduce the flame to medium-low and cook for 1 hour. Remove from flame and allow the pressure to come down. Remove cover. Place the seitan, onion, carrot, celery, mushrooms, corn, and leek in the pot with the barley.

Cover with a regular lid (not pressure cooker lid) and simmer for 10 to 15 minutes. Add soy sauce, cover, and simmer another 5 minutes. Place in serving bowls and garnish.

Fu and Vegetable Soup

1/2 pkg flat fu, soaked and sliced in 1 inch squares or thin strips
1/2 lb tofu, cubed
4 shiitake mushrooms, soaked, stems removed, and quartered
1 cup broccoli, forets
1/2 cup carrots, sliced on a thin diagonal
5 to 6 cups water
tamari soy sauce, to taste
scallion, finely chopped, for garnish

Place the water, shiitake, and fu in a pot. Cover and bring to a boil. Reduce the flame to medium-low and simmer 10 to 15 minutes. Add the vegetables, cover, and simmer for 1 to 2 minutes. Add soy sauce to taste, cover, and simmer another 5 minutes. Place in serving bowls and garnish.

White Rice Soup

1 cup white rice, washed
5 to 6 cups water
1/2 lb firm style tofu, cubed and deep-fried
1/2 cup onion, diced
1/4 cup celery, diced
1/4 cup green peas, shelled
1/4 cup sweet corn, removed from cob
2 Tbsp burdock, diced
1 Tbsp kombu, diced
4 shiitake mushrooms, soaked, stems removed, and diced
1/4 to 1/2 tsp sea salt
tamari soy sauce, to taste
scallion, chives, or parsley, finely chopped, for garnish

Place the first 10 ingredients in a pot, cover, and bring to a boil. Reduce the flame to medium-low and simmer 20 minutes. Add the sea salt and a little soy sauce. Simmer another 10 minutes. Place in serving bowls and garnish.

Chapter 7
Whole Grain Porridges and Beverages

Whole grain porridges are delicious at breakfast. In general, breakfast foods should be softer and easier to digest than the dishes served at other meals. Breakfast grains are generally cooked with more water than grain dishes served at lunch or dinner. Additional water makes the grains softer and more expanded, and thus more easily digested. Soft porridges made with whole grains are ideal as main dishes at breakfast. A variety of natural seasonings can be used when preparing breakfast porridge, including miso, sea salt, kombu, umeboshi plum, dried fruit, and whole grain sweeteners such as brown rice syrup and barley malt.

Breakfast Condiments and Garnishes

Condiment or Garnish	Flavor
Scallion (raw)	Pungent
Scallion (cooked)	Sweet
Chives	Pungent
Parsley	Bitter
Celery	Sour and bitter
Shiso	Sour and salty
Umeboshi	Sour and salty

Gomashio	Bitter and salty
Sea-vegetable powder	Bitter and salty
Nori flakes	Bitter and mildly salty
Toasted nori strips	Bitter and mildly salty
Miso condiments	Salty and sour
Roasted nuts	Bitter
Roasted nuts with salt	Bitter and salty
Roasted seeds	Bitter
Roasted seeds with salt	Bitter and salty
Raisins	Sweet
Dried fruit	Sweet, bitter, and sour
Grain sweeteners	Sweet
Amazuku	Sweet and mildly sour

In addition, condiments and garnishes help balance the energy in whole grain porridges and other dishes. They add flavor and nutrients, and increase digestibility. Brightly colored garnishes complement the soft neutral color of grain dishes. Their varied flavors also create a balance for the naturally sweet flavor of whole grains. Choosing the right garnish to balance the flavor, texture, and color of your grain dishes is an important aspect of cooking.

Soft Brown Rice (Rice Kayu)

1 cup organic brown rice, washed
5 cups water
pinch of sea salt or 1 inch piece of kombu, soaked

Place the rice, water, and sea salt or kombu in a pressure cooker. Cover and place on a high flame. Bring up to pressure. Reduce the flame to medium-low and cook for 45 to 50 minutes. Remove from the flame and allow the pressure to come down. Remove the cover and place in individual serving dishes. Garnish with chopped scallion, chives, or parsley, or sprinkle a little of your favorite condiment over each serving.

Boiled Brown Rice Kayu

1 cup organic brown rice, washed
5 cups water
pinch of sea salt or 1 inch piece of kombu, soaked

Place all ingredients in a heavy pot. Cover and bring to a boil. Reduce the flame to medium-low and simmer for 1 hour. Remove from flame and place in serving bowls. Garnish and serve.

Brown Rice Kayu with Umeboshi Plum

1 cup organic brown rice, washed
1 small to medium umeboshi plum
5 cups water

Place all ingredients in a pressure cooker, cover, and bring up to pressure. Reduce flame to medium-low and simmer for 45 to 50 minutes. Remove from flame and allow the pressure to come down. Remove cover, place in serving bowls, and garnish with toasted nori strips, chopped scallion, and a little goma-shio.

Brown Rice and Pumpkin Kayu

1 cup organic brown rice, washed
5 cups water
2 cups Hokkaido pumpkin or buttercup squash, cubed
pinch of sea salt or 1 inch piece of kombu, soaked

Place all ingredients in a pressure cooker, cover, and bring up to pressure. Reduce the flame to medium-low and simmer for 45 to 50 minutes. Remove from flame and allow the pressure to come down. Remove cover and place in serving bowls. Garnish and serve.

Quick Brown Rice Porridge

1 cup leftover, cooked brown rice
3 cups water, just to cover rice

Place rice and water in a pot, cover, and bring to a boil. Reduce the flame to medium-low and simmer for about 20 minutes until soft and creamy. Place in serving bowls and serve with your favorite garnish or condiment.

Ojiya (Miso Soft Rice)

1 cup organic brown rice, washed
5 cups water
1 inch piece of kombu, soaked and diced (use soaking water as part of water
    measurement)
3 to 4 scallion roots, finely minced
3 to 4 scallion tops, thinly sliced
3 to 4 shiitake mushrooms, soaked, stems removed, and sliced (use soaking
    water as part of water measurement)
2 level tsp barley miso, puréed

   Place the rice, kombu, shiitake, scallion roots, and water in a pressure
cooker. Cover and bring up to pressure. Reduce the flame to medium-low and
cook for 45 to 50 minutes. Remove from flame and allow pressure to come
down. Remove cover and place uncovered cooker over a low flame. Add the
miso and mix well. Cover cooker with a regular cover (not pressure cooker lid)
and simmer, without boiling, for 2 to 3 minutes. Remove cover and place in
serving bowls. Garnish with chopped scallion.

Miso Soft Rice

1 cup organic brown rice, washed
5 cups water
pinch of sea salt or 1 inch piece of kombu, soaked
3 to 4 shiitake mushrooms, soaked, stems removed, and diced (use soaking
    water as part of water measurement)
1 cup daikon, quartered and sliced thin
1/4 cup celery, slice on a thin diagonal
1/2 cup squash, cubed
1/2 cup carrot, diced
1/4 cup cabbage, diced
2 level tsp barley miso, puréed
scallion, chives, or parsley, finely chopped, for garnish

   Place the rice, water, sea salt or kombu, and shiitake in a pressure cooker.
Cover and bring up to pressure. Reduce flame to medium-low and cook for 45
minutes. Remove from flame and allow pressure to come down. Remove cover.
Add the daikon, squash, carrot, and cabbage. Cover with a regular lid, not the
pressure cooker lid, and bring to a boil. Reduce the flame to medium-low and
simmer several minutes until the vegetables are tender. Reduce the flame to

low, add the miso, and mix well. Simmer, without boiling, for 2 to 3 minutes. Place in serving bowls and garnish.

Soft Rice Porridge with Raisins

1 cup leftover, cooked brown rice
3 cups water
1/4 cup organic raisins
1/4 cup sunflower or pumpkin seeds, roasted, for garnish

Place all ingredients in a pot, cover, and bring to a boil. Reduce the flame to medium-low and simmer for 20 minutes until soft and creamy. Place in serving bowls and garnish with toasted sunflower or pumpkin seeds.

Soft Sweet Brown Rice with Chestnuts

1 cup organic sweet brown rice, washed
1/2 cup organic dried chestnuts, soaked 3 to 4 hours or dry-roasted and
    soaked 15 minutes (use soaking water as part of water measurement)
pinch of sea salt or 1 inch piece of kombu, soaked

Place all ingredients in a pressure cooker, cover, and bring up to pressure. Reduce the flame to medium-low and simmer for 45 to 50 minutes. Remove from flame and allow pressure to come down. Remove cover and place in serving bowls. Garnish and serve.

White Rice Kayu

1 cup organic white rice, rinsed
3 to 4 cups water
pinch of sea salt
1/2 cup tofu, deep-fried or pan-fried until golden and sliced in thin strips
1/4 cup celery, diced
1/4 cup carrot, diced
1/4 cup scallion, thinly sliced, for garnish
2 level tsp barley miso, puréed

Place the rice, water, and sea salt in a pressure cooker. Cover and bring up to pressure. Reduce the flame to medium-low and cook for 15 to 20 minutes. Remove from flame and allow the pressure to come down. Remove cover and add the tofu, celery, and carros. Cover with a regular lid, not the pressure cooker lid. Bring to a boil. Reduce the flame to low and simmer about 5 to 7 minutes until the vegetables are tender. Reduce the flame to low and add the miso. Mix and simmer, without boiling, for 2 to 3 minutes. Place in serving bowls and garnish with chopped scallion.

Soft Barley Porridge

1 cup organic whole barley, soaked 6 to 8 hours or overnight (use soaking
   water as part of water measurement)
5 cups water
pinch of sea salt or 1 inch piece of kombu, cooked

   Place all ingredients in a pressure cooker or heavy pot. Cover and bring up to pressure or to boil. Reduce the flame to medium-low and cook for 50 to 60 minutes if pressure cooking, or 1 hour to 1 hour and 10 minutes if boiling. Remove from the flame and, if pressure cooking, allow the pressure to come down. Place in serving bowls and garnish with your favorite condiment.

Soft Hato Mugi (Pearl Barley) Porridge

1 cup organic hato mugi, washed
4 cups water
pinch of sea salt or 1 inch piece of kombu, soaked and diced (use soaking
   water as part of water measurement)
1/2 cup sweet corn, removed from cob
1/4 cup onion, diced
3 shiitake mushrooms, soaked, stems removed, and diced (use soaking water
   as part of water measurement)
1/4 cup carrot, diced
1/4 cup leek, sliced thin

   Place the hato mugi, water, and sea salt or kombu in a pressure cooker. Cover and bring up to pressure. Reduce the flame to medium-low and cook for 45 minutes. Remove from the flame and allow the pressure to come down. Remove the cover and add the sweet corn, onion, shiitake, and carrot. Cover with a regular lid, not the pressure cooker lid. Bring to a boil, reduce the flame to medium-low, and simmer for about 15 minutes until the shiitake are tender. Add the leek and cook for 1 to 2 minutes. Remove from the flame and place in serving bowls.

Quick Rice and Barley Porridge

1 cup leftover, cooked rice and barley or rice and hato mugi
3 cups water

Place ingredients in a saucepan, cover, and bring to a boil. Reduce the flame to medium-low and simmer for 20 minutes until soft and creamy. Place in serving bowls and garnish.

Soft Millet Porridge

1 cup organic millet, washed
5 cups water
pinch of sea salt

Place ingredients in a heavy pot, cover, and bring to a boil. Reduce the flame to medium-low and simmer for 35 minutes until soft and creamy. Remove from flame and place in serving bowls. Garnish and serve.

Golden Millet Porridge

1 cup organic millet, washed
5 cups water
pinch of sea salt
1 cup winter squash, cubed
1/4 cup onion, diced
1/4 cup carrot, diced
1/4 cup cabbage, diced

Place all ingredients in a heavy pot, cover, and bring to a boil. Reduce the flame to medium-low and simmer for 35 minutes until soft and creamy. Remove from flame and place in serving bowls. Garnish and serve.

Rice, Millet, and Oat Porridge

1 cup leftover, cooked brown rice
1/4 cup organic millet, washed
1/4 cup rolled oats

pinch of sea salt
5 cups water

Place all ingredients in a heavy pot, cover, and bring to a boil. Reduce the flame to medium-low and simmer for 35 minutes until the millet is done and the porridge is soft and creamy. Remove from the flame, place in serving bowls, and garnish.

Soft Millet and Cauliflower

1 cup organic millet, washed
2 cups cauliflower, flowerets
5 cups water
pinch of sea salt
1/4 cup sunflower or pumpkin seeds, roasted, for garnish
green nori flakes, for garnish
dried shiso leaf condiment, for garnish

Place the millet, cauliflower, water, and sea salt in a heavy pot. Cover and bring to a boil. Reduce the flame to medium-low and simmer for 35 minutes. Place in serving bowls and garnish each bowl with roasted seeds, nori flakes, and shiso condiment.

Bulgur Porridge

1 cup bulgur
3 cups boiling water
pinch of sea salt

Place the bulgur and sea salt in the boiling water, stir, cover and bring to a boil again. Reduce the flame to medium-low and simmer 15 to 20 minutes. Place in serving bowls and serve with your favorite condiment or topping.

Soft Bulgur and Vegetables

1 cup bulgur
3 cups boiling water
pinch of sea salt
1/2 to 1 tsp sesame or corn oil
1/2 cup onion, diced

1/4 cup carrot, diced
1/4 cup celery, diced
1/2 cup scallion, finely chopped

Heat the oil in a saucepan. Sauté the onion for 1 to 2 minutes. Add the carrot and celery. Sauté another 2 to 3 minutes. Add the bulgur, sea salt, and boiling water. Cover and bring to a boil. Reduce the flame to medium-low and simmer for 15 minutes. Remove the cover and mix in the chopped scallion. Cover and simmer another 2 to 3 minutes. Place in serving bowls.

Quick Rice and Wheat Porridge
1 cup leftover, cooked brown rice and wheat berries
3 cups water

Place the rice and wheat in a saucepan with the water. Cover and bring to a boil. Reduce the flame to medium-low and simmer for 15 to 20 minutes until soft and creamy.

Soft Corn Grits

1 cup yellow or white corn grits
3 to 3 1/2 cups boiling water
pinch of sea salt
2 Tbsp sesame, sunflower, or pumpkin seeds, roasted
3 to 4 Tbsp brown rice syrup

Place the sea salt and corn grits in the pot of boiling water. Stir constantly to remove lumps until the water comes to a boil again. Cover, reduce the flame to medium-low, and simmer for 20 to 30 minutes until soft and creamy. Place in serving bowls and garnish with roasted seeds and a little brown rice syrup.

Polenta (Cornmeal Porridge)

1 cup cornmeal
3 cups water
pinch of sea salt
green nori flakes
powdered shiso leaf condiment

Place the water and sea salt in a saucepan, cover, and bring to a boil. Stir in the cornmeal slowly, stirring constantly to prevent lumping. Bring to a boil again. Cover, reduce the flame to medium-low, and simmer for 35 to 40 minutes. Place in serving bowls and garnish with green nori flakes and shiso condiment.

Quick Corn and Rice Porridge

1 cup sweet corn, removed from the cob
1 cup leftover cooked brown rice
3 cups water

Place all ingredients in a saucepan, cover, and bring to a boil. Reduce the flame to medium-low and simmer for 15 to 20 minutes. Place in serving bowls and garnish with your favorite natural condiment or topping.

Buckwheat Porridge

1 cup dry-roasted buckwheat groats
5 cups water
pinch of sea salt
1/4 cup scallion, finely chopped

Place the water and sea salt in a saucepan, cover, and bring to a boil. Remove the cover and stir in the buckwheat. Cover and reduce the flame to medium-low. Simmer for 20 minutes until soft and creamy. Place in serving bowls and garnish with chopped scallion.

Buckwheat and Vegetable Porridge

1 cup dry-roasted buckwheat groats
5 cups water
pinch of sea salt
1/4 cup onion, diced
1/4 cup carrot, diced
1/2 cup cabbage, diced
1/2 cup natural sauerkraut
1/4 cup leek, finely chopped
1/2 to 1 tsp sesame oil

Heat the sesame oil in a saucepan. Sauté the onion for 1 to 2 minutes. Add the carrot, cabbage, and sauerkraut. Sauté 2 to 3 minutes. Add the buckwheat, water, and sea salt. Cover and bring to a boil. Reduce the flame to medium-low and simmer for 15 minutes. Mix in the leek, cover, and simmer another 5 minutes. Place in serving bowls.

Sobagaki (Creamy Buckwheat Cereal)

1 cups dry-roasted buckwheat flour
1/2 cup onion, minced
4 cups water
pinch of sea salt
1 tsp sesame oil
1/2 tsp ginger, finely grated
2 to 3 Tbsp scallion, finely chopped
1/2 sheet nori, toasted and sliced in thin strips

Heat the oil in a saucepan. Add the onion and buckwheat flour and sauté for 1 to 2 minutes, stirring constantly. Remove from the flame and let cool for 2 to 3 minutes. Place the pan back on the flame and, stirring briskly, add the water and sea salt. Bring to a boil and simmer, uncovered, while continuing to stir, for about 10 minutes. When this dish becomes soft and creamy, place in serving bowls and garnish with a little grated ginger, chopped scallion, and a few strips of nori.

Quick Rye and Brown Rice Porridge

1 cup leftover, cooked brown rice and rye
3 cups water

Place ingredients in a saucepan, cover, and bring to a boil. Reduce the flame to medium-low and simmer for 20 minutes. Place in serving bowls and garnish with your favorite natural condiment or topping.

Boiled Whole Oats

1 cup whole oats, soaked 6 to 8 hours or overnight
4 to 5 cups water (including water used to soak oats)
pinch of sea salt

Place oats, water, and sea salt in a heavy pot, cover, and bring to a boil. Reduce the flame to medium-low and simmer for 2 to 3 hours until soft and creamy. Place in serving bowls.

Rolled Oats and Raisin Porridge

1 cup rolled oats
2 to 3 cups water
1/4 cup raisins
pinch of sea salt

Place the raisins, oats, water, and sea salt in a pot. Cover and bring to a boil. Reduce the flame to medium low and simmer for about 15 minutes until soft and creamy. Place in serving bowls.

Rolled Oats and Onion Porridge

1 cup rolled oats, dry-roasted
2 to 3 cups water
1/2 cup onion, diced
pinch of sea salt
1 Tbsp parsley, finely chopped

Place the oats, water, onion, and sea salt in a saucepan. Cover and bring to a boil. Reduce the flame to medium-low and simmer about 15 minutes until soft and creamy. Add the parsley and cook 30 seconds. Place in serving bowls.

Steel Cut Oats (Irish or Scotch Oats)

1 cup steel-cut oats
2 to 2 1/2 cups water
pinch of sea salt

Place the water and sea salt in a saucepan, cover and bring to a boil. Remove cover and stir in the oats. Reduce the flame to medium-low and simmer for 25 to 30 minutes until soft and creamy. Place in serving bowls.

Creamy Sweet Brown Rice and Dried Fruit

1 cup sweet brown rice, washed
5 cups water
pinch of sea salt
1/4 cup raisins
1/4 cup dried apricot, soaked and diced
1/4 cup dried apple, soaked and diced

Place all ingredients in a pressure cooker, cover, and bring up to pressure. Reduce the flame to medium-low and cook for 45 to 50 minutes. Remove from flame and allow the pressure to come down. Remove the cover and place in serving bowls.

Amaranth Cereal

1 cup amaranth, washed
3 cups water
pinch of sea salt

Place water and sea salt in a saucepan, cover, and bring to a boil. Reduce the flame to medium-low and simmer for 20 to 25 minutes. Place in serving bowls. For a sweeter flavor, add some raisins or dried fruit during cooking. Chopped vegetables may be added instead of dried fruit for a different flavor.

Sweet Quinoa Cereal

1 cup quinoa, washed
2 cups water
1/4 cup raisins
1/4 tsp natural cinnamon (optional)
pinch of sea salt

Place the water, sea salt, and raisins in a pot. Cover and bring to a boil. Remove the cover, and add the quinoa and cinnamon, and stir. Cover and reduce the flame to medium-low. Simmer for 10 minutes. Remove from the flame and let sit for 5 minutes. Place in serving bowls.

Teff Porridge

1/2 cup teff, washed
2 cups water
pinch of sea salt

Place the water and sea salt in a saucepan, cover, and bring to a boil. Remove the cover and stir in the teff. Cover and reduce the flame to medium-low. Simmer for 15 to 20 minutes. Place in serving bowls.

Whole Grain Beverages

A delicious, calming beverage can be made by roasting whole cereal grains and preparing them like ordinary tea. Roasted barley tea, or *mugi-cha* as it is known in Japan, is very cooling to the body and commonly enjoyed during the hotter weather. Roasted brown rice tea has a unique nutty flavor. Other grain teas, such as millet tea, oat tea, and buckwheat tea, can also be made in this way. All whole grain teas are suitable for daily use. For variety, they may be mixed with bancha tea in various proportions. Natural spring or well water are preferred for preparing teas, as well as for cooking whole grain and other dishes.

Roasted Brown Rice Tea

1/4 cup brown rice, washed and drained
1 qt water

Heat a skillet, add the rice, and dry-roast, stirring constantly, until golden brown and the rice releases a nutty fragrance. Remove the rice and place in a tea pot with the water. Bring to a boil. Reduce the flame to medium-low and simmer for about 10 to 15 minutes. Strain and drink.

Kukicha and Brown Rice Tea

1 Tbsp kukicha (twig tea)
1/4 cup roasted brown rice
1 to 1 1/2 qts water

Place ingredients in a tea pot. Bring to a boil. Reduce the flame to medium-low and simmer 5 to 10 minutes. Strain and drink.

Sencha (Green Tea) and Brown Rice Tea

1 Tbsp organic sencha
1/4 cup roasted brown rice
1 to 1 1/2 qts water

Place the brown rice and water in a tea pot. Bring to a boil. Reduce the flame to medium-low and simmer 10 minutes. Turn off the flame, add the sencha, and let steep for 1 minute. Strain and drink.

Special Brown Rice Cream

1 cup short grain brown rice, washed and drained
10 cups water
pinch of sea salt

Heat a skillet and dry-roast the rice until golden and it releases a nutty fragrance. Remove from the skillet immediately and place in a pressure cooker with the water and sea salt. Cover the cooker and bring up to pressure over a high flame. Reduce the flame to medium-low and cook for 1 1/2 hours.

Line a suribachi with 2 layers of 100 percent cotton cheesecloth. Pour the brown rice and creamy liquid, a little at a time, in the lined bowl. Bring up the corners of the cheesecloth to form a sack, and squeeze and scrape the creamy liquid out with a wooden rice paddle. The rice remaining in the sack can be used in soups and desserts. Drink the liquid hot as is or sprinkle a little condiment over and eat with a spoon.

Mugi-cha (Roasted Whole Barley Tea)

Mugi-cha is made from unmilled barley that has been dry- roasted. It can be found in most natural food stores.

1 Tbsp mugi-cha
1 qt water

Place mugi-cha and water in a tea pot. Bring to a boil. Reduce the flame to low and simmer for 5 minutes. Strain and drink.

Hato Mugi-cha (Pearl Barley Tea)

Hato mugi-cha is a tea made from pearl barley or Jobs' Tears. It can be found in many natural food stores.

2 Tbsp hato mugi-cha
1 qt water

    Place in a tea pot and bring to a boil. Reduce the flame to low and simmer about 10 minutes. Strain and drink.

Grain Coffee

Grain coffee provides a nourishing alternative to regular coffee or decaffeinated coffee which is usually processed with chemicals. Grain coffee may be prepared at home from roasted grains, beans, and chicory. George Ohsawa created a popular grain coffee known as *yannoh* made from roasted and ground brown rice, wheat, azuki beans, chickpeas, and chicory root. A variety of grain coffees is available in natural foods stores. Those made with 100 percent cereal grains, wild grasses, beans, and other vegetable-quality ingredients and containing no honey, molasses, or other strong sweeteners and fruit powders are suitable for occasional consumption.

1 cup boiling water
1 to 1 1/2 tsp grain coffee

    Place the grain coffee in a cup and pour the boiling water over it. Stir and drink.

Corn Silk Tea

4 to 5 ears of fresh organic sweet corn, remove the corn silk
1 qt water

    Place the corn silk on a bamboo mat and allow to sit for several days until completely dry. Place the corn silk in a tea pot with the water. Bring to a boil. Reduce the flame to medium-low and simmer about 10 to 15 minutes. Strain and drink hot or at room temperature.

Chapter 8
Seitan and Fu

In the Far East, whole wheat was traditionally used to make seitan or wheat gluten, a product derived from flour that is cooked in a broth of kombu sea vegetable, tamari soy sauce, and water. Seitan has a rich, dynamic taste and lends itself to a variety of dishes ranging from stews and cutlets to soups, salads, and casseroles. It is now becoming popular in the West in grain burgers and croquettes as a substitute for hamburgers, roast beef, and other animal food entrées. At home, it can be made by separating the starch and bran from the gluten in whole wheat flour. Both spring and winter wheat may be used to make seitan, though spring wheat is softer and often preferred.

Fu, another whole wheat product similar to seitan, is made from wheat gluten that has been toasted, steamed, and dried. Light in consistency, fu absorbs liquid and expands in volume when cooked. Fu may be enjoyed plain, added to soups, stews, or casseroles, or cooked together with other foods. It can be made at home or bought dried and packaged in many natural food stores.

Homemade Seitan

3 1/2 lb whole wheat bread flour
8 to 9 cups cold water
water, for rinsing gluten
1 strip kombu, 3 inches long
6 cups water, for boiling gluten
1/4 to 1/3 cup tamari soy sauce, for cooking gluten

Place the flour in a large, deep bowl or pot. Add cold water to make a dough the consistency of bread dough. Knead the dough for 5 minutes or so until it becomes stiff and harder to knead. Cover the dough with cold water and let sit for 10 minutes. It can sit longer without hurting the dough.

Knead the dough again in the soaking water for about 1 minute. The water will become cloudy and milky. Pour the cloudy water in a large jar. Save the soaking water. Pour warm water over the dough and knead again for 1 minute. Pour this water again in the jar and save. Repeat this process 2 or 3 more times, alternating between cold and warm water rinsing, but this time discard the soaking water.

Place the gluten in a colander. Pour cold water over the gluten and knead. Alternate between warm and cold water when rinsing and kneading. The alternating temperature makes it easier to wash out the bran. Continue rinsing until most of the bran has been removed and the rinsing water changes from cloudy or milky to almost clear. You should now have a ball of sticky dough or gluten. The cloudy, milky rinsing water left over after the dough is rinsed the first several times is called starch water, and is used as a thickener for stews, soups, gravies, and desserts.

Bring the water for cooking the gluten to a boil. Place the kombu in it. Separate the gluten into 4 to 5 balls and drop them in the boiling water. Boil for 4 to 5 minutes until they float when moved with a spoon. Remove the gluten and cut in slices for use in sandwiches or sweet and sour seitan, strips for stir-fries, or bite-sized chunks for soups and stews. You may even leave the gluten as is for use in a braised or seitan roast. Place the gluten back in the boiling water and add the tamari soy sauce seasoning. Bring to a boil again. Cover and reduce the flame to medium-low. Simmer for 30 to 40 minutes. The seitan is now ready to use. The salty soy sauce cooking water used for cooking the gluten is called seitan-tamari cooking water.

Seitan, Onion, and Mustard Skillet

1 lb cooked seitan, sliced or cut in strips
3 cups onions, sliced in 1/4 inch thick rounds or rings
1 Tbsp sesame oil
1 cup water
1 Tbsp natural mustard
tamari soy sauce, to taste
1/4 cup scallion or chives, finely chopped, for garnish

Heat the sesame oil in a skillet and sauté the onion rings for 3 to 4 minutes. Lay the seitan on top of the onions. Mix the water and mustard and pour in the skillet. Cover and bring to a boil. Reduce the flame to medium-low and simmer

184

for 20 minutes until the onions are very tender. Season with several drops of tamari soy sauce, mix, cover, and cook for another 3 to 5 minutes. Remove the cover, garnish with chopped scallion or chives, and place in a serving dish.

Wheat Balls (Mock Meat Balls)

1 1/2 lb cooked seitan, cubed
1/2 cup onion, minced
1/2 cup mushrooms, minced
1/4 cup green pepper, minced (optional)
1 cup whole wheat bread crumbs
2 Tbsp kuzu, diluted
light sesame or safflower oil, for deep-frying

Place a hand food mill over a mixing bowl. Place the cubes of seitan in the food mill and grind. Add the onion, mushrooms, optional green pepper, and bread crumbs. Mix thoroughly. Add the kuzu and mix again. Form the seitan mixture into about 12 balls about the size of a golf ball. Pack the balls firmly so that they hold together. Heat 2 to 3 inches of oil in a heavy deep-frying pot. Deep-fry several balls at a time until golden brown. Remove and place on paper towels to drain. Repeat until all the balls have been deep-fried.

Spaghetti with Wheat Balls and Carrot-Beet Sauce

1 lb Jerusalem artichoke or other whole grain spaghetti,
    cooked, and rinsed
1 lb carrots, washed and sliced in thin rounds
1/4 cup beets, diced
water, for cooking carrots
water, for cooking diced beet
pinch of sea salt
1/2 cup onion, diced
1/2 cup mushrooms, sliced
1/4 cup green pepper, diced (optional)
2 to 3 cloves garlic, minced (optional)
2 tsp extra virgin olive oil or light sesame oil
1/2 tsp organic, dried basil (optional)
1/4 tsp organic, dried oregano (optional)
umeboshi vinegar
12 wheat balls, deep-fried

Place the carrots in a pot with enough water to just barely cover and add a pinch of sea salt. Cover and bring to a boil. Reduce the flame to medium-low and simmer for about 10 to 15 minutes until tender. Purée the carrots, along with the cooking water, in a blender until smooth. Place the beets in a saucepan and add water to half-cover. Add a pinch of sea salt, cover, and bring to a boil.

Reduce the flame to medium-low and simmer for 10 minutes. Place the beets and juice in the blender and purée until smooth. Mix the carrot and beet purée thoroughly. The sauce should now be almost the color of tomato sauce. Heat the oil in a skillet. Sauté the garlic and onion for 1 to 2 minutes. Add the mushrooms and green pepper. Sauté for another 2 to 3 minutes. Pour the carrot-beet purée in the skillet with the sautéed vegetables. Add the basil and oregano and mix. Season to taste with umeboshi vinegar to create a slightly salty-sour flavor similar to tomato sauce. Cover and bring to a boil. Reduce the flame to medium-low and simmer for about 20 minutes or so.

Place a serving of the cooked spaghetti on each serving plate. Place 2 to 3 wheat balls on top of the spaghetti. Spoon the carrot-beet sauce over each serving of spaghetti and wheat balls and serve hot.

Swedish Wheat Balls

12 wheat balls, deep-fried
4 to 5 cups seitan tamari cooking water (see above recipe; if not
    available use 4 to 5 cups of water seasoned with 1 to 1 1/2 tsp tamari soy
    sauce for each cup of liquid)
1 cup seitan starch water (see above recipe; if not available, 1 to 1 1/2 tsp kuzu
    can be diluted and used to thicken the gravy)
1 to 2 tsp corn oil
1/2 cup onion, diced
1/2 cup mushroom, diced
1/4 cup parsley, minced

Heat the oil in a skillet. Sauté the onion for 2 to 3 minutes. Add the mushrooms and sauté for another 3 to 5 minutes. Add the seitan-tamari cooking water. Mix in the seitan starch water. Bring to a boil, stirring constantly until thick and creamy. Cover, reduce the flame to medium-low, and simmer for 10 minutes. Remove the cover, and mix in the parsley. Cook 1 minute. Pour the gravy over the wheat balls. This dish is good served either with rice, cooked pasta, or millet mashed potatoes. Serve hot.

Chinese Style Sweet and Sour Wheat Balls

12 wheat balls, deep-fried
3 cups water
2 cups apple juice
1 to 1 1/2 tsp tamari soy sauce for each cup of water (6 to 7 1/2 tsp)
2 to 2 1/2 Tbsp kuzu, diluted
1 to 1 1/2 Tbsp natural mustard
1 Tbsp brown rice vinegar

Place the water and juice in a saucepan. Mix in the soy sauce and mustard. Bring almost to a boil. Add the kuzu, stirring constantly until thick. Add the vinegar, reduce the flame to low, and simmer for 4 to 5 minutes. Pour the sauce over the wheat balls and serve with cooked noodles, brown rice, or millet.

Spicy Wheat Balls and Sauerkraut

1 1/2 lb cooked seitan, cubed
1/2 cup onion, minced
1/4 cup parsley, minced
1/2 tsp organic, dried dill
2 Tbsp natural mustard
1 cup whole wheat bread crumbs
2 Tbsp kuzu, diluted
1 lb organic sauerkraut
light sesame or safflower oil, for deep-frying

Place a hand food mill over a mixing bowl. Place the seitan in the mill and grind. Add the onion, parsley, dill, mustard, and bread crumbs. Mix thoroughly. Add the kuzu and mix again. Heat 2 to 3 inches of oil in a heavy deep-frying pot. Deep-fry several wheat balls until golden brown. Remove and drain on paper towels. Repeat until all wheat balls have been deep-fried.

Place the sauerkraut and sauerkraut juice in a saucepan, cover, and bring to a boil. Reduce the flame to low and simmer 1 to 2 minutes. Place the sauerkraut in a serving bowl. Toss in the spicy wheat balls and serve.

Sweet and Sour Seitan

1 lb cooked seitan, sliced or cut in strips
1 cup onion, sliced in 1/2 inch thick wedges

1/2 cup fresh shiitake mushrooms, sliced
1/2 cup carrot, sliced in matchsticks
1 cup broccoli, florets
1/2 cup mung bean sprouts, washed
light sesame oil
4 cups water
2 Tbsp tamari soy sauce
1/2 cup brown rice syrup
3 to 4 tsp brown rice vinegar
2 Tbsp kuzu, diluted

Heat a small amount of oil and sauté the onion for 1 minute. Add the shiitake and sauté 2 to 3 minutes. Add the water and carrot. Cover and bring to a boil. Reduce the flame to medium-low and simmer 1 to 2 minutes. Add the broccoli, cover, and simmer 1 minute. Add the sprouts and thicken with kuzu, stirring constantly. Add the soy sauce, rice syrup, and vinegar. Simmer, uncovered, 2 to 3 minutes. Serve over rice, millet, barley, or noodles.

Seitan Stroganoff

1 lb Jerusalem artichoke fettucine, cooked
1 1/2 lb cooked seitan, cut in 1/2 inch thick strips (smoked seitan is delicious in this recipe if you can find it)
2 Tbsp corn oil
1/2 cup onion, minced
1 lb mushrooms, sliced
2 Tbsp unbleached white flour or 2 Tbsp kuzu, diluted
2 cups plain soymilk
2 tsp caraway seeds (optional)
sea salt
parsley, chopped, for garnish

Heat oil in a skillet and sauté the onion for 1 to 2 minutes. Sauté the mushrooms for 2 to 3 minutes. Add the seitan, caraway seeds, and soymilk. Bring to a boil. Dilute the flour and add to the skillet, stirring constantly to prevent lumping. Season to taste with a little sea salt, cover, and reduce the flame to low. Simmer for about 10 minutes. Add the cooked fettucine and mix in. Cover and simmer for another 2 to 3 minutes until the pasta is hot. Mix in chopped parsley and place in a serving bowl. Serve hot.

Seitan Sandwiches

1 lb cooked seitan, sliced
8 to 10 slices whole wheat bread
1 small onion, sliced in thin rounds or rings
several lettuce leaves
natural mustard
tofu mayonnaise
alfalfa sprouts
organic sauerkraut
sesame oil, for frying seitan

Heat a small amount of oil in a skillet. Fry the slices of seitan 2 to 3 minutes on each side. Remove and place on a plate. Take half of the bread slices and spread a little mustard on them. On the other slices, spread a little tofu mayonnaise. Place 2 slices of seitan on 4 or 5 slices of bread. Place a little sauerkraut, a few sprouts, and lettuce leaves on top of the seitan. Place the other bread slices on top. You should now have 4 to 5 sandwiches. Slice in half and serve.

Seitan Burgers

1 1/2 lb cooked seitan, cubed
1/2 cup onion, minced
1/2 cup mushrooms, minced
1 cup fine whole wheat bread crumbs
1/4 cup parsley, minced
1/4 cup carrot, chopped fine
1/4 cup celery, minced
3 Tbsp kuzu, diluted in 4 Tbsp water
sesame or corn oil, for frying burgers

Place a hand food mill over a mixing bowl. Place the seitan in the food mill and grind. Add all the other ingredients and mix thoroughly. Form the mixture into 5 to 6 equal size patties or burger shapes. Heat oil in a skillet or griddle. Fry the burgers on one side until golden brown. Flip the burgers over and fry the other side until golden brown. Remove and place on a serving platter. The burgers may be served as is, with a gravy or sauce, with a little natural mustard, or made into a sandwich with your favorite toppings.

Seitan-Rice Burgers

1 1/2 lb cooked seitan, cubed and ground as above
2 cups cooked brown rice
1/2 cup onion, minced
1/4 cup carrot, minced
1/4 cup celery, minced
2 Tbsp parsley, minced
1/4 cup roasted sunflower or sesame seeds
1/2 cup water
3 Tbsp whole wheat pastry flour
2 tsp tamari soy sauce
sesame or corn oil, for frying burgers

Place the first 7 ingredients in a mixing bowl. Mix thoroughly. Add the flour and soy sauce and mix again. Add the water and mix again. Form the mixture into equal size patties or burgers. Heat the oil in a griddle or skillet. Place several burgers in the pan and fry on each side until golden brown. Remove and place on a serving platter. Repeat until all burgers have been fried. Place the remaining burgers on the serving platter.

Wheat Loaf with Kuzu-Mushroom Gravy

1 1/2 lb cooked seitan, cubed and ground as above
1 cup fine whole wheat bread crumbs
1 cup cooked brown rice
1/2 cup onion, minced
1/2 cup mushrooms, minced
1/4 cup green pepper, minced (optional)
1/4 cup sweet red pepper, minced (optional)
1/4 cup parsley, minced
1/2 cup water
5 Tbsp kuzu, diluted in 6 Tbsp water
2 tsp tamari soy sauce
2 Tbsp natural mustard
2 Tbsp whole wheat pastry or unbleached white flour
sesame oil

Place all ingredients in a mixing bowl and mix thoroughly. Lightly oil a loaf pan and place the mixture in the pan, pressing down firmly to form a loaf. Bake the loaf in a 350 degree F oven for 20 to 25 minutes. Remove and allow to cool slightly before slicing.

Kuzu-Mushroom Gravy

3 cups water
4 1/2 to 5 tsp tamari soy sauce
1 to 2 tsp sesame oil
1 cup mushrooms, sliced thin
1/2 cup onion, minced
2 Tbsp parsley, scallion, or chives, chopped fine
5 tsp kuzu, diluted in 6 tsp water

Heat the oil in a skillet. Sauté the onion for 1 to 2 minutes. Add the mushrooms and sauté for 3 to 4 minutes. Add the water and soy sauce. Cover, bring to a boil, and reduce the flame to medium-low. Simmer for 5 minutes. Reduce the flame to low and add the kuzu, stirring constantly until the sauce becomes thick . Turn off the flame and add the parsley, scallion, or chives, and mix. Place 1 to 2 slices of wheat loaf on each serving plate and ladle the gravy over them. Serve hot.

Seitan and Vegetable Kebabs

4 to 5 broccoli, florets
4 to 5 cauliflower, florets
4 to 5 mushrooms
4 to 5 pieces of carrot, cut in bite-sized chunks
4 to 5 red radishes
4 to 5 onion wedges
4 to 5 small Brussels sprouts
8 to 10 pieces cooked seitan, cut in 2 inch squares
water, for cooking vegetables
dark sesame oil, for sautéing mushrooms
tamari soy sauce
4 to 5 bamboo skewers

Place 2 inches of water in a saucepan, cover, and bring to a boil. Boil the vegetables in the following order for recommended time: onion, 1 minute, carrot, 2 minutes, cauliflower, 2 to 2 1/2 minutes, broccoli, 2 minutes, Brussels sprouts, 2 to 3 minutes, and red radishes, 2 minutes. Place on a platter, keeping each vegetable separate.

Heat a small amount of oil in a skillet. Sauté the mushrooms for 2 to 3 minutes. Add several drops of soy sauce and sauté for 1 more minute. Remove and place on the platter with the other vegetables. Arrange 1 or 2 pieces of seitan and 1 piece of each type of vegetable on each of the bamboo skewers. Set aside while you prepare the following sauce.

Sauce

1 cup water
1/4 cup brown rice syrup
1 tsp natural mustard
2 tsp tamari soy sauce

Place all ingredients in a saucepan and bring almost to a boil. Reduce the flame to low and simmer for 2 to 3 minutes. Remove from the flame. With a pastry or oil brush, brush the sauce over each kebab. Place on a cookie sheet and broil for 2 to 3 minutes, brushing each with sauce once more during cooking. Remove and place on a serving platter.

Stuffed Seitan Croquettes with Gravy

These croquettes are made with homemade seitan. It is well worth the effort as they have a very rich flavor.

2 cups homemade wheat gluten (seitan)
2 carrots, sliced in 2 inch lengths
1 piece daikon, 4 to 6 inches long, sliced in 1/2 inch thick rounds
1 piece burdock, sliced in 2 inch lengths
light sesame or safflower oil, for deep-frying croquettes
1 piece kombu, 2 to 3 inches long, soaked and diced
water
tamari soy sauce, to taste
1 cup seitan starch water
1 tsp fresh ginger juice

Separate the gluten into 8 to 10 balls. Pull the balls of gluten apart in flat pieces. Wrap a piece of carrot, burdock, or daikon up inside of each piece. Press the gluten firmly with your fingers so that the vegetables are completely surrounded by it. Heat 2 to 3 inches of oil in a heavy deep-frying pot and deep-fry several pieces of gluten at a time until they are golden brown and puff up. Remove and drain on paper towels. Repeat until all gluten has been fried.

Place the fried stuffed gluten in a pot on top of the kombu. Add enough cold water to just cover. Season the liquid with enough soy sauce for a slightly salty flavor. Cover and bring to a boil. Reduce the flame to medium-low and simmer for 30 to 35 minutes. Remove the cover and add the seitan starch water, stirring constantly until thick and smooth. Cover and simmer for another 10 minutes. Add the ginger juice and simmer 1 minute. Remove and place the seitan and gravy in a serving dish.

Tempura Seitan Kebabs

1 1/2 lb cooked seitan, cut in 3 inch long by 1 inch wide chunks
1/2 cup whole wheat pastry flour
1/2 cup corn flour
2 tsp kuzu, diluted in 3 tsp water
1/8 tsp sea salt
1 Tbsp natural mustard
2 Tbsp parsley, minced
1 to 1 1/4 cups cold water
bamboo skewers
light sesame or safflower oil, for deep-frying

Place the flours, sea salt, and parsley in a mixing bowl and mix. Add the water, kuzu, and mustard. Mix again. Place 1 piece of seitan on each bamboo skewer. Heat 2 to 3 inches of oil in a heavy deep-frying pot. Dip each skewer in the batter, completely coating the seitan. Deep-fry, holding the uncovered end of the skewer, until the batter is golden brown around the seitan. Remove and drain. Repeat until all seitan has been fried. Place on a serving platter and prepare the following dip sauce.

Sauce

1 cup water
2 to 3 tsp tamari soy sauce
1 tsp fresh ginger juice

Place the water and soy sauce in a saucepan and bring almost to a boil. Reduce the flame to low, and simmer 2 to 3 minutes. Add the ginger juice and remove from the flame. Pour in individual dipping bowls. Dip the kebabs in the dipping sauce before eating. Serve hot.

Seitan Cutlets with Mushroom Gravy

1 1/2 lb cooked seitan, sliced in 1/2 inch thick slices
1/2 cup corn flour
1/8 tsp sea salt

corn oil, for frying seitan
2 cups water
3 tsp tamari soy sauce
1 cup mushrooms, sliced
4 tsp kuzu, diluted in 5 tsp water
parsley, choped, for garnish

Place the flour and sea salt in a mixing bowl and mix. Roll the slices of seitan in the flour to completely coat them. Heat a small amount of oil in a skillet or griddle. Fry the coated seitan slices on both sides until golden brown. Remove and place on a serving platter.

To prepare the gravy, place the water, mushrooms, and soy sauce in a saucepan. Cover and bring to a boil. Reduce the flame to medium-low and simmer for 5 to 7 minutes. Reduce the flame to low and add the kuzu, stirring constantly to prevent lumping. When thick, mix in the parsley and remove from the flame. Place in a serving bowl. Spoon the gravy over the cutlets when served.

Seitan Boiled Dinner

2 cups homemade gluten
6 cups water
3 Tbsp tamari soy sauce
l strip kombu, 2 inches long, soaked and diced
dark sesame oil
3 carrots, sliced in half lengthwise, then in 2 inch lengths
1 parsnip, sliced in half lengthwise, then in 2 inch lengths
5 small onions, peeled and sliced in half
5 to 6 mushrooms, leave whole
2 stalks celery, sliced in 2 inch lengths
1/2 small head cabbage, sliced in wedges
5 to 6 albi (small taro) potatoes, peeled and washed, halved
1/2 cup rutabaga, sliced in chunks

Place water in a pot, cover, and bring to a boil. Remove the cover and place the gluten (leave in one large chunk) in the boiling water. Boil, uncovered, for about 5 minutes. Season the water with tamari soy sauce and add the kombu. Cover and bring to a boil again. Reduce the flame to medium-low and simmer for 35 to 40 minutes. Remove the whole piece of cooked seitan, and drain. Save the cooking water.

Heat a small amount of oil in a heavy stock pot. Place the whole piece of seitan in the pot and fry on each side until slightly browned. Place 2 inches of seitan-tamari cooking water in the pot. Place the vegetables around the seitan roast, keeping each type in its own section. Cover and bring to a boil. Reduce the flame to medium-low and simmer for 25 to 30 minutes until the vegetables are very tender.

Remove the seitan roast and place on a serving platter. Slice the seitan in 1/4 to 1/2 inch thick slices. Arrange the vegetables around the roast on the platter. If you wish you may thicken the cooking water with a little kuzu or seitan starch water to make a gravy, which can be ladled over the seitan and vegetables when served.

Seitan Stuffed Cabbage

4 to 6 cabbage leaves, left whole
4 to 6 pieces cooked seitan, 2 to 3 inches long by 1 inch thick
1/3 cup sauerkraut
1 cup carrot, cut in matchsticks
water
tamari soy sauce
1 strip kombu, 2 inches long, soaked

Take each cabbage leaf and cut out the thick base. Place 2 inches of water in a pot, cover, and bring to a boil. Remove the cover and place the cabbage leaves in the pot. Cover and cook for 1 to 2 minutes. Remove and drain. Take each leaf and place a piece of seitan, a tablespoonful of sauerkraut, and 2 tablespoonfuls of carrot in the center. Roll up the leaves and fasten together with a toothpick to keep from falling apart.

Place the kombu in a heavy skillet. Place the stuffed cabbage in the skillet. Add enough cabbage cooking water to the skillet to half- cover the rolls. Place a few drops of soy sauce in the water. Cover the skillet and bring to a boil. Reduce the flame to medium-low and simmer for 20 minutes until the cabbage is tender. Remove and place in a serving dish.

Seitan Stuffed Mushrooms

8 to 10 large stuffing mushrooms, stems removed
1/2 cup cooked seitan, finely minced or ground
1 Tbsp onion, finely minced
1 Tbsp carrot, finely minced
1 tsp parsley, finely minced
1/4 cup fine whole wheat bread crumbs
2 Tbsp finely grated mochi

Place the seitan, onion, carrot, parsley, bread crumbs, and mochi in a mixing bowl. Mix thoroughly. Stuff each mushroom with the stuffing. Place the mushrooms on a cookie sheet and broil several minutes until the mushrooms are tender and juicy. Remove and place on a serving platter. Serve hot.

Seitan-Vegetable Pastry Rolls

2 cups cooked seitan, sliced in thin strips
1/2 cup onion, diced
1 cup mushrooms, sliced
1/2 cup carrot, matchsticks
1 cup leek, sliced
sesame oil

Heat a small amount of oil in a skillet. Sauté the onion for 1 minute. Add the mushrooms, carrot, leek, and seitan. Sauté for another 3 to 4 minutes. Remove from the flame and prepare the following dough.

Pastry Dough

2 cups whole wheat pastry flour
1/4 tsp sea salt
1/4 cup corn oil
1/3 to 1/2 cup water

To prepare the pastry dough, mix the flour and salt in a mixing bowl. Add the corn oil, mixing it in well, by sifting it in your hands using a rubbing motion. Add the water and form into a ball of dough. Knead for 2 to 3 minutes. Place in the refrigerator for 1/2 hour. Remove and divide in half. Flour a table or cutting board and roll out half of the dough as if you were making a pie crust. Place half of the seitan and vegetables on the crust, spreading it evenly around. Roll up the crust into a log or cylinder shape. Roll out the rest of the dough, place seitan and vegetables on it, and roll up. Seal the ends of the rolls by pressing together with a fork. Take the fork and poke several air holes in the top of the rolls.

Place on a lightly oiled baking sheet and bake at 350 degrees F for about 30 to 35 minutes until the crust is golden brown. Remove and slice. Place on a serving platter.

Stuffed Squash or Hokkaido Pumpkin

1 large buttercup squash or Hokkaido pumpkin
1 1/2 cups whole wheat bread cubes
1/2 cup onion, diced
1 1/2 cups cooked seitan, cubed
4 to 5 mushrooms, diced
1/4 cup celery, diced
1/2 cup water
1 tsp organic dried sage (optional)
tamari soy sauce
corn oil

Cut out the top of the squash as you would when making a Jack-O'-Lantern. Clean out the seeds. Heat a small amount of oil in a skillet and sauté the onion for 1 to 2 minutes. Add the mushrooms and celery. Sauté another 3 to 4 minutes. Place in a mixing bowl. Add the bread cubes, seitan, water, and sage. Sprinkle several drops of soy sauce over the ingredients. Mix thoroughly. Place the stuffing inside the hollowed-out squash. Place the top of the squash on top. Lightly oil the skin of the squash. Bake at 450 degrees F for about 30 to 35 minutes or until tender. Test with a fork or bamboo skewer or chopstick to see whether or not the squash is done. Remove and place on a serving plate. Slice or scoop out squash and stuffing to serve.

Seitan and Vegetable Stir-Fry

1 cup cooked seitan, sliced in strips
2 cups kale, chopped
1/2 cup carrot, cut in matchsticks
water
sesame oil

Heat a small amount of oil in a skillet. Sauté the carrot for 1 minute. Add the seitan and sauté for another 2 minutes. Add the kale and a small amount of water, cover, and simmer for about 2 minutes until the kale is tender but still bright green. Remove the cover and cook off any liquid. Place in a serving dish.

Fu and Vegetable Stir-Fry

5 to 6 rounds of whole wheat fu or flat fu, soaked 10 minutes,
  liquid squeezed out and sliced in bite-sized chunks
1 cup onion, sliced in half-moons
5 fresh shiitake mushrooms, sliced
1 cup carrot, sliced in thin diagonals
1 1/2 cup green string beans, sliced in half
sesame oil
tamari soy sauce, to taste

Heat a small amount of oil in a skillet. Sauté the onion for 1 to 2 minutes. Add the shiitake and sauté another 2 to 3 minutes. Add the carrot, green beans, and fu. Sauté until the carrot is almost done, stirring occasionally. Add several drops of soy sauce for a slightly salty flavor and cook another 4 to 5 minutes. Place in a serving bowl.

Boiled Fu and Vegetables

6 pieces round whole wheat fu, soaked and sliced
1/2 lb tofu, cubed
5 shiitake mushrooms, soaked, stems removed, and sliced
1 cup broccoli, florets
1/2 cup carrot, sliced on a thin diagonal
water
tamari soy sauce, to taste

Place the fu and shiitake in a pot. Add water to half-cover. Cover and bring to a boil. Reduce the flame to medium-low and simmer for 10 minutes until the shiitake are tender. Add the carrot and broccoli, cover, and simmer another 1 to 1 1/2 minutes. Add the tofu and season with a little tamari soy sauce to taste. Cover and cook for another 1 to 2 minutes. Remove and place in a serving dish.

Baked Beans and Fu

1 cup navy, northern, or white kidney beans, soaked 6 to 8 hours, discard
  soaking water
2 cups water, for cooking beans
1 strip kombu 2 inches long, soaked and diced
1 cup onion, diced

1 pkg. bonito flakes (optional)
5 pieces round fu, soaked and cubed
1 Tbsp natural mustard
1/8 to 1/4 tsp sea salt
barley malt or rice syrup, to taste

Place the beans and kombu in a pressure cooker. Bring to a boil, uncovered. Simmer for 10 minutes. Cover and bring up to pressure. Reduce the flame to medium-low and cook for 45 to 50 minutes. Remove from the flame and allow the pressure to come down. Remove the cover.

Place the onion, bonito flakes, fu, mustard, and sea salt in the cooker with the beans and mix. Add enough barley malt or rice syrup for a sweet flavor and mix. Pour the beans in a casserole or baking dish and cover. Bake at 350 degrees F for 30 to 35 minutes or until the onions are done. Remove the cover and brown the top of the beans by baking for several more minutes. If the beans are too watery, bake a little longer to allow liquid to evaporate. Be careful not to let the beans get too dry as they do harden after cooling off.

Fu and Green Peas

1 pkg. round whole wheat fu, soaked and cubed
1 to 1 1/2 cups fresh green peas, shelled
4 shiitake mushrooms, soaked, stems removed, and sliced
1/2 cup onion, diced
3 cups water
2 1/2 to 3 Tbsp kuzu, diluted in 4 Tbsp water
tamari soy sauce, to taste

Place the fu, shiitake, and water in a pot, cover, and bring to a boil. Reduce the flame to medium-low and simmer for about 10 minutes until the shiitake are tender. Add the onion and green peas, cover, and simmer for another 4 to 5 minutes. Reduce the flame to low and add the kuzu, stirring constantly to prevent lumping. When the liquid is thickened, season with a little tamari soy sauce to taste. Simmer another 2 to 3 minutes. Place in a serving bowl.

Deep-Fried Fu and Squash

1 small buttercup squash, seeds and skin removed, and sliced
   in chunks
6 rounds whole wheat fu, broken in bite-sized pieces
light sesame or safflower oil, for deep-frying fu

water
tamari soy sauce

Heat the oil in a heavy deep-frying pot. Deep-fry the fu until golden. Remove and drain. Place the fu and squash in a pot with enough water to half-cover the ingredients. Cover and bring to a boil. Reduce the flame to medium-low and simmer for 10 minutes or so. Remove the cover. Season with a little soy sauce and mash the squash chunks with a potato masher. Cover and simmer over a low flame for 5 more minutes. Remove and place in a serving bowl.

Vegetarian Sukiyaki (Fu, Seitan, and Vegetable Skillet)

In this traditional Japanese dish, tofu, seitan, and fu are used in place of animal food. This dish is very attractive and delicious. The ingredients are cooked together in a cast iron skillet and served in the skillet. The ingredients are placed in separate sections and cooked in a kombu-shiitake mushroom broth. A variety of vegetables with different colors can be used to make a visually appealing dish. Cooked noodles or pan-fried mochi can be added to the skillet for a quick one-dish meal. Sukiyaki may be served with or without a dip sauce. Typical sauces include tamari soy sauce and ginger, tamari soy sauce and grated daikon, tofu cream, and umeboshi-tahini sauce.

This dish is usually prepared at the table on a portable burner. One or two ingredients are placed in the skillet to cook, then removed. Other ingredients are added to the skillet as needed. It can also be prepared on the stove and served as is at the table.

6 cups water
1 strip kombu, 2 inches long, soaked
2 Tbsp tamari soy sauce
5 shiitake mushrooms, soaked, stems removed, and quartered
1 Tbsp mirin or sake (optional)
4 to 5 pieces daikon, sliced in 1/2 inch thick rounds
1/2 lb tofu, sliced in cubes
4 to 5 slices cooked seitan, cut in strips
4 to 5 broccoli, florets
1/2 cup Chinese cabbage, sliced in 1 inch pieces
4 to 5 carrot slices, cut in 1/4 inch thick diagonals
4 to 5 buttercup squash slices, 1/4 inch thick
4 to 5 butternut squash slices, 1/4 inch thick
1 medium onion, sliced in 1/4 inch thick rounds or rings
4 to 5 pieces round fu, soaked and cut in half
4 to 5 pieces mochi, 2 inches by 3 inches, pan-fried until golden

Place the water, kombu, shiitake, and daikon in a pot, cover, and bring to a boil. Reduce the flame to medium-low and cook for 15 minutes. Remove the daikon and set aside.

Pour the cooking water from the daikon, shiitake, and kombu in a 12 inch cast iron skillet. Season with tamari soy sauce and mirin or sake. Place the cooked daikon in one section of the skillet. Next, place the fu, onion, carrot, and squash in the skillet, keeping them in separate sections. Cover and bring to a boil. Reduce the flame to medium-low and simmer for 2 to 3 minutes until the squash in tender. Remove the cover and add the broccoli. Cover and cook 1 minute. Remove the cover and add the tofu, mochi, and Chinese cabbage. Cook, uncovered, for 1 to 2 minutes until done. The colors of the vegetables should be very bright and the green vegetables slightly crisp. Remove from the burner and place on the table. Serve hot with the following dip sauce.

Dip Sauce

1 cup water
1 1/2 tsp tamari soy sauce
1/2 tsp ginger juice
1 Tbsp scallion, finely chopped

Place the water and soy sauce in a saucepan and bring almost to a boil. Reduce the flame to low and simmer for 2 to 3 minutes. Add the ginger juice and scallion. Simmer 30 seconds. Remove and place in individual dipping bowls. Place vegetables and other ingredients in the dip sauce before eating.

Baked Fu, Wakame, and Onions

1/2 pkg. flat fu, soaked 10 minutes and sliced
1/2 cup wakame, soaked and sliced
2 cups onion, sliced in thin half-moons
3 to 4 Tbsp organic roasted tahini
1/3 to 1/2 cup water
tamari soy sauce

Mix the fu, onion, and wakame in a mixing bowl. Dilute the tahini with water and season with several drops of soy sauce. Pour the mixture over the fu. Mix well. Place the fu, onion, and wakame in a covered casserole dish. Bake at 350 degrees F for 25 to 30 minutes. Remove the cover and bake for another 5 minutes or so. Remove and serve.

Chapter 9
Noodles and Pasta

In the Far East, whole wheat was traditionally used to make noodles. Noodles made completely with whole wheat are known in Japanese as udon or in Chinese as mien. A lighter wheat noodle called somen is also available and more suitable for use during warmer weather or in hot climates. Noodles that are made primarily with buckwheat and only partially with whole wheat are called soba.

Pasta and noodles are very delicious, come in many varieties, and are usually more digestible than flour prepared in baked form. Western pasta include whole wheat spaghetti noodles, lasagna, elbows, shells, and spirals and usually come without seasoning so the cook can add a pinch of sea salt to the water on the stove. Eastern noodles include, in addition to udon, soba, and somen, saifun, clear cellophane noodles made from mung bean threads; maifun, rice flour noodles; ramen, either udon or soba that has been deep-fried; and various green-colored noodles made with flour combined with mugwort, artichoke flour, or green tea. Oriental noodles customarily include sea salt and do not require further seasoning during cooking. Pasta and noodles made with eggs, white flour, or other refined ingredients and seasonings are best avoided except on rare social occasions.

Almost everyone loves to eat noodles and pasta. Besides being very easy to digest, they are light and fun to eat. They can be eaten for breakfast, lunch, or dinner, or as a snack.

Basic Udon, Somen, or Soba

In Japan, noodles are cooked differently than they are in the West. No salt is added to the cooking water because there is salt in the noodle dough. Western pastas usually do not contain salt. The largest difference is in the actual cooking process. To keep Oriental-style noodles firm or al dente, and to lock in nutrients and flavor, add cold water to the boiling noodles several times during the cooking process. The number of times you need to add cold water varies with the type of noodle being cooked. This is called "shocking" the noodles. After you add cold water, bring the water to a boil again. Then add cold water again. This simple process improves the texture and flavor of the noodles.

8 oz. udon, somen, or soba
2 quarts water

Place the water in a pot, cover, and bring to a boil. Remove the cover. Place the noodles in the water, stir, and bring to a boil again. Pour a little cold water over the noodles to stop the cooking action. Bring to a boil again. Pour cold water over the noodles 2 to 3 more times, each time waiting until the water comes to a boil again. Check the noodles by breaking one in half. If the outside is brown and the inside white, continue cooking the noodles until they are the same color all the way through. However, the noodles should still retain a degree of firmness. Remove from the burner, pour in a colander or strainer, and rinse under cold water. The noodles are now ready to eat with a little soy sauce and chopped scallion. They can also be fried, added to soup or broth, or used in salads and other dishes.

Basic Pasta

Western style pasta, including naturally made semolina, Jerusalem artichoke, corn, brown rice, spelt, or whole wheat pasta, can be boiled in water with a little sea salt until done. Several drops of sesame oil can sometimes be added to the cooking water to prevent the pasta from sticking together. For those who wish to limit the intake of oil, simply boil the pasta in salted water without oil. Stir the pasta periodically to prevent sticking and rinse when done.

8 oz. natural semolina or whole grain pasta
2 quarts water
pinch of sea salt

Place the water and sea salt in a pot, cover, and bring to a boil. Remove the cover and place the pasta in the water. Stir and cook several minutes, periodically checking the pasta by breaking a piece in half. The pasta is done when it is the same color all the way through. If the center of the pasta is white or lighter than the outside, continue cooking until done. Drain the water and serve hot with your favorite sauce, or place in a colander and rinse under cold water to prevent sticking until you use them to prepare another dish.

Fried Udon, Somen, or Soba

1 lb udon, somen, or soba, cooked
1 Tbsp light or dark sesame oil
1 to ½ Tbsp tamari soy sauce
1 cup scallion or chives, finely chopped

Heat the oil in a skillet. Add the udon, somen, or soba and the soy sauce. Stir the noodles every few seconds until they are hot to prevent burning. Add the chopped scallion or chives. Stir again for another minute or so until the scallion or chives are done. Remove and place in a serving dish.

Winter Fried Noodles and Vegetables

1 lb udon, somen, or soba, cooked
1 Tbsp dark sesame oil
1 cup onion, sliced in thin half-moons
1/4 cup burdock, sliced in thin matchsticks
1/2 cup carrot, sliced in thin matchsticks
1/2 cup cabbage, shredded
1 to 2 Tbsp tamari soy sauce
1/4 cup scallion or parsley, finely chopped
1 tsp fresh ginger juice

Heat the oil in a skillet. Add the onion and sauté for 1 to 2 minutes. Add the burdock and sauté for 1 to 2 minutes. Add the carrots and cabbage. Place the cooked noodles on top and turn the flame to low. Cover and cook for 5 to 7 minutes until the noodles are hot and the vegetables are done. Add the tamari soy sauce, mix, and cover. Cook for 2 to 3 minutes. Add the scallion or parsley and ginger juice. Cover and cook another minute or so. Place in a serving dish.

Summer Fried Noodles and Vegetables

1 lb udon or somen, cooked
1 lb firm style tofu, cubed
1 Tbsp sesame oil
1/2 cup onion, sliced in thin half-moons
1/2 cup carrot, sliced in thin matchsticks
1/4 cup sweet corn, removed from cob
1/4 cup snow peas, sliced in half
1/4 cup scallion, sliced thin
1 1/2 to 2 Tbsp tamari soy sauce

Heat oil in a skillet. Sauté the onion for 1 to 2 minutes. Add the tofu, corn, carrot, and cooked noodles. Sprinkle the soy sauce over the noodles. Cover, reduce the flame to medium-low, and cook 5 to 7 minutes until the vegetables are done and the noodles are hot. Remove the cover, add the snow peas and scallion. Cover and cook for 1 to 2 minutes. Remove cover and mix. Place in a serving dish.

Pasta Salad with Umeboshi-Tahini Dressing

8 oz. whole wheat or Jerusalem artichoke shells, elbows, ziti, or
    rigatoni, cooked
1 cup chickpeas, cooked
1/2 cup cucumber, quartered and sliced thin
1/2 cup red onion, sliced in thin half or quarter-moons
1/4 cup celery, diced
1/4 cup red radish, sliced in thin rounds or half-moons
1/2 cup green peas, cooked 2 to 3 minutes
1 cup red leaf lettuce, sliced in 1 inch pieces
2 Tbsp parsley, minced

Place all of the above ingredients in a mixing bowl and toss. Prepare the dressing below.

Umeboshi-Tahini Dressing

2 to 3 umeboshi plums, pits removed
2 to 3 Tbsp organic, roasted tahini
1 Tbsp onion, finely grated
1 cup water

Purée the umeboshi in a suribachi until smooth. Add the grated onion and tahini. Purée again. Gradually pour the water in the suribachi and purée until smooth and creamy. Pour the dressing over the salad just before serving. Place in a serving bowl.

Pasta Salad with Creamy Tofu Dressing

8 oz. whole grain elbows, shells, ziti, or rigatoni, cooked
1/2 cup green beans, sliced in 1 inch lengths
1/2 cup yellow wax beans, sliced in 1 inch lengths
1/4 cup red radish, sliced in thin half-moons
1/4 cup summer squash, sliced in thin quarters
1/2 cup leek, sliced in 1/2 inch rounds
1/4 cup green peas, removed from pods
1 cup black olives, pits removed and sliced
water, for boiling vegetables

Place 2 inches of water in a saucepan, cover, and bring to a boil. Boil the vegetables separately in the following order: summer squash for 1 to 1 1/2 minutes; yellow wax beans for 2 to 3 minutes; green peas for 2 to 3 minutes; green beans for 2 to 3 minutes; leek for 2 minutes; and red radish for 1 minute. Place the cooked pasta, cooked vegetables, and olives in a mixing bowl and prepare the following dressing.

Creamy Tofu Dressing

1 lb firm style tofu, drained
4 Tbsp umeboshi vinegar
2 Tbsp onion, finely grated
2 Tbsp parsley, minced
1/2 cup water
1/2 tsp tamari soy sauce

Place all the ingredients in a blender and purée until smooth and creamy. Just before serving, pour the dressing over the salad ingredients, mix well, and place in a serving bowl.

Pasta Salad with Pumpkin Seed Dressing

8 oz. any whole grain pasta or Japanese noodles, cooked
1/2 cup onion, sliced in thin half-moons

1 cup broccoli, florets
1/2 cup cauliflower, florets
1/2 cup carrot, sliced in thin half-moons
water, for cooking vegetables

Place 2 inches of water in a saucepan, cover, and bring to a boil. Boil the vegetables separately in the following order: onion for 1 minute; carrot for 2 minutes; cauliflower for 2 to 3 minutes; and broccoli for 2 minutes. Place the vegetables and cooked pasta or noodles in a mixing bowl and prepare the dressing.

Pumpkin Seed Dressing

1 cup pumpkin seeds, washed and roasted
1/4 cup parsley, minced
2 Tbsp onion, finely grated
3 Tbsp umeboshi vinegar
3/4 cup water

Place the pumpkin seeds in a suribachi and grind until half-crushed. Add the parsley and onion. Grind for 1 minute. Add the umeboshi vinegar and water and grind again to thoroughly mix. Just before serving the salad, mix in the dressing and place the salad in a serving bowl.

Bean, Pasta, and Dandelion Salad

8 oz. whole grain shells or elbows, cooked
1 cup organic kidney beans, cooked
1 cup organic chickpeas, cooked
1 cup green beans, sliced in 2 inch lengths
water, for boiling green beans
2 cups fresh dandelion greens, chopped
1 tsp. sesame or extra-virgin olive oil
1/2 tsp tamari soy sauce
3 umeboshi plums, pits removed
2 Tbsp onion, finely grated
2 Tbsp parsley, finely minced
3/4 cup water

Place 2 inches of water in a saucepan, cover, and bring to a boil. Boil the green beans for 2 to 3 minutes, remove, and drain. Boil the dandelion greens for 1 minute, remove, and drain. Heat oil in a skillet and add dandelion. Add soy sauce and sauté for 1 to 2 minutes. Remove and place in a mixing bowl. Place the cooked pasta, kidney beans, chickpeas, and green beans in the mixing bowl. Place the umeboshi in a suribachi and purée until smooth. Add the onion and parsley. Grind for 1 to 2 minutes. Add the water and purée again. Pour the umeboshi dressing over the salad ingredients, mix thoroughly, and let sit for 30 minutes. Place in a serving bowl.

Spaghetti with Peanut-Mustard Pesto

8 oz. whole wheat or Jerusalem artichoke spaghetti, cooked
1/2 cup kale, chopped
1/4 cup carrot, sliced in thin matchsticks
water, for cooking vegetables

Place the pasta in a mixing bowl. Place 2 inches of water in a saucepan, cover, and bring to a boil. Boil the carrot for 1 minute, remove, and place in the mixing bowl. Boil the kale for 1 1/2 to 2 minutes, remove, and place in the mixing bowl. Prepare the peanut-mustard pesto below.

Peanut-Mustard Pesto

1/2 cup organic roasted peanuts
1 Tbsp natural mustard
1/3 cup scallion or chives, chopped
1 Tbsp tamari soy sauce
1/2 cup water
1 Tbsp fresh lemon juice

Place the ingredients in a blender and purée until smooth and creamy. Just before serving, pour the pesto sauce over the salad ingredients, mix thoroughly, and place in a serving dish.

Soba Sushi

8 oz. ito soba or jinenjo soba, cooked
4 to 5 sheets of nori, toasted
4 to 5 scallions, roots and hard white bases removed
2 Tbsp tan sesame seeds, roasted
4 slices firm style tofu, 1/4 to 1/2 inch thick, deep-fried

208

Kombu-Bonito Flake Dip Sauce

1 cup water
2 inches kombu, soaked
1 to 1 1/2 Tbsp tamari soy sauce
2 Tbsp bonito flakes

Place the water, kombu, soy sauce, and bonito flakes in a saucepan and heat. Reduce flame to low and simmer for 3 to 4 minutes. Remove from the flame and place in individual small bowls. Set aside until the sushi is ready.

Slice the deep-fried tofu in 1/4-1/2 inch thick strips and place on a plate. Place a bamboo sushi mat on your cutting board. Place a sheet of nori on the mat with the smooth shiny side down. Divide the cooked soba into 4 to 5 bunches. Spread one bunch of soba evenly across the width of the nori, so that it is about 1/4 inch thick on the sheet. Leave 2 inches of the upper end of the nori uncovered. Leave 1 inch at the lower end, closest to you, uncovered. Use a knife to trim any noodles that may be hanging over the edges.

Place 1/4 of the tofu strips end to end in a straight line across the width of the center of the soba. Place a raw scallion on top of the tofu strips. Sprinkle a few sesame seeds over the tofu and scallion. Use the bamboo mat to roll the nori and soba into a log-shaped roll. Stop rolling when you get to the uncovered area at the far end of the nori. Moisten the area with a little cold water and continue rolling. You should now have a log- or cylinder-shaped roll. Wrap the mat completely around the roll and gently squeeze to seal the nori together. Remove the roll from the mat and place it on the cutting board. Repeat until all ingredients have been used. You should now have 4 to 5 rolls.

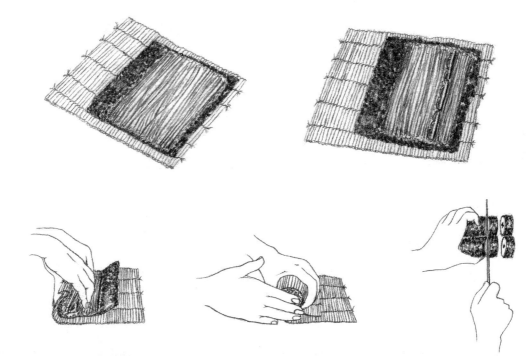

Slice each roll in half, making 2 equal-sized pieces. Then slice each half in half and each quarter in half, so that you have 8 equal-sized pieces of soba hand-rolled sushi. Repeat until all the rolls have been sliced. You should now have 32 to 40 pieces of soba sushi. Arrange the sushi on a serving platter with the soba ends facing up. Dip the sushi in the dip sauce as you eat.

Linguine with Fresh White Clam Sauce

1 lb Jerusalem artichoke or natural linguine or udon, cooked
1 qt. shucked clams, chopped in pieces
1 pt. fresh clam juice
2 to 3 Tbsp extra virgin olive oil
4 cloves garlic, minced (optional)
2 small onions or shallots, minced
1 1/2 cups water
1/4 cup parsley, minced
sea salt, to taste

Heat the oil in a large skillet. Add the garlic and onions or shallots. Sauté for 2 to 3 minutes. Add the water and clam juice. Season to taste with sea salt, cover, and reduce the flame to low. Simmer for 10 minutes. Add the clams and parsley. Simmer 3 to 4 minutes until the clams are done. Do not overcook as this will cause the clams to become tough. Remove from the flame. Place the cooked pasta in a serving dish and pour the clam sauce over it. Serve hot.

Tofu Stuffed Shells

1 dozen large whole wheat stuffing shells, cooked al dente
1 lb firm style tofu, ground in a hand food mill
3 Tbsp onion, finely grated
1 tsp sesame oil
1/2 cup green string beans, sliced very thin
1/2 cup sweet corn, removed from the cob
1 Tbsp parsley, finely minced
2 Tbsp umeboshi vinegar
2 tsp tamari soy sauce

Heat the oil in a skillet. Add the string beans and corn. Sauté for 2 to 3 minutes. Remove and place in a mixing bowl. Place the tofu, onion, parsley, umeboshi vinegar, and soy sauce in the mixing bowl and mix thoroughly. Stuff each shell with tofu stuffing and place in a baking or casserole dish. Prepare sauce.

Mushroom Kuzu Sauce

2 cups mushrooms, sliced thin
1/2 cup onion, diced
3 cups water
1 strip kombu, 2 inches long
4 tsp kuzu, diluted
4 to 4 1/2 tsp tamari soy sauce

Place the water, onion, kombu, and mushrooms in a saucepan. Cover and bring to a boil. Reduce the flame to medium-low and simmer for 4 to 5 minutes. Remove the kombu and set aside. Add the kuzu, stirring constantly to prevent lumping, until the sauce is thick and translucent. Season with soy sauce. Pour the sauce over the stuffed shells, cover, and bake at 350 degrees F for 20 to 25 minutes. Remove the cover and bake 5 more minutes. Remove and serve hot.

Shrimp and Vegetable Chow Mien

1 pkg. (8 oz.) udon or rice noodles, cooked and drained
light sesame or safflower oil, for deep-frying
1 lb medium shrimp, shelled and veins removed (optional; you may
    substitute fresh tofu slices or cubes or cooked seitan strips)
5 cups water, including water used to soak kombu
1 strip kombu, 2 to 3 inches long, soaked
1 cup carrot, sliced in matchsticks
1 bunch scallion, sliced in 2 inch lengths
1 cup mung bean sprouts, rinsed
1 cup snow peas, stems removed
3 to 4 Tbsp kuzu, diluted
1 1/2 to 2 Tbsp tamari soy sauce
2 tsp fresh ginger juice

Heat the oil in a heavy deep-frying pot. Deep-fry cooked noodles, a small amount at a time, until golden brown. Remove and drain on paper towels. Repeat until all noodles have been deep-fried. Place the noodles in a bowl.

Place the water in a pot with the kombu. Cover and bring to a boil. Reduce the flame to medium-low and simmer for 3 to 4 minutes. Remove the kombu and set aside for future use. Add the shrimp and carrots. Cover and simmer 1 minute. Add the scallions, mung bean sprouts, and snow peas. Cover and cook 1 minute. Add the diluted kuzu, stirring constantly, until the sauce becomes thick and translucent. Turn the flame to low. Add the soy sauce and ginger juice. Simmer 1 to 2 minutes. Remove from burner. Place the deep-fried noodles in individual serving bowls and ladle the shrimp-vegetable sauce over them. Serve hot.

Udon with Chinese Style Vegetable-Kuzu Sauce

1 pkg. (8 oz.) udon, cooked
1/2 lb firm style tofu, cubed
sesame or safflower oil, for deep-frying
4 cups water, including kombu soaking water
1 strip kombu, 2 to 3 inches long, soaked
1 cup onion, sliced in 1/2 inch thick wedges
1/2 cup mushrooms, quartered
1/2 cup carrot, sliced in thick matchsticks
1/4 cup celery, sliced in thick diagonals
1 cup broccoli, florets
3 to 4 Tbsp kuzu, diluted
1 to 2 Tbsp tamari soy sauce

Heat the oil in a heavy deep-frying pot. Deep-fry the tofu cubes until golden brown. Remove and drain on paper towels. Place the water and kombu in a pot, cover, and bring to a boil. Reduce the flame to medium-low and simmer for 4 to 5 minutes. Remove the kombu and set aside for future use.

Turn the flame to high and add the onion, mushrooms, carrot, celery, and broccoli. Reduce the flame to medium-low, cover, and simmer for 1 minute. Add the tofu and simmer another 1 minute. Reduce the flame to low, add the diluted kuzu, stirring constantly to prevent lumping, until the liquid is thick and translucent. Add the soy sauce and simmer for another 1 to 2 minutes. Pour the sauce over the cooked udon and serve hot.

Nabeyaki Udon

Nabeyaki is a traditional dish from Japan in which either udon or soba are cooked and served in a special earthenware casserole dish called *do-nabe*. The noodles are cooked and garnished with vegetables and other foods. The ingredients in nabeyaki are similar to those used in sukiyaki. However, sukiyaki is served in a cast iron skillet or pot rather than in a pot made of earthenware.

1/2 lb udon (any kind), cooked al dente
5 to 6 cups water, including kombu soaking water
1 strip kombu, 2 to 3 inches long, soaked

5 to 6 shiitake mushrooms, soaked, stems removed, and quartered
1/2 cup daikon, sliced in thin rounds
1/2 cup carrot, sliced on a long, thin diagonal
2 Tbsp tamari soy sauce
1 lb fresh tofu, cubed
1 bunch watercress, washed
2 cups Chinese cabbage, sliced in 1 inch wide diagonals

Place the kombu and shiitake in a pot with water. Cover and bring to a boil. Reduce the flame to medium-low and simmer for about 15 minutes until the shiitake are tender. Remove the kombu and set aside. Reduce the flame to low and simmer with soy sauce. Cover and simmer for 2 to 3 minutes. Place the kombu-shiitake broth in the nabe along with the shiitake. Place the cooked udon in the broth. Arrange the carrot, daikon, and tofu in separate sections on top of the udon, leaving room for the watercress and Chinese cabbage to be added later.

Put the lid on the nabe and place over a medium flame. Bring to a boil. Cook for 3 to 4 minutes. Remove the cover and place the watercress and Chinese cabbage on top of the udon. Cover and simmer for several minutes until the watercress and Chinese cabbage are tender but still bright green. Remove the cover and place the pot on a pad at the table. Serve hot. Each person can serve himself from the nabe, taking vegetables and noodles as he desires.

Baked Noodles and Vegetables with Bechamel Sauce

1 lb udon, cooked al dente, rinsed
1 cup onions, diced
1/2 cup celery, diced
1 lb mushrooms, sliced
1 cup broccoli, cut in small florets
1 cup cauliflower, cut in small florets
1/2 cup Brussels sprouts, halved
3/4 cup unbleached white flour
4 cups water, or kombu or vegetable stock
1 to 2 Tbsp corn oil
3 Tbsp tamari soy sauce
scallion, chives, or parsley, finely chopped, for garnish

Heat the oil in a skillet. Add the onion, mushrooms, and celery. Sauté for 3 to 4 minutes. Add the flour and sauté for another 2 minutes, making sure the flour completely coats the vegetables. Add the water, a small amount at a time, stirring constantly to prevent lumping. When smooth and thick, add the broccoli, cauliflower, and Brussels sprouts. Cover and simmer for 2 minutes. Season with soy sauce.

Place the cooked udon in a baking dish, and pour the vegetables and bechamel sauce over the noodles. Cover and bake at 375 degrees F for 30 to 35 minutes. Remove the cover and brown the top for another 5 to 7 minutes. Garnish with chopped scallion, chives, or parsley. Serve hot.

Chapter 10
Breads, Pastries, and Desserts

Aside from being eaten in their whole form, for thousands of years whole grains have been crushed into flour and used to prepare breads, pastries, desserts, and other baked goods. Bread made from whole wheat, unrefined sea salt, and water has been a staple in India, the Middle East, and Western cultures for centuries. There are several principal varieties including: 1) flat bread such as chapati and pita; 2) round or rectangular loaves that naturally ferment and rise from wild yeast in the air or a sourdough starter; and 3) sprouted wheat bread. Traditional breads were not made with baker's yeast, oil, sugar, or other ingredients usually added to modern breads. Loaves of naturally fermented bread kept year round without spoiling, their taste improved with aging, and they could be reconstituted very simply by soaking and steaming.

Macrobiotic bakers have revived the traditional art of making sourdough wheat and rye, and when properly made, these naturally fermented breads, like miso, can have a beneficial effect on digestion and assimilation of nutrients in the body. An assortment of other high-quality breads can also be made combining wheat with softly cooked whole grains or with flour made from barley, rice, buckwheat, corn, millet, or oats. A small amount of unrefined natural vegetable oil or a natural sweetener such as rice syrup may sometimes be added to make breads. Good quality bread is preferably served plain, toasted in the oven, or steamed rather than toasted in electric toasters or microwave ovens. Unyeasted, whole grain sourdough bread is preferred over yeasted bread for regular consumption.

In addition to bread, a variety of baked goods can be made using whole wheat flour and all natural ingredients. These include crackers, pizza, pancakes, muffins, rolls, biscuits, bagels, donuts, pies, cakes, and cookies. Whole grains and grain products can also be used to prepare a variety of appetizing desserts. Couscous, or partially refined wheat, makes a delicious couscous cake that can be prepared with a natural fruit topping. Amazake is a rice-based sweetener made from sweet brown rice and a bacterial starter that is allowed to ferment into a thick liquid. This starter, known as *koji*, is made from rice inoculated with bacteria and is also used to make other fermented foods including miso, tamari soy sauce, natto, and sake (the traditional rice wine). Brown rice, sweet rice, and amazake can be used to make naturally sweet puddings which are wonderfully sweet and soothing.

Rice Kayu Bread (1 loaf)

2 cups organic whole wheat flour
1/4 tsp sea salt
2 cups leftover soft brown rice
water (optional; see instructions)

Mix the flour and sea salt. Add the soft brown rice and form into a ball of dough. If the rice is soft enough, you do not need to add extra water. If the rice is a little dry, add small amounts of cold water until you are able to form a firm ball of dough. Knead the dough about 350 to 400 times. This will take about 15 to 20 minutes. The dough should be soft and smooth. As you are kneading, occasionally sprinkle a little flour on the dough to prevent it from sticking to the bowl.

Oil a standard medium-sized loaf pan with a little corn or sesame oil and sprinkle a little flour in it. This will help prevent the bread from sticking to the pan. Form the dough into a loaf and place in the floured pan. Lightly press the edges of the dough down to form a rounded loaf. Make a shallow slit in the top center of the dough with a knife. Cover the pan with a clean, damp hand towel. Place the covered pan in a warm place, such as the oven with the pilot light or inside light bulb on, or near a warm radiator. Let the dough rise for 8 to 10 hours, occasionally moistening the towel with warm water as it dries out. Remove the towel from the loaf pan.

Place the dough in a 200 to 250 degree F oven for about 30 minutes. Increase the temperature to 350 degrees F and bake for another 60 or 75 minutes. When the bread is done, remove from the oven. Remove the bread from the pan and place on a rack to cool.

Brown Rice Bread (1 loaf)

2 cups leftover cooked brown rice
2 cups organic whole wheat flour
1/4 tsp sea salt
1 Tbsp light sesame or corn oil (optional)
1 1/4 cups water

Mix the flour and sea salt. Add the rice and sift the flour and rice through your hands   with a rubbing motion. Continue until the rice is completely coated with the flour. Add the oil and again sift the flour, rice, and oil through your hands until the oil is completely mixed in.

Add the water gradually to form a ball of dough. Knead the dough about 350 to 400 times (approximately 15 to 20 minutes). When the dough becomes moist and sticky, sprinkle a small amount of flour on it and continue kneading. This may happen 4 or 5 times during the kneading process.

Oil a medium-sized standard loaf pan with a little corn or sesame oil. Sprinkle a little flour over the oiled pan. Form the dough into a loaf and place in the pan. Press the dough down all along the edges of the pan to create a rounded effect and then make a shallow slit down the center of the dough with a knife. Place a clean, damp towel over the pan and let sit in a warm place for 8 to 10 hours.

Bake at 200 to 250 degrees F for 30 minutes and then raise the temperature to 350 degrees F. Continue baking for another 1 hour and 10 minutes. Remove from the oven. Remove the bread from the pan and place on a rack to cool before slicing.

Raisin-Rice Bread (1 loaf)

2 cups leftover cooked brown rice
2 cups organic whole wheat flour
1/4 tsp sea salt
1 Tbsp sesame or corn oil (optional)
1 1/4 to 1 1/2 cups water
2 cups organic raisins

Boil the raisins in the water for about ten minutes. Allow to cool. Mix the flour and sea salt. Add the rice and sift together with your hands. Add the oil and sift again. Add the cooled water and raisins. Form into a ball and knead about 350 to 400 times, adding a little flour from time to time to prevent sticking. Oil a loaf pan with a little sesame or corn oil and then flour the pan. Shape the dough into a loaf and place in the pan. Cover with a damp towel and place in a warm place for 8 to 10 hours to rise.

Bake at 200 to 250 degrees F for 30 minutes. Then raise the temperature to 350 degrees F and continue baking for 1 hour and 10 minutes longer. Remove from the pan and allow to cool.

No-Bake Rice Bread

2 cups leftover cooked brown rice or any other whole grain
2 cups organic whole wheat flour
1 1/4 to 1 1/2 cups warm water
1/2 tsp sea salt

Mix flour, sea salt, and rice, rubbing between your hands to evenly mix. Add water gradually to form a dough. Knead 350 to 400 times. Place in a lightly oiled bowl, cover with a warm damp cloth, and let sit in a warm place for 8 to 10 hours. Press down and form into a loaf.

Place 1 inch of water in a pressure cooker. It is best to use a large 5 or 7 quart pressure cooker for this process. Place a steamer or rack in the bottom of the pressure cooker. Place the dough in a lightly oiled loaf pan that will fit inside the pressure cooker. Place the pan on top of the rack in the pressure cooker. Remove the pressure gauge from the lid and place the lid on the cooker. Bring to a boil and steam the bread for about 45 minutes to 1 hour. Remove the cover and add water if necessary to maintain 1 inch of water in the bottom of the cooker.

Place the pressure gauge on the lid, cover the cooker, and bring up to pressure. Reduce the flame to medium-low to low and cook for another 1 1/2 to 2 hours. Remove from the flame and allow the pressure to come down. Remove the cover. Remove the pan and set aside to cool to room temperature. Pressure-steamed bread is more moist than oven baked bread but as it cools it becomes more firm.

Whole Wheat Bread (1 loaf)

4 cups organic whole wheat flour
1/4 tsp sea salt
2 Tbsp sesame or corn oil
water

Mix the flour and sea salt. Add the oil and thoroughly mix with the flour by sifting or rubbing between your hands. Add enough cold water to form a ball of dough. Knead the dough about 350 to 400 times.

Oil a loaf pan and form the dough into the shape of a loaf. Place in the pan and press down the edges to form a loaf. Make a shallow slit in the center of the loaf with a knife. Cover the pan with a clean damp towel and let sit in a warm place for 8 to 10 hours to rise. Bake at 300 degrees F for 15 to 20 minutes. Then raise the temperature to 350 degrees F and continue baking for another 1 hour and 15 minutes or so. Remove from the loaf pan and place on a rack to cool.

Whole Wheat Sourdough Bread (2 loaves)

Whole wheat sourdough bread is made by preparing a starter which is allowed to ferment prior to combining with the bread.

Sourdough Starter

1 cup organic whole wheat flour
water

Place the flour in a glass or ceramic bowl. Add enough cold water to create a thick batter. Cover the bowl with a piece of cheesecloth and let the starter ferment for 3 to 4 days in a warm place. As the starter begins to ferment, it will form bubbles and turn sour. This starter may be added to any of the whole grain bread recipes above or below. The amount of water used in each recipe needs to be adjusted to compensate for the water content of the starter.

whole wheat sourdough starter
5 cups organic whole wheat flour
1/2 tsp sea salt
2 cups water

Pour the starter in a bowl, add 2 cups of water, and stir. Stir in 2 1/2 cups of whole wheat flour so as to create a loose, almost pourable, dough. Place the uncovered bowl in a warm place and let sit for 2 hours. Remove 1 1/2 cups of the starter from the bowl and place in a glass jar and refrigerate. This can be used as a starter for other sourdough recipes.

Mix in the remaining 2 1/2 cups of whole wheat flour and the sea salt with the starter remaining in the bowl. Form a ball of dough. If necessary, you may add additional flour so the the mixture can be formed into a ball and kneaded. Place the dough on a flour board or table and knead until smooth. This may take 10 to 15 minutes of kneading, so that the texture is smooth and elastic.

Oil a bowl and place the dough in it. Cover the bowl with a warm, damp cloth and set aside in a warm place for 6 to 8 hours or overnight. Punch the dough down, knead it well for several minutes, and then divide it in half. Form the two halves into loaves and place them in lightly oiled loaf pans. Place the loaves in a warm place for 2 to 3 hours to rise.

Bake at 200 to 250 degrees F for 20 minutes or so then raise the temperature to 350 degrees F. Continue baking for about 1 hour. Tap the loaves with your fingers or a spoon. It they make a hollow sound when tapped, they are done. Remove the bread from the pans and place on a rack to cool.

Sourdough Olive Bread (2 loaves)

2 cups organic black olives, sliced or diced

Follow the recipe above for plain sourdough bread until before the last time you knead the dough. Then add the olives, knead, and follow the instructions again. Rise and bake as instructed.

Sourdough Nut Bread (2 loaves)

1 cup organic raisins
1/2 cup organic almonds, roasted and chopped
1/2 cup organic walnuts or pecans, roasted and chopped
2 Tbsp grated lemon rind
1 tsp organic cinnamon

Follow the recipe for plain sourdough bread until before the last kneading. Add all of the ingredients, knead again as instructed, and follow the rising and baking directions above.

Amazake Bread (1 loaf)

2 cups organic whole wheat flour
2 cups homemade amazake, unblended (see recipe later in this chapter)
1/2 tsp sea salt
1/4 cup sesame or corn oil (optional)
water

Mix the flour and sea salt. Add the oil and sift it through your hands to mix with the flour and sea salt. Add the amazake and mix again. Add enough cold water to form a stiff ball of dough. Knead on a floured surface 350 to 400 times until smooth and elastic.

Oil a loaf pan and form the dough into a loaf. Place in the pan and press the edges down. Cover the pan with a warm, damp towel and set in a warm place to rise for 8 to 12 hours. Bake at 250 degrees F for 15 to 20 minutes, then raise the temperature to 350 degrees F and continue baking 1 hour 15 minutes or so. Remove from the pan and place on a rack to cool.

Barley-Wheat Bread (1 large or 2 small loaves)

2 cups organic barley flour
4 cups organic whole wheat flour
1 tsp sea salt
1/4 cup corn or light sesame oil
3 1/4 to 3 1/2 cups warm or boiling water

Mix the flours and sea salt. Add the oil and rub it between your hands to evenly and thoroughly mix with the flour and salt. Add the water and mix, forming the dough into a ball. Knead the dough 350 to 400 times, or for approximately 15 to 20 minutes, until smooth and elastic. Place the dough in an oiled loaf pan. Make a shallow slit in the top of the loaf. Cover with a warm, damp towel and let sit in a warm place for 8 to 10 hours. Bake at 300 degrees F for 15 minutes and then raise the temperature to 350 degrees F and continue baking for 1 hour or so. Remove and place on a rack to cool.

Barley and Millet Bread (2 loaves)

5 cups organic whole wheat flour
1 1/2 cups organic barley flour
1 1/2 cups organic millet flour
1/4 cup corn or light sesame oil
1 tsp sea salt
water (about 4 cups)

Combine the flours and sea salt. Add the oil and rub between your hands to evenly mix with the flour. Add enough water to form into a ball of dough. Knead 350 to 400 times. Shape into loaves and place in oiled loaf pans. Cover with a warm, damp towel and let sit for 8 to 10 hours. Bake at 300 degrees F for 15 minutes and then raise the temperature to 350 degrees F and continue baking for another 1 hour and 15 minutes. Remove from the pans and place on a rack to cool.

Rye Bread (2 loaves)

5 cups organic whole wheat flour
3 cups organic rye flour
1 tsp sea salt
1/4 cup corn or light sesame oil
water (about 4 cups)

Combine the flours and sea salt. Add the oil and rub between your hands to evenly mix with the flour. Add enough water to form into a ball of dough. Knead 350 to 400 times. Shape into loaves and place in oiled loaf pans. Cover with a warm, damp towel and let sit for 8 to 10 hours. Bake at 300 degrees F for 15 minutes and then raise the temperature to 350 degrees F and continue baking for another 1 hour and 15 minutes. Remove from the pans and place on a rack to cool.

Corn Bread

3 cups organic cornmeal
1 cup organic whole wheat pastry flour
1/4 tsp sea salt
1/4 cup corn oil
2 1/2 to 3 cups cold water

Mix the flours and sea salt. Add the oil and mix by rubbing the flour and oil between your hands. Add the water and mix again. Pre-heat the oven to 375 degrees F. Oil a cake pan with a small amount of corn oil and place the empty pan in the oven to heat the oil for about 5 minutes. Remove the hot pan and pour the batter in it. Bake for 1 hour and 35 to 40 minutes. Remove and allow to cool before slicing.

Skillet Corn Bread

3 cups organic cornmeal
1 cup organic whole wheat pastry flour
1/4 tsp sea salt
2 cups cooked brown rice
1 cup fresh sweet corn, removed from cob
2 Tbsp corn oil
2 1/2 to 3 cups water

Mix the flours and sea salt. Add the brown rice, oil, and sweet corn. Rub the ingredients together with your hands to evenly mix. Add the water and mix again. Oil a cast iron skillet with corn oil, liberally coating the sides and bottom. Heat the oil over a high flame until it sizzles but does not smoke. Pour the batter in the hot skillet. Cover and reduce the flame to low. Cook for 30 to 40 minutes until the bottom and sides are browned and the inside is done.

Remove the skillet from the flame. Place a plate on top of the skillet. Turn the skillet over, holding the plate under it and let the corn bread slide onto the plate with the browned crust facing up. Slice and serve.

Steamed Bread

4 to 5 slices whole grain sourdough or unleavened bread
water

Place about 1/2 to 1 inch of water in a pot. Place a steamer basket inside or on top of the pot, whichever applies for the type of steamer you are using. Cover the pot and bring the water to a boil. Place the slices of bread in the steamer and cover the pot again. Steam for 4 to 5 minutes until the bread is hot and moist. Remove and serve with your favorite natural spread, jam, or jelly.

Steamed Bread with Miso-Tahini Spread

4 to 5 slices of whole grain sourdough or unleavened bread, steamed
3 Tbsp organic tahini
1 to 1 1/2 tsp organic barley miso
2 to 3 Tbsp scallion or chives, finely chopped
1 Tbsp water

Place the tahini and miso in a skillet. Add the water and mix thoroughly. Heat the mixture over a high flame, stirring constantly to prevent burning. Add the scallion or chives and mix in. Cook for 1 to 2 minutes over a medium-low flame. Remove from flame and place in a small bowl. Spread the miso-tahini spread on the slices of steamed bread and serve.

Whole Wheat Chapati (1 dozen)

5 cups organic whole wheat flour, sifted
2 cups warm water
1 tsp sea salt

Mix the flour and sea salt. Slowly add the water and form the dough into a ball. Knead on a floured board or table for about 10 minutes until smooth and elastic. Shape the dough into balls about the size of a golf ball. Roll out the balls until very thin. Lightly oil a griddle or cast iron skillet and heat. Cook the chapatis on one side until small bumps or blisters appear. Flip them over and fry the other side for 1 to 2 minutes. Remove and repeat until all the chapatis have been fried.

Puri (Deep-Fried Chapati)

chapati dough
light sesame or safflower oil, for deep-frying

Roll out the chapati dough as instructed above. Place 2 to 3 inches of oil in a heavy deep-frying pot and heat. Drop one chapati at a time in the hot oil, gently holding it under the oil with a spoon or chopstick until it puffs up. Then let the chapati rise to the surface. Brown and turn over and brown the other side. Remove and drain on paper towels. Repeat until all the chapatis have been deep-fried.

Pita Bread

2 cups organic unbleached white flour
1 cup organic whole wheat flour, sifted
1/4 tsp sea salt
1 cup sourdough starter (see previous recipe)
3 cups water
1/4 cup corn oil

Place the sourdough starter in a glass or ceramic bowl. Add water and half of the above flour. Mix well, forming a thick batter or "sponge." Cover the bowl with a warm, damp towel and set aside in a warm place for about 8 hours or until the batter starts to bubble. Remove 1 cup of the "sponge," place in a glass jar and refrigerate. This can be used as a starter for your next batch of pita or other sourdough bread.

Mix the sea salt and corn oil with the remaining starter. Gradually mix in the remaining flour mixture and form into a moist but firm dough. Knead the dough on a floured board or table for about 10 minutes. Place the dough in a lightly oiled glass or ceramic bowl and cover with a warm, damp towel. Set aside in a warm place for about 1 1/2 to 2 hours.

Punch down the dough and knead for 5 minutes until smooth. Form the dough into balls about the size of a tennis ball. Cover the balls and let sit for about 15 to 20 minutes. Roll out the balls so that they are about 1/8 to 1/4 inch thick. Pre-heat the oven to 475 degrees F. Place the rolled-out dough on lightly oiled cookie sheets. Place on the lower rack of your oven and bake for about 10 minutes until they puff up and form pockets. Remove and repeat until all the dough has been baked. Allow to cool to room temperature. Store in a tightly sealed container to keep soft.

Sprouted Wheat and Raisin Bread

1 lb organic whole wheat berries
1/2 tsp sea salt
1/2 cup organic raisins, soaked
1/2 cup organic almonds, roasted and chopped
water

To prepare sprouted wheat bread, you will need a large glass jar, cotton cheesecloth, and a rubber band. Wash the wheat berries and place in glass jar. Cover with water and let soak overnight. Pour off the water, rinse, and drain. Cover the jar with the cheesecloth, securing it with the rubber band. Place the jar upside down in a bowl and let sit overnight. Rinse and drain the berries again. Place the jar upside down in the bowl again and let sit overnight. Repeat one more night if necessary.

When the sprouts are about 1 inch long, remove and grind them as finely as possible in a hand grinder, blender, or food processor. Grind twice if necessary. Mix in the sea salt, raisins, and roasted almonds. Knead the dough for about 5 minutes. Form into a loaf about 1 inch thick and 6 to 8 inches long. Place in an oiled shallow baking dish or casserole. Cover the pan or dish and bake at 200 degrees F for 4 hours. Remove the cover during the last 20 minutes of cooking. The bread will shrink from the sides of the pan and form a hard crust on the outside. The inside should be very moist and sweet. Remove and allow to cool. To store, refrigerate.

As a variation, substitute rye berries for wheat berries, omit the fruit or nuts, add roasted seeds, add diced onions, or add soaked, chopped dried fruit to the ground sprouted berries.

Yeasted Whole Wheat Bread

3 cups organic unbleached white flour
3 cups organic whole wheat flour, sifted
2 Tbsp natural dry yeast

1/4 to 1/2 cup warm water
1 Tbsp powdered brown rice syrup
2 cups hot water or hot plain soymilk
1 1/2 tsp sea salt

Dissolve the yeast in 1/4 to 1/2 cup warm water. Mix in the powdered rice syrup. Let sit for about 10 minutes. Combine the hot water or soymilk and salt in a mixing bowl. When cooled slightly, mix in the yeast mixture. Add the unbleached white flour and beat thoroughly. Stir in the whole wheat flour. Form a dough and knead for 5 minutes. Place in an oiled bowl and turn to coat with oil. Cover the bowl with a warm, damp towel and allow to sit in a warm place until double in size. Remove and divide the dough in half. Form into loaves and place in lightly oiled loaf pans. Cover and allow to sit until double in size again.

Bake at 400 degrees F for about 10 minutes. Then reduce the temperature to 350 degrees F and continue baking for another 40 minutes or so. Remove the loaves from the pans and tap the bottom. The bread is done when it makes a hollow sound. If not done, place back in the oven and bake a few minutes longer. Remove and allow to cool.

Cinnamon-Raisin Doughnuts (12 doughnuts)

2 1/4 cups organic unbleached white flour
1 cup organic whole wheat flour, sifted
1/4 cup warm water (about 80 degrees F)
1 Tbsp natural dried yeast
2 Tbsp corn oil
1 tsp sea salt
1 cup warm water
1 cup organic raisins, soaked 1/2 hour
1 tsp organic cinnamon
1/2 cup powdered brown rice syrup
light sesame or safflower oil, for deep-frying

Combine the yeast, 1/4 cup warm water, and oil. Dissolve and let sit for 5 to 10 minutes. Combine the flours, sea salt, and raisins. Mix gradually with the yeast mixture. Add the remaining water and form into a ball of dough. Knead on a floured surface for 10 minutes. Place the dough in a lightly oil bowl, turn the dough to coat the other side with oil, and cover with a warm, damp towel. Allow to sit in a warm place to rise for 2 hours or until double in size. Punch down, cover, and let rise for another 1 hour. Punch down again. Roll out the dough to a thickness of 1/3 to 1/2 inch on a floured surface. Cut the dough

226

with a doughnut cutter into 2 to 3 inch circles. Set the doughnuts and doughnut centers aside for about 10 minutes.

Heat oil in a heavy deep-frying pot (about 375 degrees F) and deep-fry 2 to 3 doughnuts at a time until golden brown on both sides. Remove and drain on paper towels. Repeat until all doughnuts and doughnut centers have been fried. Combine the brown rice powder and cinnamon in a paper bag. Place 2 to 3 doughnuts and centers in the bag. Close the bag and shake to coat with the powdered mixture. Remove and place on a serving platter. Repeat until all doughnuts and centers have been dusted.

Sourdough Waffles (8 to 10 waffles)

1 1/2 cups organic whole wheat pastry flour
1 cup organic whole wheat flour
2 Tbsp sesame or corn oil
1/4 tsp sea salt
1 cup leftover soft rice
1 cup sourdough starter, sour noodle water, or sour seitan-starch water
1 cup cold water
light sesame or corn oil, for frying

Combine the flours and sea salt. Mix in all of the remaining ingredients. Place in a covered glass or ceramic bowl and let sit overnight in a warm place to rise. Make sure that the bowl is large enough to allow for the batter to rise. Oil a waffle iron and heat. Place the batter in the waffle sections and close the top. Cook until golden brown. Remove and repeat until all batter has been cooked. Serve with your favorite natural syrup or fruit topping.

Rice and Corn Waffles (8 to 10 waffles)

1 cup organic whole wheat pastry flour
1 cup organic cornmeal
1/2 cup organic whole wheat flour
1 cup cooked brown rice
1/4 tsp sea salt
2 Tbsp corn oil
2 cups water
light sesame or corn oil, for frying

Combine the flours, rice, and sea salt. Add the oil and water. Mix well. Oil a waffle iron and heat. Spoon batter in the waffle sections and close the top.

Cook several minutes until golden brown. Remove and repeat until all batter has been cooked. Serve with your favorite natural syrup or fruit topping.

Sourdough Pancakes (8 to 10 pancakes)

1 cups organic whole wheat pastry flour
1 cup organic cornmeal
1/2 cup organic rolled oats
1/4 tsp sea salt
1 cup sourdough starter
2 cups water
2 Tbsp corn oil
light sesame or corn oil, for frying

Combine the flours and salt. Mix in the starter, water, and oil. Place in a large mixing bowl, cover with a towel, and let sit in a warm place to rise overnight. The batter should be pourable, not too thick or watery. Adjust the water content if necessary. Oil a pancake griddle and heat. Ladle 3 to 4 batches of batter on to the hot griddle. Fry until golden brown and air bubbles form on top of the pancake. Flip over and fry the other side until golden. Remove and repeat until all pancakes are fried. Serve hot with your favorite natural syrup or fruit topping.

Leavened Fruit Pancakes (8 to 10 pancakes)

1 cup organic whole wheat pancakes
1 cup organic cornmeal
1/2 tsp sea salt
2 tsp non-aluminum baking powder
2 Tbsp corn oil
1 cup thinly sliced apple, pear, peach, strawberries, or whole berries
1/2 tsp organic cinnamon
1 1/2 to 2 cups water
light sesame or corn oil, for frying

Combine the flours, sea salt, baking powder, and cinnamon. Mix in the oil and water. Add the fruit and mix again. Oil a pancake griddle and heat. Ladle 3 to 4 pancakes on to the griddle and fry until golden brown. Flip over and fry the other side. Remove and repeat until all the batter has been fried. Serve with you favorite natural syrup or fruit topping.

228

Leavened Buckwheat Pancakes

2 cups organic buckwheat flour
1/2 tsp sea salt
2 tsp non-aluminum baking powder
2 Tbsp corn oil
1 1/2 to 2 cups water
light sesame or corn oil, for frying

Combine the flour, salt, and baking powder. Mix in the oil and water. Oil a pancake griddle and heat. Ladle 3 to 4 pancakes on to the griddle and fry until golden. Flip over and fry the other side until golden. Remove and repeat until all batter has been fried. Serve with your favorite natural syrup or fruit topping.

Unleavened Rice Pancakes (8 to 10)

1 cup leftover cooked brown rice
1 cup organic whole wheat pastry flour
1/2 cup organic brown rice flour
1/4 tsp sea salt
1 1/2 to 2 cups water
light sesame oil, for frying

Combine the flours and sea salt. Add the water and mix thoroughly. Oil a griddle and heat. Ladle out 3 to 4 pancakes and fry until golden. Flip over and fry the other side. Remove and repeat until all batter has been fried. Serve with the tamari-ginger sauce described above or another other favorite topping.

Tofu French Toast (8 to 10 slices)

8 to 10 slices whole grain bread
1 lb firm style tofu, drained
1/2 cup water
1 tsp tamari soy sauce
corn oil

Place the tofu, water, and soy sauce in a blender and purée until smooth and creamy. Pour in a mixing bowl. Oil a pancake griddle and heat. Dip 3 to 4 slices of bread in the tofu mixture, coating both sides. Place on the hot griddle and fry each side until golden brown. Remove and repeat until all slices have been fried. Serve with your favorite vegetable or fruit topping, or natural jam or syrup.

Whole Wheat Crepes with Vegetable Filling
(9 crepes)

2 cups organic whole wheat pastry flour
1/4 tsp sea salt
2 cups water
light sesame or corn oil, for frying

Mix the flour and sea salt in a mixing bowl. Gradually add water to create a thin batter, stirring to remove lumps. For a lighter batter, blend in a blender or mix with an egg beater. Lightly oil a crepe pan or griddle and heat. Pour a small amount of batter on to the griddle and with a quick, gentle, circular motion, smooth out the batter with a spoon until the batter is very thin and round in shape. Cook on one side until tiny bubbles appear on the surface. Flip the crepe over and fry the other side for 1 minute. Remove and place on a platter. Repeat until all batter has been fried.

Vegetable Filling

1/4 cup onion, sliced in thin half-moons
1/2 cup mushrooms, thinly sliced
1/4 cup green pepper, diced
2 Tbsp burdock, sliced in thin matchsticks
1/4 cup carrot, sliced in thin matchsticks
1/2 cup green cabbage, finely shredded
dark sesame oil
water
tamari soy sauce

Heat a small amount of oil in a skillet. Add the onion and sauté for 1 to 2 minutes. Next, add the mushrooms and green pepper and sauté for 2 to 3 minutes. Finally, add the burdock, carrot, and cabbage. Place a small amount of water in the skillet so that it barely covers the bottom. Bring to a boil, cover, and reduce the flame to medium-low. Cook for several minutes until the vegetables are tender. Remove the cover and season with several drops of soy sauce. Continue to cook until all of the liquid has evaporated. Place 2 Tbsp of vegetable filling on top of each crepe and roll up, forming a cylinder. Place on a serving platter.

Buckwheat Crepes with Fruit Filling

1 cup organic whole wheat flour
1 cup organic buckwheat flour
2 cups water
1/4 tsp sea salt
light sesame oil, for frying

Combine the flours and sea salt. Add the water, stirring constantly to create a thin batter. Lightly oil a crepe pan or griddle and heat. Pour in a small amount of batter on the pan and smooth out with a spoon in an even circular motion. Continue until the batter is very thin. Cook on one side until tiny air bubbles appear on the surface. Flip the crepe over and fry the other side. Remove and place on a platter. Repeat until all batter has been fried. Prepare the following filling for the crepes:

Fruit Filling

2 cups cherries, pitted and halved, or other fruit, sliced
water
pinch of sea salt
3 to 4 tsp barley malt or rice syrup
1 heaping Tbsp kuzu, diluted in 2 Tbsp water

Place about 1/8 inch of water in a saucepan, and add the fruit and sea salt. Add the syrup and bring to a boil. Cover and reduce the flame to medium-low. Simmer until soft. Reduce the flame to low and add the kuzu, a small amount at a time, stirring constantly until thick. When thick, remove and place inside or on top of each crepe. If inside, roll up the crepes and serve. Any type of fruit, fresh or dried, can be used to make filling. Dried fruit should be soaked and sliced before cooking.

Couscous Cake with Dried Fruit Topping

2 cups organic whole wheat couscous
3 1/2 cups apple juice
2 cups dried apples, soaked and sliced
1 cup Turkish or northern dried apricots, soaked and sliced
1/4 cup raisins, soaked
5 cups fruit soaking water and apple juice combination
4 1/2 Tbsp kuzu, diluted
pinch of sea salt

Place the 3 1/2 cups of apple juice in a pan with a pinch of sea salt. Cover and bring to a boil. Remove the cover and add the couscous. Stir, cover, and reduce the flame to low. Simmer for 20 minutes. Place the dried fruit, water, and a pinch of sea salt in another pan. Cover and bring to a boil. Reduce the flame to low and simmer for about 5 to 7 minutes. Remove the cover. Add the kuzu, stirring constantly, until thick.

Remove the couscous and place in a glass baking dish or cake pan. With slightly wet hands, press the couscous down firmly in the pan or dish, moistening your hands with cold water several times to avoid burning your fingers. Spread the fruit topping evenly over the top of the couscous cake. Set aside and allow to cool to room temperature or refrigerate to slightly chill. Slice and serve. Fresh fruit may be used in place of dried fruit for a lighter topping.

Strawberry Kanten Couscous Cake

2 cups yellow (French or Moroccan) couscous
2 cups apple juice
pinch of sea salt

Place the apple juice and sea salt in a pan, cover and bring to a boil. Stir in the couscous. Cover and turn the flame off. Let sit for 5 minutes. Remove and place the couscous in a glass cake pan. With moistened hands, press the couscous down firmly in the pan. Prepare the following topping:

Strawberry Kanten Topping

2 cups fresh strawberries, washed, tops removed, and sliced in half
3 cups apple juice
pinch of sea salt
3 to 4 heaping Tbsp agar-agar flakes (read directions on package)

Place the water, agar flakes, and pinch of sea salt in a pan. Stir and turn the flame to high. Bring to a boil, stirring occasionally. Reduce the flame to low and cook 2 to 3 minutes. Remove from the flame and add the strawberries. Let the liquid cool off a little and then pour it over the couscous cake. If the liquid is too hot, it will cause the couscous to absorb the liquid and expand. Place the cake in the refrigerator and let sit until the kanten jells. When done, the bottom of the cake and the strawberry topping should both be firm. Slice and serve chilled or room temperature. Any type of fruit can be used to make the kanten topping.

Basic Whole Wheat Pie Crust (2 crusts)

4 cups organic whole wheat pastry flour
1/4 tsp sea salt
1/4 cup corn oil
3/4 to 1 cup cold water

     Combine the flour and sea salt in a large mixing bowl. Add the oil and sift it through your hands, using a rubbing motion, to evenly mix. Add the water gradually to form a dough. The dough should not be sticky. If it is, add a little more flour. Form into a ball and quickly knead for 2 to 3 minutes. Let the dough sit for a few minutes before rolling out. Divide the dough in half and roll out on a floured surface until about 1/8 inch thick. Roll out the other half in the same manner. Use one crust for the bottom and one for the top of the pie.

Whole Wheat and Unbleached White Flour Crust

For a slightly lighter crust try combining different flours with whole wheat pastry flour, such as unbleached white, rice, oat, or corn flour.

2 cups organic whole wheat pastry flour
2 cups organic unbleached white flour
1/4 cup corn oil
1/4 tsp sea salt
3/4 to 1 cup cold water

     Combine the flours and sea salt. Sift in the oil in the same manner as above. Add the water and form into a ball of dough. Knead 2 to 3 minutes and roll out as above.

Pressed Oat and Seed Crust

1 cup organic whole wheat pastry flour
1 cup organic rolled oats
1/4 tsp sea salt
1/4 cup tan sesame seeds, toasted
1/4 cup corn oil
barley malt, brown rice syrup, or maple syrup
water or apple juice

     Combine the flour, oats, sea salt, and seeds in a mixing bowl. Add enough sweetener for a slightly sweet flavor and mix. Gradually add the oil, rubbing the mixture between your hands to evenly mix, until crumbly. Add a small amount of water or apple juice, just enough to hold together slightly. Do not add too much or the crust will not be soft and flaky. Pre-bake at 375 degrees F for 10 to 15 minutes before filling.

Apple Pie (1 large)

10 to 12 medium, organic cortland apples, peeled, cored, and sliced (you may substitute any other type of baking apple)
1/2 cup brown rice syrup or combination of barley malt and rice syrup
1/2 tsp organic cinnamon
1/4 tsp sea salt
2 to 3 Tbsp arrowroot or unbleached white flour
basic whole wheat pie crust (see above recipe)

Mix the apples, syrup, cinnamon, salt, and arrowroot or unbleached white flour. Roll out one pie crust and place it in a pie plate. Place the filling in the pie plate. Roll out the other crust. Dip your fingers in cold water and moisten the edges of the crust in the pie plate. Place the top crust on over the filling. To seal the crusts together, moisten a fork and press all around the edges of the pie plate or pinch together with your thumbs. Trim the excess dough from the edges of the pie plate. Make 4 small slits in the center of the crust with a fork or paring knife so that the crust does not crack when baking.

Bake at 375 degrees F for approximately 30 to 35 minutes until the crust is golden brown and the apples are tender (poke with a fork to test.) Remove and allow to cool before slicing.

Blueberry or Cherry Pie (1 large)

2 qts. blueberries, washed, or 4 cups cherries, pitted and halved
pinch of sea salt
1/8 to 1/4 cup water
1/4 to 1/2 cup brown rice syrup
kuzu, diluted
basic whole wheat pie dough (reduce recipe by half)

Place the blueberries or cherries in a saucepan. Add the salt and water. Bring to a boil. Reduce the flame to low, cover, and simmer 2 to 3 minutes. Add the brown rice syrup to taste. Dilute a small amount of kuzu and gradually add it to the fruit, stirring constantly to prevent lumping, until fairly thick. Allow to

234

cool slightly.

     Roll out the pie crust on a floured surface and place it in a pie plate. Press the edges of the crust down with a fork. Trim the excess dough off the sides of the pie plate with a knife. Take the fork and poke several air holes in the crust in the pie plate. Bake the empty crust at 375 degrees F for 10 minutes. Remove and place the fruit filling in the pre-baked pie shell. Place the pie in the oven and bake again for 25 to 30 minutes until the crust is golden. Remove and allow to cool before slicing.

Pumpkin Pie (1 large)

1 medium-sized baking pumpkin, halved and seeds removed
1 cup vanilla soymilk
1/4 to 1/2 cup maple syrup
2 Tbsp agar agar flakes
1 Tbsp kuzu, diluted
pinch of sea salt
1/2 to 3/4 tsp allspice
1 tsp vanilla
1/4 cup roasted walnuts or pecans, finely chopped
basic whole wheat pie crust dough (reduce recipe by half)
sesame or corn oil

     Oil a baking sheet and place the pumpkin upside down on it. Bake at 400 degrees F for 35 to 40 minutes until soft. Test with a fork. Remove from the oven and scoop out the pumpkin. Measure out about 4 cups of pumpkin. Place the pumpkin in a blender or food processor with the soymilk, maple syrup, and sea salt. Purée until smooth and creamy. Remove the purée and place in a pot. Add the agar flakes, stir, and cover. Bring to a boil. Reduce the flame to low and simmer for about 5 minutes. Remove the cover and slowly add the diluted kuzu, stirring constantly to prevent lumping. Simmer for another 1 to 2 minutes. Turn off the flame and add the vanilla and allspice. Mix well and allow to cool.

     Roll out the pie crust on a floured surface and place in a pie plate. With a fork, press the edges of the crust down and trim off the excess dough with a paring knife. Poke several holes in the bottom of the crust with a fork. Pre-bake the pie shell at 375 degrees F for about 10 minutes. Remove and pour the pumpkin mixture in the shell. Sprinkle the chopped walnuts or pecans over the pumpkin purée. Bake again for another 20 minutes or so until the crust is golden brown. Remove and allow to cool before slicing.

Squash Pie

1 medium buttercup squash or Hokkaido pumpkin, skin and seeds removed
   and cubed
1 cup water
pinch of sea salt
1/2 tsp cinnamon
1/2 cup barley malt
1/2 cup roasted walnuts, finely chopped
basic whole wheat pie crust dough (reduce the recipe by half)

Place the squash in a pot with the water and sea salt, cover, and bring to a
boil. Reduce the flame to low and simmer for 7 to 10 minutes until tender. Purée the squash in a hand food mill, using most of the water from cooking. The
purée should be quite thick. Place the purée in a pot and add the barley malt
and cinnamon. Mix, cover, and bring to a boil. Reduce the flame to low and
simmer 3 to 5 minutes. Remove.

Roll out the crust and place in a pie plate. Press the edges of the dough
down with a fork and trim the excess dough off with a paring knife. Poke several holes in the bottom of the crust with a fork. Pre-bake the crust at 375 degrees F for 10 minutes. Remove and place the purée in the pie shell. Smooth out
and sprinkle the chopped nuts evenly over the purée. Bake again for another 20
minutes or so until the crust is golden brown. Remove and allow to cool before
slicing.

Lemon Pie

4 cups organic apple juice
4 to 5 Tbsp agar agar flakes
2 to 3 Tbsp kuzu, diluted
pinch of sea salt
juice of 1 1/2 to 2 lemons
1 tsp vanilla
maple syrup or brown rice syrup
basic whole wheat pie crust dough (reduce recipe by half)

Place the apple juice, agar flakes, and sea salt in a pot. Stir occasionally and
bring to a boil. Add the lemon juice, vanilla, and enough syrup to taste for
sweetness, making sure not to add so much that it overpowers the flavor of the
lemons. Add the diluted kuzu, stirring constantly. Remove and allow to cool almost room temperature.

Roll out the pie crust and place in a pie plate. Press the edges of the dough down with a fork and trim off the excess dough. Poke several holes in the bottom of the pie crust with a fork. Pre-bake the crust at 375 degrees F for 25 to 30 minutes until golden brown. Remove and pour the lemon-kanten mixture in it. Set aside in a cool place to jell. When jelled, slice. For a meringue-like topping, thicken amazake or vanilla soymilk with diluted kuzu until very thick. Blend and spread on top of the jelled lemon filling.

Vegetable Pie (1 large or 2 medium pies)

1/2 cup onion, diced
1 cup carrot, diced
1 cup leek, sliced
1 cup mushrooms, sliced
1 cup green peas
1/2 cup celery, diced
2 cups taro potato, peeled and cubed
1 Tbsp corn oil
1/4 cup unbleached white flour
8 cups water
sea salt
tamari soy sauce
basic whole wheat pie crust (see previous recipe)

Place the corn oil in a pot and heat. Sauté the onion for 2 to 3 minutes. Add the remaining vegetables and sauté for another 3 to 4 minutes. Mix in a small amount of unbleached white flour and sauté for another 1 to 2 minutes until all vegetables are coated with the flour.

Slowly add water, stirring constantly to dissolve the flour, without producing lumps. The liquid should become quite thick. If not, dissolve a little more flour in water and add to the liquid until thick. Season with a little sea salt and tamari soy sauce for desired taste. Cover and bring to a boil. Reduce the flame to low and simmer until the vegetables are tender. Remove from the flame and allow to cool.

Roll out the pie crust on a floured surface and place in the pie plate or plates. Press down the edges with a fork and trim off any excess dough. Poke several holes in the bottom crust with a fork. Pre-bake the bottom crust for 10 minutes at 375 degrees F. Remove and pour the cooled vegetable filling in the pre-baked shell or shells. Roll out the top crusts on a floured surface and place over the filled pie or pies. Seal the edges with a fork. Poke several holes in the center of the top crust with a fork. Place in the oven and bake for another 30 to 40 minutes until the crust is golden brown. Remove and allow to cool slightly before slicing.

Basic Whole Wheat Crackers

2 cups organic whole wheat pastry flour
1/4 to 1/2 tsp sea salt
1/4 cup corn oil
1/2 cup water

Mix the flour and sea salt. Add the oil and mix in by rubbing between your hands until evenly distributed. Add water and form a dough. If too sticky, sprinkle a little more flour on the dough. Knead for 3 to 4 minutes. Roll our the dough on a floured surface until about 1/4 inch thick. Cut into rectangular shapes 2 inches long by 1 1/2 inches wide, either with a knife or fluted pastry wheel. Lightly oil a baking sheet, and place the cracker dough on it. Bake at 375 degrees F for about 20 to 25 minutes until golden brown. Remove and allow to cool.

Sesame or Poppy Seed Crackers

2 cups organic whole wheat pastry flour
1/4 to 1/2 tsp sea salt
1/4 cup corn oil
1/4 to 1/2 cup poppy seeds or tan sesame seeds, roasted
1/2 cup water

Combine the flour, sea salt, and seeds. Add the oil and mix by rubbing between your hands. Add water and form into a ball of dough. Knead for 3 to 4 minutes. Roll out the dough on a floured surface and cut into desired shapes. Place on a lightly oiled baking sheet and bake at 375 degrees F for 20 to 25 minutes until golden brown. Remove and allow to cool.

Strawberry Shortcake

1 qt fresh strawberries, washed, stems removed, and halved
1/4 cup organic maple syrup
1 1/2 cups unbleached white flour
1/2 cup whole wheat pastry flour
2 tsp non-aluminum baking powder
1/2 tsp sea salt
1/4 cup corn oil
1 to 1 1/2 cups water

Combine the flours, baking powder, and sea salt in a mixing bowl. Add the oil and mix in thoroughly by rubbing between your hands. Gradually add the water, mixing constantly until thick. Oil a baking sheet and with a spoon, place the biscuit mixture in mounds (about 1 heaping tablespoonful per biscuit) on the sheet. Bake at 400 degrees F about 20 to 25 minutes until golden. Remove. Place half of the strawberries and the maple syrup in a blender and purée. Pour the purée over the other half of the sliced strawberries and mix. Place 1 to 2 biscuits in each serving bowl and spoon the strawberry mixture over. Serve.

Apple-Raisin Strudel

8 medium organic baking apples, washed, cored, and sliced
1/2 cup organic raisins
1/4 cup roasted walnuts, chopped
1 to 2 Tbsp arrowroot or unbleached white flour
1/4 to 1/3 cup barley malt
1/2 tsp organic cinnamon (optional)
1 tsp lemon juice
pinch of sea salt
basic whole wheat pie crust dough (reduce recipe by half)

Place the apples in a large mixing bowl. Mix in the remaining ingredients. Roll out the pie crust dough on a floured surface. Place the apple mixture on one half of the crust. Dip your fingers in cold water and moisten the edges of the crust. Fold the dough in half, covering the apples. Press the edges of the dough down with a fork to seal or pinch together with your thumbs. Trim off any excess dough. Poke several air holes in the top of the crust. Oil a baking sheet and place the strudel on it. Bake at 375 degrees F for 30 to 40 minutes until the crust is golden brown and the apples are tender. Test with a fork or bamboo skewer. Remove, allow to cool, and slice.

Unleavened Cinnamon Rolls

1 cup roasted walnuts, finely chopped
1 tsp organic cinnamon
1/4 to 1/3 cup barley malt
basic whole wheat pie crust dough (reduce recipe by half)
water
sesame or corn oil

Roll out the crust on a floured surface. Place the barley malt on it. Moisten your fingers and spread the barley malt evenly over the pie crust. Sprinkle the cinnamon evenly on top of the barley malt and spread around with your fingers. Sprinkle the walnuts evenly on top. Moisten the edges of the dough with water. Roll the dough up in a log or cylinder shape with the walnut mixture forming a spiral on the inside. Press the ends of the roll together with a fork to seal and trim off any excess dough. Poke several air holes in the top of the roll with a fork.

Oil a baking or cookie sheet and place the roll on it. Bake at 375 degrees F for about 30 minutes until golden brown. Remove and allow to cool. Slice in 1 inch thick rounds and place on a serving plate with the spiral design of the walnut mixture facing up.

Hijiki Rolls

1 basic whole wheat pie crust
1 1/2 cups cooked hijiki with vegetables
corn oil
whole wheat pastry flour

Roll our the pie crust on a floured surface. Place the cooked hijiki and vegetables on the rolled dough, evenly covering all but the edges of the dough. Roll up the dough in a log or cylinder shape. Seal the ends of the roll by pressing down with a fork. Trim off the excess dough. With a fork, poke several air holes in the crust, covering the entire length of the roll. Oil a baking sheet and place the roll on it. Bake at 375 degrees F for 25 to 30 minutes until golden brown. Remove and slice in 2 inch thick rounds and serve.

Carrot Pastry Rolls

1 basic whole wheat pie crust, rolled out
2 medium-sized carrots, washed and left whole
corn oil

Roll the carrots up inside the pie dough, creating a log or cylinder shape. Oil a baking dish and place the roll on it. Bake at 375 degrees F for 25 to 30 minutes until the pastry is golden brown and the carrots are tender. Remove and slice into rounds and serve. Instead of carrots, use whole burdock root, parsnip, or leeks.

Sourdough Muffins (8 to 10 muffins)

1 cup sourdough starter (see recipe)
3 cups organic whole wheat pastry flour
3 cups water
1 cup barley malt
1 cup raisins
1 cup walnuts, roasted and chopped
1/4 cup corn oil
1 Tbsp pure vanilla extract
1/4 tsp sea salt

Combine the flour, starter, and water. Cover with a damp towel and set aside for 6 to 8 hours in a warm place. Add the remaining ingredients and a little more pastry flour to make a loose but not quite a pourable dough. Let sit for 1 more hour in a warm place. Oil muffin tins and fill with dough. Pre-heat the oven to 350 degrees F and bake for 40 to 50 minutes.

Unleavened Apple Muffins (10 to 12 muffins)

2 cups whole wheat pastry flour
1 cup whole wheat flour
1/4 cup corn oil
1/4 tsp sea salt
3 apples, washed, cored, and diced
1 3/4 cup apple juice
1/4 tsp organic cinnamon

Combine the dry ingredients. Add the oil and mix well. Add juice and mix. Add the apples and mix again. Pre-heat oven to 350 degrees F. Oil and fill the muffin tins to the top with batter. Bake for 40 minutes or until golden brown. Peaches or blueberries may be substituted for apples.

Unleavened Corn Muffins (12 muffins)

3 cups corn meal
1 1/2 cups whole wheat pastry flour
1/4 tsp sea salt
1 cup barley malt or brown rice syrup

1/4 cup corn oil
1 1/2 to 2 cups water

Combine dry ingredients. Add the oil and barley malt and mix well. Add water and mix again. Oil muffin tins and fill sections to the top. Pre-heat the oven to 350 degrees F and bake for about 30 minutes until golden.

Blueberry Muffins (12 to 15 muffins)

1 1/2 cups unbleached white flour
1/2 cups whole wheat pastry flour
2 to 3 Tbsp maple syrup
1/2 tsp sea salt
2 tsp non-aluminum baking powder
1/4 cup corn oil
1 cup blueberries
3/4 to 1 cup water

Combine the flours, sea salt, and baking powder. Add the maple syrup, corn oil, and water. Mix in the blueberries. Oil muffin tins and fill sections to three-quarters full. Pre-heat oven to 400 degrees F and bake for 20 to 25 minutes until golden.

Corn Muffins (12 to 15 muffins)

1 1/2 cups corn flour or meal
1/2 cup whole wheat pastry flour
1/4 cup maple syrup
1/2 tsp sea salt
2 tsp non-aluminum baking powder
1/4 cup corn oil
3/4 to 1 cup water

Combine the flours, sea salt, and baking powder. Mix in the maple syrup, oil, and water. Mix thoroughly. Oil muffin tins and fill to three-quarters full. Pre-heat oven to 400 degrees F and bake for 20 to 25 minutes until golden.

242

Golden Layer Cake

1 1/2 cups unbleached white flour
1/2 cup whole wheat pastry flour
1/4 tsp sea salt
1/4 cup natural tofu mayonaisse
1/4 cup organic maple syrup
1/4 cup corn oil
1 to 2 tsp pure vanilla extract
3/4 cup water or vanilla soymilk
2 to 3 tsp non-aluminum baking powder

Combine the flours, sea salt, and baking powder. Add the oil, tofu mayonnaise, syrup, corn oil, and vanilla. Mix well. Add the water or soymilk to create a thick but pourable batter. Oil cake pan(s) and pour the batter in it. Pre-heat oven to 375 degrees F and bake 25 to 30 minutes until golden. Remove and allow to cool before adding your favorite natural topping or frosting.

Carrot Cake

1 cup whole wheat pastry flour
1 cup unbleached white flour
1/4 tsp sea salt
2 to 3 tsp non-aluminum baking powder
1/4 cup corn oil
1 cup organic raisins
1 to 1 1/2 cups coarsely grated carrot
1/2 cup organic maple syrup
1 tsp organic cinnamon or allspice
3/4 cup water

Combine the flours, sea salt, baking powder, and cinnamon. Mix in the oil, raisins, carrot, and syrup. Add the water and mix thoroughly. Oil cake pan(s). Pre-heat oven to 375 degree F and bake for 25 to 30 minutes. Remove and allow to cool.

Peanut Butter Squares

1 cup organic peanut butter

2 cups whole wheat pastry flour
1/2 cup organic maple syrup
2 to 3 tsp non-aluminum baking powder
water
corn oil

Combine the flour and baking powder. Mix in the peanut butter and syrup. Add enough water to make a thick batter. The batter should be more like cookie batter than a pourable cake batter. Oil a baking sheet and spread the batter evenly on the sheet. Pre-heat the oven to 375 degrees F and bake for 25 to 30 minutes. Remove and allow to cool slightly before slicing in squares.

Apple-Pear Crunch

2 to 3 organic baking apples, washed, cored, and sliced
2 to 3 organic pears, washed, cored, and sliced
2 cups apple juice
1 Tbsp kuzu, diluted
1 cup organic rolled oats
1/4 cup walnuts, roasted and chopped
1/4 cup almonds, roasted and chopped
1/4 cup filberts or hazelnuts, roasted and chopped
2 to 3 Tbsp brown rice syrup
2 to 3 Tbsp barley malt
pinch of sea salt

Place the apples, pears, apple juice, and sea salt in a pot. Cover and bring to a boil. Reduce the flame to low and simmer several minutes until the fruit is tender. Add the diluted kuzu, stirring constantly, until the juice is thick and translucent. Heat a dry skillet and roast the oats for several minutes, stirring constantly to prevent burning and to evenly roast. Place the oats and nuts in a mixing bowl.

Heat the syrup in a saucepan. When it comes to a boil, reduce to low and simmer for 2 to 3 minutes. Remove and pour the hot syrup over the oat-nut mixture. Mix thoroughly. Place the cooked fruit in a baking or casserole dish and sprinkle the crunch mixture on top. Bake at 375 degrees F for about 10 minutes until the crunch is slightly browned.

No-Bake Crunch Topping

1 cup organic rolled oats

1/4 cup walnuts, roasted and chopped
1/4 cup almonds, roasted and chopped
1/4 cup pecans, roasted and chopped
2 to 3 Tbsp brown rice syrup
2 to 3 Tbsp barley malt

Heat a skillet and dry-roast the oats for several minutes, stirring constantly to prevent burning and to evenly roast. Mix in the roasted, chopped nuts. Add the syrups and stir to mix thoroughly. Roast all the ingredients for 3 to 4 more minutes, stirring constantly, until the syrup begins to harden around the oat-nut mixture. Remove and crumble on top of any stewed fruit.

In place of nuts, you may substitute equal amounts of roasted sesame, pumpkin, and sunflower seeds and combine with the oats and syrup.

Rice Crispy Bars

2 cups natural brown rice crispy cereal
1/4 cup brown rice syrup
1/4 cup barley malt
1/4 cup organic raisins
1/4 cup nuts or seeds, roasted and chopped

Place the rice syrup and barley malt in a saucepan and bring to a boil, stirring constantly. Reduce the flame to low and simmer for about 5 to 7 minutes. Place the rice cereal, raisins, and chopped nuts or seeds in a mixing bowl. Pour the hot syrup over and mix well.

Take a small glass baking dish or bread pan and rinse it under cold water. Do not dry it. Place the mixture in the moistened dish. Wet your hands slightly with cold water and press the mixture down firmly in the dish. Place in the refrigerator or freezer for 30 minutes or until the syrup cools and hardens around the cereal-nut mixture. Remove and slice in squares or bars.

Macro-Jacks

4 cups popped popcorn
1/4 cup brown rice syrup
1/4 cup barley malt
1/2 cup roasted peanuts

Place the brown rice syrup and barley malt in a saucepan and heat. Place the popped corn and peanuts in a mixing bowl. Pour the hot syrup over the mixture and mix thoroughly. Spread the mixture evenly on a baking or cookie sheet. Pre-heat the oven to 350 degrees F and bake for about 5 to 7 minutes or until the syrup hardens around the corn and turns slightly brown like caramel. Be careful not to brown too long or burn. Remove from the oven and immediately place the Macro-Jacks in a serving bowl.

Homemade Amazake

Amazake is a natural sweetener, dessert, or sweet drink made from fermented brown rice, sweet brown rice or other whole grains. It can be used as a sweetener for cookies, cakes, breads, pancakes, donuts, frostings, or toppings. It can also be used to make pickles, puddings, and custards. Serve it blended as a hot or chilled drink.

4 cups sweet brown rice or short grain brown rice, washed
8 cups water
1 to 3 cups rice koji
pinch of sea salt

Place the rice and water in a pressure cooker. Set the uncovered cooker aside and let the rice soak overnight. Then place the cover on the cooker and bring up to pressure over a high flame. Reduce the flame to medium-low, place a flame deflector under the pot, and cook for 40 to 45 minutes. Remove from the burner and allow the pressure to come down. Remove the cover and place the rice in a large ceramic bowl. Mix thoroughly for 10 to 20 minutes with a wooden spoon or rice paddle until the rice is cool enough to poke your fingers into.

Mix 1 to 3 cups of rice koji in with the warm rice. For a sweeter taste, use 3 cups of koji, and for a mild taste, use 1 cup. Cover the dish with a towel and set aside in a warm place for 8 to 10 hours. The temperature should not exceed 140 degrees F. The amazake can also be put in the oven with the inside light on. Periodically turn the oven on to the lowest setting for 5 minutes or so, then turn it off. Stir the rice and koji mixture every hour or hour and a half. Remove and place in a pot. Add the sea salt and heat to stop the fermentation process. Dilute with spring water and blend in a blender for a rich, sweet drink or eat as is. You may refrigerate to store.

Amazake Pudding (Plain)

2 qts amazake
4 to 5 tsp kuzu, diluted

raisins ornuts, roasted and chopped, for garnish

Place the amazake and kuzu in a saucepan. Bring to a boil, stirring constantly to prevent lumping. Reduce the flame to low and simmer 1 to 2 minutes. Remove and pour in individual dessert cups. Garnish with raisins and/or chopped nuts. Serve hot or slightly chilled.

Amazake Fruit Pudding

1 qt plain amazake
1 cup peaches, pits removed and sliced
4 to 5 tsp kuzu, diluted

Place the amazake and peaches in a saucepan. Bring to a boil, and reduce the flame to low. Slowly add the kuzu, stirring constantly, until the pudding becomes thick. Simmer 2 to 3 minutes. Place in individual dessert cups and serve hot or chilled. Other local seasonal fruits such as apples, pears, nectarines, tangerines, and berries can be substituted for peaches.

Brown Rice Pudding

1 cup cooked brown rice
2 cups water or apple juice
1/4 cup barley malt or brown rice syrup
2 Tbsp organic raisins
1/4 cup fresh apples washed, cored, peeled, and sliced
1 Tbsp organic roasted tahini
1/4 tsp organic cinnamon (optional)
pinch of sea salt

Place the brown rice, water or juice, sea salt, and raisins in a pressure cooker and cook for 20 to 25 minutes. Let the pressure come down and remove the cover. Add the syrup, apples, tahini, and cinnamon, and mix. Place on the burner and simmer several minutes or place in a lightly oil baking dish, cover, and bake at 375 degrees F for 30 to 40 minutes. Remove the cover and slightly brown the top. Serve hot.

White Rice Pudding

1 cup cooked organic white rice

1 cup water
1/4 cup organic maple syrup
1/4 cup organic raisins
2 tsp pure vanilla extract
2 Tbsp organic roasted tahini
1/4 tsp organic cinnamon
pinch of sea salt

Place the rice, water, raisins, and sea salt in a saucepan. Cover and bring to a boil. Reduce the flame to low and simmer for about 10 minutes. Mix in the syrup, vanilla, tahini, and cinnamon. Cover and simmer for another 10 minutes. Remove, place in individual dessert cups, and chill slightly.

Indian Pudding

2 cups plain soymilk or water
2 cups apples, cored, peeled, and diced
1/2 cup yellow cornmeal
1/2 cup maple syrup or 3/4 cup barley malt
1 tsp organic cinnamon
1 tsp ginger juice
pinch of sea salt
1 tsp corn oil
1/4 cup organic raisins
1 Tbsp kuzu, diluted

Place the soymilk or water in a saucepan and bring to a boil. Place in a double boiler with the cornmeal and a pinch of sea salt, beating with a whisk to prevent lumping. Bring to a boil, reduce the flame to medium-low, and simmer 20 minutes until thick. Stir almost constantly. Place the syrup, apples, cinnamon, ginger juice, corn oil, kuzu, and raisins in the pot with the cornmeal and mix thoroughly. Lightly oil a baking dish and pour the corn mixture in it. Cover and bake at 300 to 325 degrees F for about 1 1/2 hours or so. Serve hot.

Peanut Butter Cookies (12)

3 cups whole wheat pastry flour
1/2 tsp sea salt
1/4 cup corn oil
1 cup barley malt
1/4 cup apple juice

1 cup peanut butter
1/2 to 1 tsp pure vanilla extract

Combine flour and sea salt in a mixing bowl. Combine the oil, barley malt, juice, peanut butter, and vanilla in another mixing bowl. Stir in the flour mixture to form a thick paste or dough. Lightly oil a baking dish and spoon out small amounts of dough on to it. Press the dough down with a fork. Bake at 350 degrees F for about 10 to 15 minutes until the bottom of each cookie is slightly browned. Remove and allow to cool several minutes.

Strawberry or Raspberry Drop Cookies (12)

3 cups whole wheat pastry flour
1/2 tsp sea salt
1/2 tsp organic cinnamon
1 cup barley malt
1/2 cup organic maple syrup
1/4 cup corn oil
1 tsp pure vanilla extract
1 1/2 to 2 tsp baking soda
natural strawberry or raspberry jam

Combine the flour, sea salt, cinnamon, and baking soda. Mix in the barley malt, maple syrup, corn oil, and vanilla to make a thick, firm dough. Place the bowl in the refrigerator and chill for 30 to 40 minutes. Oil a cookie sheet and spoon the dough out on the sheet. Make an indentation in the center of each cookie with a teaspoon or your thumb. Fill each indentation with jam. Bake at 325 to 350 degrees F for about 20 to 25 minutes until browned. Remove and allow to cool.

Oatmeal Raisin Cookies (24)

3 cups rolled oats
1 1/2 cups whole wheat pastry flour
1/4 tsp sea salt
1/4 cup corn oil
1 cup water
1 cup brown rice syrup or barley malt
1 cup organic raisins
1 cup walnuts or pecans, roasted and chopped

Combine the oats, flour, sea salt, raisins, and nuts. Mix in the oil, water, and syrup to make a thick batter. Lightly oil a cookie sheet and spoon the batter on to the sheet. Pat down each cookie with a spoon. Do not make cookies too thick as these do not rise and take longer to bake. Each cookie should be about 2 inches in diameter and about 1/4 inch thick. Pre-heat oven and bake at 375 degrees F for 25 to 30 minutes until golden brown.

Sweet Rice Cookies (12)

1 cup sweet rice flour
1 1/2 cups whole wheat pastry flour
1/2 cup tan sesame seeds, roasted
1/2 cup sunflower seeds, roasted
1 cup apple juice
1/2 cup brown rice syrup or barley malt
2 Tbsp corn oil
1 cup raisins or currents
1/4 tsp sea salt

Combine the flours, seeds, raisins, and sea salt. Add the oil and mix well by rubbing the ingredients through your hands. Add the apple juice and syrup and mix again. Place a tablespoonful at a time of the batter on an oiled cookie sheet, spreading out each cookie so that it is about 1/8 inch thick. Pre-heat oven and bake at 350 degrees F for about 25 minutes until golden brown. Remove and cool.

Resources

One Peaceful World is an international information network and friendship society devoted to the realization of one healthy, peaceful world. Activities include educational and spiritual tours, assemblies and forums, international food aid and development, and publishing. Membership is $30/year for individuals and $50 for families and includes a subscription to the One Peaceful World Newsletter and a free book from One Peaceful World Press. For further information, contact:

One Peaceful World
Box 10, Becket, MA 01223
(413) 623—2322
Fax (413) 623—8827
e-mail opw@macrobiotics.org

The Kushi Institute offers ongoing classes and seminars including cooking classes and workshops presented by Wendy Esko. For information, contact:

Kushi Institute
Box 7, Becket MA 01223
(413) 623—5741
Fax (413) 623—8827
e-mail kushi@macrobiotics.org

Recommended Reading

1. *Amber Waves of Grain: American Macrobiotic Cooking*, Alex and Gale Jack (Japan Publications, 1992).

2. *Aveline Kushi's Complete Gu ide to Macrobiotic Cooking*, Aveline Kushi with Alex Jack (Warner Books, 1985).

3. *Aveline: The Life and Dream of the Woman Behind Macrobiotics Today*, Aveline Kushi,with Alex Jack (Japan Publications, 1989).

4. *Aveline Kushi's Wonderful World of Salads*, Aveline Kushi and Wendy Esko (Japan Publications, 1989).

5. *The Changing Seasons Cookbook, Aveline Kushi and Wendy Esko* (Avery Publishing Group, 1985).

6. *Diet for Natural Beauty*, Aveline Kushi and Wendy Esko (Japan Publications, 1991).

7. *Eat Your Veggies*, Wendy Esko (One Peaceful World Press, 1997).

8. *Food Governs Your Destiny: The Teachings of Namboku Mizuno*, Michio and Aveline Kushi, with Alex Jack (Japan Publications, 1990).

9. *The Good Morning Macrobiotic Breakfast Book*, Aveline Kushi and Wendy Esko(Avery Publishing Group, 1991).

10. *Introducing Macrobiotic Cooking*, Wendy Esko (Japan Publications, 1978).

11. *The Macrobiotic Cancer Prevention Cookbook*, Aveline Kushi and Wendy Esko (Avery Publishing Group, 1988).

12. *Macrobiotic Cooking for Everyone*, Wendy and Edward Esko (Japan Publications, 1980).

13. *Macrobiotic Diet*, Michio and Aveline Kushi with Alex Jack (Japan Publications, revised edition, 1993).

14. *The New Pasta Cuisine*, Aveline Kushi and Wendy Esko (Japan Publications, 1992).

15. *The Quick and Natural Macrobiotic Cookbook,* Aveline Kushi and Wendy Esko (Contemporary Books, 1989).

16. *Raising Healthy Kids*, Michio and Aveline Kushi with Wendy and Edward Esko (Avery Publishing Group, 1994).

17. *Rice Is Nice*, Wendy Esko (One Peaceful World Press, 1995).

18. *Soup du Jour*, Wendy Esko (One Peaceful World Press, 1996).

About the Authors

Aveline Kushi has taught a generation of macrobiotic and natural foods cooks, as well as offered seminars and classes in family and child care, and traditional arts and culture. She has written and illustrated several books including *Aveline Kushi's Complete Guide to Macrobiotic Cooking* and her autobiography, *Aveline: The Life and Dream of the Woman Behind Macrobiotics Today*. She is the mother of five children and numerous grandchildren and takes an active role in macrobiotic education and development.

Wendy Esko teaches macrobiotic cooking at the Kushi Institute and around the world. She is the author of *Introducing Macrobiotic Cooking*, co-author with Aveline Kushi of *The Changing Seasons Macrobiotic Cookbook*, and author of *Rice Is Nice, Soup du Jour*, and many other books. Wendy is a co-founder of KINA, a natural products company that distributes, under the *Ki Essentials* label, *Rice Country* and *Basmati Glycerine Soap* with organic rice bran. Wendy lives with her husband, Edward, also a macrobiotic teacher and author, and eight children in Becket, Mass.

Recipe Index